YOUNG CHILDREN AT SCHOOL
IN THE INNER CITY

YOUNG CHILDREN AT SCHOOL
IN THE INNER CITY

Barbara Tizard, Peter Blatchford, Jessica Burke,
Clare Farquhar, and Ian Plewis

Thomas Coram Research Unit,
41 Brunswick Square,
London, WC1N 1AZ

LAWRENCE ERLBAUM ASSOCIATES, PUBLISHERS
Hove and London (UK)   Hillsdale (USA)

Lawrence Erlbaum Associates Ltd., Publishers
27 Palmeira Mansions
Church Road
Hove
East Sussex, BN3 2FA
U.K.

British Library Cataloguing in Publication Data

Young children at school in the inner city.
1. Great Britain. Urban regions. Inner
areas. Primary schools. Students. Academic
achievement. Social factors
I. Tizard, Barbara
372.1'264

ISBN 0-86377-095-9
ISBN 0-86377-096-7 Pbk

Typeset by Ponting–Green Publishing Services
Printed and bound by A. Wheaton & Co. Ltd., Exeter

Contents

Foreword

This research was carried out with a grant from the Economic and Social Research Council, at an ESRC Designated Research Centre, the Thomas Coram Research Unit. The Unit is a department of the Institute of Education, London.

The book is jointly authored by the research team, all of whom contributed to the writing. We are very grateful to the Inner London Education Authority and the schools, teachers, parents, and children in our study who enabled us to carry out the work. We are also very grateful to our two Advisory Committees, one of educational researchers, the other of educationalists of Afro-Caribbean origin. Although both groups offered us valuable comments and advice, neither can in any way be held responsible for what we have done or written. Finally, we received a great deal of support and help from the two secretaries involved, Maria Harrison and Patricia McGuane.

1 Background to the Study

INTRODUCTION

This book is concerned with young children's attainment and progress in school. More particularly, it is concerned with factors in the school and home that affect attainment and progress. Of course, children's attainment depends a great deal on their own individual abilities and personalities, but to a large extent these characteristics must be accepted as given. From a practical point of view, it is more useful to know in what way schools and parents can affect children's progress.

Most parents are deeply concerned that their children should acquire a good grasp of the basic reading, writing, and number skills during their first years at school. As we shall see, the great majority are not content to leave this process to the teacher, but want to know how best they can contribute themselves. They are anxious that the school their children attend is one where they will not only be happy, but where they will also make good progress. Surprisingly, although definite opinions on these issues abound, there is little firm research evidence about which educational practices in the home and the school contribute to early progress. Is it important, for example, for children to make good progress in reading in their first year at school? Does the amount of progress children make depend on the school they attend? How much do teachers' expectations of children affect their progress? Should parents try to teach children to read and write before ever they start school, or is it better at this stage to concentrate on reading them stories? Once they have started at school, how important is it for parents to help with school work at home? Most of these questions can only be answered by following children for several years, starting before school entry, and trying to assess the impact of different parental and teacher practices on progress.

Our study was planned not only to tackle these questions, but also to throw light on the reasons for the differences in educational achievement of boys and girls, and for the underachievement of black British children of Afro-Caribbean origin. We use the term "Afro-Caribbean" in preference to "West Indian", with its overtones of colonialism, except when referring to the work of earlier writers. For brevity, we often refer to these children and their parents as "black" or "black British". We do *not* use the term black to include other ethnic groups, such as Asians. It is important to remember that virtually all black children of Afro-Caribbean origin, and many of their parents, were born in Britain. These children are a minority of British ethnic minority children nationally, the largest groups being of Indian and Pakistani origin. However, black people of Afro-Caribbean origin are, to a considerable extent, concentrated in the London area. In London infant schools, pupils of Afro-Caribbean origin form much the largest minority group, with 12% of pupils, the next largest group being of Bangladeshi origin. Only 53% of London infant school pupils in 1982 were of white British origin (I.L.E.A., 1983).

At the time that we began our study in 1982 there was considerable public concern and discussion about the underachievement of children of Afro-Caribbean origin, and about the underachievement of girls in maths, which had led to a number of initiatives by local and central government. In 1979 the Government set up a Committee of Inquiry into the Education of Children from Ethnic Minority Groups, charged with considering the factors contributing to the underattainment of ethnic minority children and the remedial action required. This produced an interim report, the Rampton Report, in 1981, called *West Indian children in our schools*, and a final report in 1985, the Swann Report. At about the same time a number of local authorities had adopted policies intended to counter race and gender inequalities in school achievement.

Since these inequalities had been recognised from at least the sixties (see review in Taylor, 1981; also Terman & Tyler, 1954), the question arises of why government took 20 years to respond to the findings. The answer requires consideration of the socio-political context in which the initiatives developed, and we will briefly highlight some of the developments in the seventies which appear to be relevant. From the late 1960s, the growth in the women's movement, accompanied by the growth of Women's Studies and Women's Centres in universities, stimulated both feminist research on gender and education and pressure for positive action against sex discrimination in education. The Sex Discrimination Act, passed in 1975, and the Equal Opportunities Commission set up in 1975 were partial victories for this movement.

The 1970s were also marked by increasing pressure from Asian and Afro-Caribbean parent and community groups for a better educational deal for their children. Since the mid-sixties, parents' groups had been set up in North London to fight the policy of bussing black children away from "ghetto" schools and of "banding" children according to academic ability (see discussion in Carter, 1986).

An important landmark in their struggle was the publication in 1971 of Bernard Coard's study, *How the West Indian child is made educationally sub-normal in the British school system.* D.E.S. figures for 1970 showed that West Indian children were indeed over-represented in E.S.N. schools, by a ratio of 4:1 (Taylor, 1981). Coard called on the West Indian community to set up supplementary schools which would give extra help to children suffering from the inadequacies of the British school system. A few such schools already existed, but their numbers expanded throughout the seventies. Stone has pointed out that the idea of supplementary education was readily accepted by West Indian parents, since most ambitious parents in the Caribbean expect to pay for extra tuition for their children (Stone, 1981). Other landmarks of black pressure for improved education in the seventies included the setting up of the Caribbean Teachers' Association and the Haringey Black Parents' Group. Pressure from these groups, supported by largely white groups, such as All London Teachers Against Racism and Facism (A.L.T.A.R.F.), and the National Association for Multi-racial Education (N.A.M.E.) shifted the National Union of Teachers towards formulating an anti-racist policy, and resulted from 1977 in policy initiatives on multicultural education and anti-racism by a number of local education authorities, including the Inner London Education Authority (Carter, 1986; Gundara, 1986).

These events took place in the context of heightened racism and of a series of violent street confrontations between the police and black youths. Gilroy has documented the changing attitude of officialdom and the media to crime in the West Indian community, from a concern in the sixties with a minority who were involved in drug trafficking and vice offences to the current widely-held view that West Indians are a high crime group, prone to mugging, rioting, and other forms of street violence (Gilroy, 1986). Recurrent fears have been expressed by politicians from the mid-seventies onwards that the inner cities are "powder kegs", liable to explode into violence. The growth of the Rastafari movement in the seventies has been seen as another indication of the alienation of some sectors of the black community from dominant white values. It seems likely that fear of violence from alienated black youth played an important role in putting the issue of the educational underachievement of children of Afro-Caribbean origin on the agenda of local and central government by the late seventies.

THE CAUSES OF UNDERACHIEVEMENT

Social Class

In this section, we start by discussing the evidence on the underachievement of working-class children, which has been the subject of study for many years. Although our project was not directly concerned with social class differences, indirectly the issue is very relevant, since most researchers have seen social class as one of the major causes of the underachievement of children of Afro-Caribbean origin.

Social class is usually assessed by occupation, the major divide being between middle-class or white-collar workers and working-class or manual workers. This classification of social class is one of the most powerful descriptive tools at the social scientist's disposal. The basic framework of children's lives—from their chances of surviving the first year of life to the age at which they are likely to marry, the number of children they are likely to have, and their chances of dying from various diseases—is strongly related to the social class of their parents. Studies of childrearing carried out in Nottingham show that every aspect of childrearing, from the likelihood of children sucking their thumbs to the kind of punishment they receive, is related to social class (Newson & Newson, 1968).

Social class differences are particularly striking in education. The most extensive evidence comes from nationwide longitudinal studies of birth cohorts, including the National Child Development Study (Davie, Butler, & Goldstein, 1972). The most recent of these studies, the Child Health and Education Study (C.H.E.S.) has followed all British children born during the week 5–11 April 1970. At the age of 10, the most socially disadvantaged children had average reading scores one standard deviation (15 points on a standardised test) behind the most advantaged children (Osborn & Milbank, 1987).

Further recent evidence comes from a longitudinal study of nearly 2000 children aged 7 to 11 years in 50 London junior schools, carried out between 1980 and 1984 (I.L.E.A., 1986). At age 7 there was a difference of nearly 10 months in both reading and mathematics "age" between children whose fathers were in manual work and those in non-manual occupations. Social class differences of this kind have been found in many countries, including those of Eastern Europe (Firkowska et al., 1978).

A disproportionate number of black British children have fathers who are manual workers. Brown (1984) showed that only 15% of men of Caribbean origin are in non-manual occupations, compared with 42% of white male workers. Many have therefore argued that all or most of their children's underachievement can be attributed to this social class difference. The issue will be discussed later in the chapter.

Ethnic Group

Most studies have found that children in certain ethnic groups on average achieve as well as, or better than, white British children, whilst others do worse.

The most recent I.L.E.A. (1986) study of junior school children, aged 7 to 11, referred to earlier, found that children of Caribbean and Cypriot origin had lower reading attainments than white children, whilst children from some Asian groups, e.g. Gujerati speakers (mainly East African Indians) and children of Chinese origin (mainly from Hong Kong), had above average reading scores. A similar pattern of ethnic differences emerged from an earlier study of 31,000 pupils in inner London, born between September 1959 and September 1960 (Mabey, 1981).

There have been far fewer studies of mathematical attainment in different ethnic groups, but almost all have found that children of Caribbean origin do less well than white children (e.g. London Borough of Redbridge, 1978). The I.L.E.A. Junior School survey (I.L.E.A., 1986) found that children of Caribbean and Cypriot origin scored below the mean in maths as well as reading throughout the junior school, although this was not the case with practical maths, involving understanding of weight, volume, etc.

The underachievement of children of Afro-Caribbean origin continues in the secondary school. The most recent evidence from the Inner London Education Authority (I.L.E.A., 1987) shows that at the end of the fifth year of secondary schooling a number of ethnic minority children, particularly those of Indian, Pakistani, and South East Asian origin, were more successful in "O" and "C.S.E." level examinations than white British children. Children of Caribbean, Turkish, and Bangladeshi origin, on the other hand, did less well. It was not, however, the case that children of Caribbean origin did worse at all levels than white children. Table 1.1 abstracts some of the data to show that they were more likely to take public examinations than white British children, and to obtain at least one lower grade result. But they were less likely than white British children to achieve at the highest level, that is five or more CSE or O passes with the highest grades.

The same report records a definite improvement in the examination performance of pupils of Caribbean origin between 1976 and 1986. Nearly 5% of these pupils achieved 5 or more high-grade C.S.E. or O level passes in 1986, compared with under 2% in 1976, and 27% achieved between 1 and 4 high–level passes, compared with 21% in 1976. This gain was larger

TABLE 1.1
C.S.E. and O level Achievement: I.L.E.A. Pupils 1986

| | Percentage of Pupils Achieving... | | | |
	No Exams Taken	*1+ C.S.E. 2/5 or O D/E*	*5+ C.S.E. 1 or O A/C*	*No. of Pupils*
African	12.2	40.9	14.2	386
Arab	18.7	48.0	10.6	123
Bangladeshi	32.1	36.5	3.6	535
Caribbean	14.0	40.0	4.6	2649
English, Scottish, Welsh	22.9	35.6	9.4	7985
Greek	11.8	33.5	15.9	170
Indian	9.8	33.1	20.7	387
Irish	21.5	33.5	11.4	1037
Pakistani	9.8	38.1	16.1	255
SE Asian	12.9	33.1	16.0	326
Turkish	25.3	35.1	6.0	285
Other Black	17.8	40.0	12.6	135
Other European	14.9	27.8	21.0	649
Other White	26.7	28.3	16.7	120
All	20.1	37.9	9.8	15,042

Note: Not all the table columns have been reprinted.

than that made by any other ethnic group. (It should be noted that national, as opposed to London, surveys [e.g. Swann, 1985] have found white English and Welsh children performing relatively better, probably because of social class differences in the samples.)

Public examination results are a less valid index of attainment than standardised tests, since results depend to a considerable extent on the class into which the child is "streamed" at school, a decision made on a variety of considerations, including prejudice, as well as by the child's ability. On the other hand, they are very important to the individual concerned, since they play an important role in determining job prospects. Brown (1984) has shown that of West Indian male employees with at least one O level, 42% are in non-manual jobs, whilst only 5% of those with no O levels are in non-manual jobs. The extent of the discrimination they face is shown by the corresponding figures for white male employees—61% of those with an O level are in non-manual jobs, compared with 22% of those without.

There are other positive aspects of the attainments of British children of Afro-Caribbean origin which are important to note, and which suggest that their attitude to the education system differs from that of white working class children. Both Maughan and Rutter (1986) and various I.L.E.A. studies (I.L.E.A., 1986) have shown that, contrary to widespread belief, pupils of Afro-Caribbean origin have a better attendance record at school than white pupils. They also show greater persistence and involvement in secondary education, and are more likely than white pupils to get C.S.E. and O levels after the fifth form at school, and to move on to further education and vocational courses after leaving school, although less likely to go to university.

Gender[1]

The gap between girls' and boys' educational attainment is of a different kind and magnitude to that between children of different social class and ethnic group. Until the age of 16, girls' overall educational attainments are slightly higher than those of boys. The I.L.E.A. ethnic background and examination results survey of 1985 showed that girls in every ethnic group got better O level and C.S.E. results than boys (I.L.E.A., 1987). National figures show that in 1984/85 59% of girls leaving school had at least one O level or equivalent at grade A–C, compared with 53% of boys. Almost the same proportion of girls as boys—14% compared with 15%—left school with two or more A levels. From this point onwards, the educational underachievement of women becomes more marked. Women formed less than half—42%—of those awarded first degrees in the U.K. in 1984 (Great Britain, 1987).

A particular cause of concern is that girls tend to underachieve compared to boys in maths and maths-related subjects. This means that they are more likely than boys to be debarred from a wide range of skilled and professional jobs. Male superiority in maths has been accepted as a fact for so long, both by the general public and by the research world (Maccoby & Jacklin, 1974) that it is quite surprising to find that the differences in attainment at school level are rather small. In 1984/1985 more boys than girls (33% compared with 28%) left school with a maths G.C.E. O level grade A–C or equivalent. The sex difference for physics was larger. By the A level stage the gap widens considerably, with three times as many boys as girls studying A level maths. And in 1983 twice as many men as women obtained first degrees in science, and over ten times as many men obtained first degrees in engineering and technology (Great Britain, 1987).

The reasons for these differences are not fully understood, and it seems

---

[1] We use the term "gender" to refer to the social differentiation of men and women, as in gender role and gender stereotypes, and "sex" to refer to biological differentiation. Since the groups in our study were selected by sex, we refer to the differences between the groups, e.g. in their attainment, as sex differences.

likely that many more factors than attainment in maths are involved. However, it is known that the sex difference in attainment on mathematical tests increases during the school years. The Assessment of Performance Unit, which monitors attainment nationwide, found that 11-year-old boys consistently obtained higher scores in the majority of sub-categories of the mathematics tests given, whilst girls did better at only two, computation and generalised arithmetic (Great Britain, 1982a). The difference was small, but a similar, more pronounced, pattern was found at age 15, where girls were particularly under-represented amongst the higher attaining children (Great Britain, 1982b).

At and below the age of 11 there is conflicting evidence about whether a sex difference in maths attainment is present at all. Both the National Child Development Study of 7-year-olds and the C.H.E.S. survey of 10-year-olds found that girls did significantly worse at arithmetic problems than boys. In contrast, the I.L.E.A. Junior School Study, referred to earlier, found no significant sex difference in any of the three junior school years in either written or practical mathematics attainment.

Some have argued that the conflicting findings about sex differences in mathematics attainment in younger children depend on the type of questions set (e.g. Shuard, Note 1). There is certainly considerable evidence that at a later age boys excel on problems involving scale, proportion, and spatial problems, whereas girls excel on more abstract deductive problems (Pattison & Grieve, 1984). At any rate, it is generally agreed that, below the age of 11 the inferiority of girls in maths, if it exists, is very small. On the other hand, their superiority to boys from an early age in reading and writing is well established. The influence of the underlying current concerns of researchers is shown by the fact that before the seventies the sex difference that tended to be highlighted was the relative underachievement of boys in reading, rather than the current concern with the underachievement of girls in maths (see, for example, Douglas, 1964).

RELATIVE INFLUENCE OF SOCIAL CLASS, ETHNIC GROUP, AND SEX ON TEST SCORES

From studies that have presented data that allow one to compare the size of sex, social class, and ethnic group differences in attainment, it is clear that the social class difference is much the largest. The C.H.E.S study found that the sex difference in educational scores was less than a third of that of the social class difference. They did not present data on ethnic group (Osborn & Milbank, 1987). From the I.L.E.A. Junior School Study (1986) it is possible to make all three comparisons. Girls' attainment in writing and reading was markedly better than that of boys throughout the junior school. In the first year of junior school, this sex difference was larger than the difference between the black and white children. By the end of junior school, the difference between the black and white groups in reading was bigger than that between the sexes. However, social class differences were twice as large (Table 1.2).

THE RELATIONSHIP BETWEEN ETHNIC GROUP, SOCIAL CLASS, SEX, AND UNDERACHIEVEMENT

There is a good deal of evidence to show that British children of Afro-Caribbean origin are on average more likely to grow up in working-class families, in materially more disadvantaged circumstances than white children (Brown, 1984). The level of unemployment amongst black workers is higher, incomes of employed workers are lower, and the housing allocated to black families is of poorer quality. Since research has repeatedly shown that children from working-class and materially disadvantaged homes do worse at school, the question arises whether the low attainment of children of Afro-Caribbean origin as a group simply reflects this association. Two recent studies referred to earlier have tackled this question statistically. They both concluded that, after taking social class into account, children of Afro-Caribbean origin still scored lower than white children. In the first I.L.E.A. study (Mabey, 1981) the difference in reading scores between white children and those of Afro-Caribbean origin was halved when it was adjusted to take account of social background factors. However, a small

TABLE 1.2
Comparison of Sex, Ethnic Group and Social
Class Differences in Attainment

	Reading	Maths
(a) 1st Year Juniors (7/8-year-olds)		
Sex	0.38	0.08
Ethnic Group	0.30	0.49
Social Class	0.83	0.74
(b) 3rd Year Juniors (10/11-year-olds)		
Sex	0.34	0.15
Ethnic Group	0.39	0.43
Social Class	1.08	0.86

Note: These are standard deviation units. Hence, the social class difference in 11 year old reading was 15 points on a standardised test, the sex and ethnic differences about 5 points. The information was given to us by the I.L.E.A. Research and Statistics Division from their Junior School Study data.

difference remained. In the more recent I.L.E.A. Junior School Study ethnic group differences were still present after other background factors had been taken into account—including mother's and father's occupation (i.e. social class), eligibility for free meals (i.e. low income), family size, and nursery school experience (I.L.E.A., 1986).

These statistical attempts to control for social background are not totally convincing. One of us (Plewis, 1987) has pointed out that the social indicators used are generally so coarse-grained that they conceal real differences in living conditions. For example, "equating" for social class usually means that all manual workers are equated, although some will be highly skilled and well paid, others unskilled and poorly paid. On average, families of Afro-Caribbean origin are likely to be more materially disadvantaged than the white families they are equated with.

Further, other differences between Afro-Caribbean and white families, not controlled for statistically, may be important for educational attainment. For example, as Yule and his colleagues pointed out, black children may live in more deprived areas and attend schools with lower standards than white children (Yule, Berger, Rutter, & Yule, 1975). No study has so far controlled for family background factors *and* school and area. It therefore remains uncertain whether or not the underachievement of children of Afro-Caribbean origin can fully be accounted for by social class and attendance at schools with lower standards.

However, there is another reason why "equating" black and white families for social class may be unsatisfactory. In a white population, the occupational level of the father is highly predictive of the education level of the child, for complex sociological reasons to do with the parents' educational level and their attitudes both to education and many other matters. In a black population, these associations may, for historical reasons, be different. We have already pointed out that Afro-Caribbean manual workers are likely to have higher educational qualifications than white manual workers, and we shall demonstrate important differences in attitude to education between the Afro-Caribbean and white parents in our sample. Hence parental occupation may be a much less accurate predictor of child's educational level in black than in white families.

So far we have discussed the associations between sex, social class, ethnic group, and underachievement separately, since this is how they have usually been studied. Grant and Sleeter (1986) recently analysed 71 articles in educational journals which were directly concerned with these issues. The great majority focused almost entirely on either sex, or ethnic group, or social class, and only three articles focused on all three variables. Thus it is usually impossible to tell from the published accounts of research whether, for example, both black and white British girls tend to underachieve in maths, or whether black middle-class British children underachieve relative to white middle-class British children.

There is, however, some evidence, reviewed by Tomlinson (1983), which suggests that, amongst children of Afro-Caribbean origin, girls have higher educational achievements than black boys, especially in reading. Both Sharpe (1976) and Fuller (1980) found that teenage girls of Afro-Caribbean origin placed great importance on acquiring educational qualifications. There is thus a hint that, just as social class may have different associations in the black and the white communities, so gender may have different connotations for black and white children.

Explanations for Ethnic Differences in Attainment: Blaming the Victim

The great majority of white researchers have assumed that the cause of underachievement, insofar as it is not explained by social class, is located in the "problems" of children of Afro-Caribbean origin and their families. This assumption is clearly shown by the fact that they have chosen to investigate factors in the child and the home, and not teachers and school processes. During the sixties and seventies the children's failure to progress was widely blamed on their own characteristics, especially their use of Creole and their negative self-image, although by the end of this period both these explanations were much less frequently heard. This is because research showed that children of Afro-Caribbean origin born in Britain are likely to have a reasonable command of the syntax of standard English, as well as a form of Creole. They appear able to switch from one code to another, and the great majority do not have difficulties in reading or writing arising from the influence of Creole.

There is now considerable evidence that the self-esteem of children of Afro-Caribbean origin is not lower than that of white children, hence this explanation of their educational failure can no longer be sustained (see reviews in Milner, 1983; Stone, 1981). Stone argues that in a racist society: "black people create alternative sources of selfhood through political, social, literary and musical styles, and do not simply introject the negative views of white society". She argues that attributing educational failure to the supposed identity problems of black children has led teachers to act like therapists or social workers, to the neglect of their primary task of teaching.

Other explanations of underachievement have concentrated on the supposed inadequacies of the Afro-Caribbean family. The usual approach has been to show differences between black and white families, to assume that the white family behaviour or structure is superior, and then to argue that it is these differences which account for underachievement at school. Studies that have found fewer problems in black families, e.g. Earls and Richman's (1980) finding that white parents reported more frequent and severe behaviour problems in four-year-olds than West Indian parents did, have generally been overlooked.

In some studies of black and white families the differences between them are very subjectively assessed. For example, Scarr, Capanulo, Ferdmass, Tower, and Caplan (1983) asked health visitors to rate the amount of "developmentally appropriate stimulation" and "the quality of the mother-child relationship" in white and ethnic minority families. All the ethnic minority groups were said to be inferior in the provision of developmentally appropriate stimulation (especially toys), and the West Indian and Pakistani families were said to be "relatively poor in the quality of the mother-child relationship". The view that toys are necessary for developmental stimulation, and that a particular (British) style of mother-child interaction is superior to other styles of interaction, are both examples of ethnocentric thinking that is widespread amongst professionals.

In other studies assessment was more objective, but there was a surprising readiness to go well beyond the evidence collected in concluding that West Indian childrearing practices were deficient. Thus Rutter et al. (1975) concluded that: "there are aspects of the patterns of child-rearing in some West Indian families which give cause for concern ... we found somewhat less interaction between parents and children in West Indian families", although they noted that this difference "fell well short of statistical significance". They went on to observe that "this is probably not very important in itself, but it appears from what we observed (in anecdotal fashion) in the homes and from what others have written ... that some parents did not understand the importance of play in children's learning, and consequently did not always provide the optimal conditions for early cognitive growth and development". Like other authors, they reported that more children in West Indian than white families had experienced childminding by nonrelatives. They concluded that: "it would be expected that the ill-effects (resulting) would mainly involve cognitive development", whilst acknowledging that evidence of these ill-effects was not available. It is entirely reasonable to discuss non-significant findings and anecdotal evidence if this appears to support other evidence. Our point is that discussions such as the one quoted indicate the researcher's prior expectations that black childrearing patterns are deficient.

Research reports like these and others (e.g. Pollak; 1972, 1979) assume that modern middle-class Western childrearing practices provide "the optimal conditions for growth and development", despite the evidence both from the past and from the wide variety of contemporary cultures that educational success can develop from a great range of family patterns and practices.

The same fallacy underlies the argument of those who see the origins of underachievement in the structure of the West Indian family. The Western nuclear family, with father working, mother at home, and a small number of children, is assumed by many white professionals and researchers to be ideal. It is argued that the West Indian family, typified as "matriarchal", headed by a single mother, who goes out to work, and has a number of children, leads to the neglect of the children's education. Again, this argument rests on assumptions which are unproven, or have been refuted. The children of working mothers do not, on average, underachieve at school (Hoffman, 1974), and the underachievement of the children of single mothers has been shown to relate to poverty, not single parent status as such (Essen & Wedge, 1982).

Finally, almost all comparisons of Afro-Caribbean and white families assume that Afro-Caribbean families are homogeneous, and share an identical lifestyle. Generalisations are made to an extent that would not be found in discussing white families, as in Taylor's (1981) summing up of her discussion of West Indian families in Britain. "Such, then, is the natural family background of the child of West Indian origin starting school."

Explanations for Underachievement: Racism

The realisation that their children were underachieving at school caused great concern to the Afro-Caribbean community, many of whom had been drawn to England by the prospect of improving their credentials and skills (Carter, 1986). Their leaders were not prepared to accept the view that the fault lay in themselves and their children, but instead blamed poor teaching, low standards in schools, and racism in schools and society.

Since there are very few researchers who are of Afro-Caribbean origin, the black point of view has not been tested and elaborated by research workers to the same extent as the feminist viewpoint (see next section). Instead, it has been expressed primarily by pressure from black parents' and teachers' groups, and by the initiative of Afro-Caribbean parents in setting up supplementary schools. The pressure of black community groups was crucial in determining that the report of the Rampton Committee and the subsequent Swann Report highlighted the role of racism in underachievement, and that it largely ignored the issue of the supposed inadequacies of West Indian family life. But neither Swann nor Rampton were able to draw on any substantial research concerned with the issue of how black children's achievements were influenced by racism, although they suggested that low teacher expectations, an ethnocentric curriculum, and teachers' stereotyped attitudes might be responsible.

Explanations for Underachievement: Girls and Maths

In many respects the discussions about the underachievment of girls in maths parallel those about children of Afro-Caribbean origin. One difference is that whilst the argument that children of Afro-Caribbean origin are genetically less intelligent than white is no longer given academic credence, genetic explanations of sex differences are still prevalent.

A second difference between educational research on ethnic group and gender is that because of the existence of a body of feminist researchers, a considerable amount of research has addressed the issue of the ways in which schools may create or foster gender inequalities. In contrast, there has been very little research on whether schools may create or foster underachievement in children of Afro-Caribbean origin.

A number of sociologists have discussed, for example, ways in which teachers treat girls and boys in primary school differently. They have argued that teachers subtly encourage girls to be dependent, passive and conforming, anxious for approval, and unwilling to court possible failure. Active, aggressive behaviour, although discouraged in all children, is more often tolerated in boys as "natural". Paradoxically, because boys are more likely to escape the teachers' moulding, they are seen by them as more interesting and stimulating than girls, and both for this reason and because of their worse behaviour, they demand and receive more of the teacher's attention. Others have argued that when boys are criticised at school it tends to be for their bad behaviour, whereas girls tend to be more often criticised for poor work. Girls thus come to internalise the teachers' view of themselves as relatively uninteresting, and also lose confidence in their ability. Thus, although girls are academically more successful than boys at primary school, this is said to be at the price of low self-confidence and of avoiding intellectual challenges. Mathematical problems, which are seen by girls as difficult, arouse anxiety and fear of failure in them (see Clarricoats, 1978; Delamont, 1980; French, 1984; Weiner, 1980).

Most of these ideas have been developed by sociologists on the basis of talking to a small number of teachers, or observing in a very small number of classrooms. It is not known how many teachers behave in these ways, or how many girls respond in the ways described. It does, however, seem to have been established that girls perceive maths as more difficult than boys do, and have lower expectations of success, even when their performance is objectively equivalent (see discussion in Huston, 1983). There is also considerable evidence that girls get less of the teachers' attention in class than boys. The recent author of a meta-analytic review concludes that this statement holds true for all age groups, social classes and ethnic groups, across all subjects, and with both male and female teachers. She states that it also holds true for different types of contact, whether criticism of behaviour, praise, or instruction, (Kelly, in press). However, it should be said that most of this research is from the U.S.A., and not all British research has produced similar findings (see Galton, Simon & Croll, 1980).

SCHOOL INFLUENCES ON ATTAINMENT IN GENERAL

So far this discussion has been concerned with the educational under-achievement of particular groups of children, and it may seem to have strayed a long way from the issue of what factors in the school affect the attainment and progress of all children. Yet it is clear that a greater understanding of factors affecting progress in general may throw light on the underachievement of particular groups, and also that the reverse may be true. In this sector of the chapter we discuss briefly some recent issues raised by educational researchers that may contribute to understanding ethnic and sex underachievement.

Teacher Expectations

The issue of whether teachers' expectations affect progress assumed prominence with the publication of the controversial "Pygmalion in the Classroom" study in the late sixties (Rosenthal & Jacobson, 1968). In this experiment, teachers were (falsely) told that certain of their pupils were "late bloomers", and likely to make remarkable intellectual improvement over the course of the year. At the end of the year, those children did indeed make significantly higher I.Q. gains than the others. The researchers concluded that the false information set up expectations in the teachers, which influenced their behaviour towards those pupils in such a way as to improve their performance. The study has been much criticised on methodological grounds, but it did set in train a considerable body of research about the effects of naturally occurring expectations. It is now well established that those children whom teachers expect to do well do indeed tend to do so (see review by Brophy, 1983). However, the impor-tant issue is whether this is because teachers judge children's academic potential accurately, or whether in some cases they *cause* under or overa-chievement, by basing their expectations on considerations other than children's academic potential. In this way, the expectations become a self-fulfilling prophecy.

An early and influential study of one U.S. kindergarten teacher showed how this could happen (Rist, 1970). In this case, the teacher's expectations were influenced by her knowledge of the children's social background, and by such indicators of social class as clothing and use of standard American English. These factors, according to Rist, influenced her allocation of children to fast and slow learning groups in the first days of the school year. Subsequently, most of her attention and interest was directed to the "fast learners", who did indeed make most progress. In consequence, this initial discrimination between pupils was perpetuated in subsequent years.

The study makes compelling reading, but similar, less well-known case studies of primary teachers failed to find evidence of bias of this kind (e.g. Carew & Lightfoot, 1979). However, a number of larger-scale, quantitative studies, which have taken into account the child's achievement at the beginning of the year, have found some evidence of the effect of a self-fulfilling prophecy (see review in Brophy, 1983). Some of these studies suggest that teachers' judgements of children's potential are biased by the child's social behaviour in class. That is, children seen by the teacher as well-behaved and a pleasure to have in the class tend to be judged as of higher academic potential than their test results indicate, and vice versa (Crano & Mellon, 1978). One British study in junior schools found that it is below-average children who are most likely to be affected in their progress by their teacher's low expectations of them (Galton & Delafield, 1981).

If teachers' expectations affect children's progress, how large is this influence? Brophy considers a best estimate is in the region of 5–10% of the variance, whilst Smith, in a meta-analysis of expectation research, reports an effect of 0.38 standard deviation units (see Brophy, 1983). That is, on a standardised reading test teachers' expectations are likely to make a difference of about 5 points either way to a child's progress. This is about the same size as many reported sex and ethnic differences, but much smaller than social class differences (see Table 1.2).

Clearly, if it could be shown that teachers tend to have low expectations of children of Afro-Caribbean origin, or of girls in maths, and boys in reading, and that these expectations tend to become a self-fulfilling prophecy, then the underachievement of these groups of children could, at least in part, be explained. A meta-analysis of North American research suggests that teachers' expectations are to some extent influenced by social class and race, but less often by sex (Dusek & Joseph, 1983). There appears to have been no British research on the influence of children's ethnic group on teachers' expectations, perhaps because most researchers have looked to the home for explanations of ethnic underachievement.

A further important question is how teachers' expectations are translated into pupils' achievement. Complex models have been advanced by Cooper (1985) and Rogers (1982). Some researchers have approached this question by observing the ways in which teachers interact with children of whom they have high and low expectations (see review by Brophy & Good, 1974). Typically, children of whom teachers have high expectations have been found to receive more praise from them, and more contact with them. A British study found that children seen by teachers as low-achieving not only received less praise and more criticism, but also less feedback from the teachers. This, they suggest, led to disruptive behaviour in an attempt to get more of the teacher's attention (Galton & Delafield, 1981). Others have suggested that teachers' expectations may affect achievement through such administrative decisions as, for example, placement in higher or lower streams, and in the case of secondary school, decisions about which examinations to enter children for. If it could be shown that bias against girls or children of Afro-Caribbean origin on the part of the teacher is associated with the slower progress of these groups, then an important mechanism in the process of ethnic and sex underachievement would have been disclosed.

Curriculum and Progress

Very little research has considered the relationship between children's achievement and the extent and depth of the curriculum taught to them. But this issue may be of particular relevance in British primary schools, for two reasons. As we explain in Chapter 3, at the time of writing Britain had no centrally regulated school curriculum—each school, usually each teacher, may cover what ground they like in the course of a year. Further, especially in the infant school, learning is usually individualised, children being encouraged to work on their own, at their own pace. Some official unease has been expressed by school inspectors that this may result in high ability children "not being stretched" (H.M.I., 1978). Research by Bennett and his colleagues in classes of six-and seven-year-olds suggests that this may well be the case (Bennett, Desforges, Cockburn & Wilson, 1984). Paradoxically, they found that high-attaining children were given less *new* knowledge and more practice in familiar skills than their low-attaining peers in the same class. Whereas the teachers quickly recognised when a task was proving too difficult for a child, they were said to be "totally blind to tasks whose demands were too easy". From the teachers' point of view, the children were busy, and they assumed that if children were busy, then the work given them was at an appropriate level.

Bennett and his colleagues found that there were enormous differences in the content of what was taught in different classes, with some classes covering almost twice as many areas as others. Equally, enormous differences were found in what was taught to different children in the same class. They point out that the "work at your own rate" philosophy of the British primary school (Bennett et al., 1984): "precluded many low attainers from experiencing a wide range of content met by their more academically advanced peers in the same classroom". They quote an example of the mathematical curricula taught to a high- and a low-attaining child in the same class. Only one subject, clock time, which was taught as a class lesson, was studied in common. That apart, the children followed a totally different curriculum.

This individualised approach allows the teacher to match the work set to the children to their abilities. It is, however, clear that such an approach also allows great scope for a teacher's expectations to operate. Children of whom she has low expectations may not be given the opportunity to acquire the skills taught to others of whom her expectations are higher, and one early U.S. study found experimental evidence that this is the case (Beez, 1968).

It is possible, therefore, that any ethnic or sex bias of the teacher could affect children's achievement by means of the curriculum offered them.

Problem Behaviour and Progress

There is a well-established relationship between aggressive and overactive behaviour and reading retardation (Yule & Rutter, 1985). The Isle of Wight studies, for example, found that one third of children with school behaviour problems of this kind were severely retarded in reading, compared with only 4% in the general child population (Rutter, Tizard, & Whitmore, 1970). It has often been argued that school failure leads to problem behaviour, perhaps through creating antagonism to school, or damage to the child's self-esteem (Rutter et al., 1970). The evidence is now rather stronger that, at least in the first years at school, the converse may be the case. Aggressive and overactive behaviour has been shown in several studies to precede reading difficulties, and to be present at school entry, in association with poor performance on reading readiness tests (see Richman, Stevenson, & Graham, 1982; McMichael, 1979; McGee, Williams, Share, Anderson, & Silva, 1986). It is also possible that a third factor, for example, temperament, may be the cause of both behaviour problems and reading difficulties (see Richman et al., 1982; Yule & Rutter, 1985).

We have already described the evidence that boys and working-class children tend to be less successful at reading. It is also the case that these groups of children are more often described as being active, restless, and aggressive than are either girls or middle-class children (see MacFarlane, Allen, & Honzik, 1954; Schaffer, Meyer-Bahlburg, & Stokman, 1980; Rutter et al., 1970). Children of Afro-Caribbean origin, as we have seen, tend to have lower reading scores than white children, but in their case the association with conduct disorder is less clear-cut. They are said to show more conduct disorder than white children at school (I.L.E.A., 1986), but not at home (Earls & Richman, 1980; Rutter et al., 1974). There is also some evidence of a sex difference amongst children of Afro-Caribbean origin in reading attainment, but not in the frequency of behaviour problems (Wolkind & Rutter, 1985). We have already pointed out that both sex and social class may have different connotations in black and white groups, and this evidence suggests that the processes linking reading backwardness and problem behaviour may also differ in different ethnic groups. That is, even if it proves to be the case that problem behaviour causes reading backwardness in white children, it cannot be assumed that this will be the case for black children.

Although correlation studies can never on their own reach a final understanding of these complex processes, it seemed to us that any study of ethnic and sex differences in educational progress should include an attempt to tease out the relationship between progress and the frequency of behaviour problems.

Classroom Interaction and Progress

One of the dominant trends in educational research in the United States has been the study of classroom interaction and behaviour—based on systematic observation of teachers and pupils—and their associations with children's educational progress. Over the past two decades there have been many of these so-called "process-product" studies (see reviews by Brophy, 1979; Dunkin & Biddle, 1974; Good, 1979; Rosenshine, 1977), including three studies of the first grades in school (Brophy & Evertson, 1977; Soar, 1977; Stallings, 1975). These studies have by no means produced consistent results, but they tend to show that there is a relationship between the amount of time children are "on-task", and the frequency of their instructional contacts with teachers, with their educational attainment.

It is an open question whether such results are relevant to, or would also be found in, British infant schools. To date there have been next to no "process-product" studies in British infant schools. There has been one major study at the junior school level which, like the American studies, used a systematic observation study to obtain measures of teacher and pupil behaviour. This was the ORACLE study (Galton et al., 1980; Galton & Simon, 1980).

Because there is some evidence that differences in classroom interaction are associated with progress, we thought it possible that ethnic and sex differences in progress might be associated with differences in the time that these groups spent "on and off task", and the amount of instruction they received from the teachers. Accordingly, we decided to include in our study observations of these variables, and of other aspects of classroom interaction that might reflect possible prejudice or bias.

School Differences

Several recent studies (e.g. Rutter, Maughan, Mortimore, & Ouston, 1979; I.L.E.A., 1986) have suggested that there are important differences between schools that may affect children's progress. If black children, or one particular sex, are disproportionately concentrated in schools where progress tends to be slow, this could in part, at least, account for ethnic or sex underachievement. Because, as explained in Chapter 2, the design of our study did not allow us to come to firm conclusions about different rates of progress in different schools and classes, we will not discuss this issue further. Nevertheless, as we shall show, our evidence does suggest that this may indeed be an important factor in progress.

Parental Influences on Literacy

Research on factors within the home associated with the development of literacy has stemmed from concern with the underattainment of white working-class children. The research hypotheses and underlying assumptions were very similar to those made about children of Afro-Caribbean origin. In the sixties, educationalists believed that working-class parents lacked interest in, and support for, schooling, and lacked knowledge of, and contact with, the school (e.g. Plowden, 1967; Jackson & Marsden, 1962). Through the influence of psychologists, the emphasis then shifted to the particular importance of the first five years of life, and the relative failure of working-class parents to read to their young children, play with them, or talk to them in stimulating ways. Working-class parents are thus held responsible for the underachievement of their own children, just as black parents are.

Social class differences in parents' childrearing practices and relationships with school undoubtedly exist, but there is very little evidence that they are a major factor in accounting for differences in the children's school achievement. However, there is some evidence that parental influence on school achievement may operate via a much more direct route—early help with reading. In the late seventies, a survey of seven-year-olds in a working-class area of outer London showed that higher reading attainment was much more strongly associated with parental help in learning to read than with such "middle-class" practices as reading to children (Hewison & Tizard, 1980). Wells and his colleagues in Bristol found that the strongest association with school attainment at age seven was the child's knowledge of written language at school entry. Wells found that the extent of this knowledge was related to the number of books owned by the child, and to the children's and parents' interest in books (Wells, 1985).

If it is the case that Afro-Caribbean parents, and the parents of boys, show less support for schooling and literacy than white parents, and the parents of girls, then ethnic and sex differences in reading attainment could at least in part be explained.

OUR OWN RESEARCH APPROACH

No researcher is free of prejudice or unexamined assumptions; these influence both one's choice of questions to study and one's method of tackling them. In our case we tried to avoid seeing the issues entirely through the eyes of white researchers, by including a researcher of Afro-Caribbean origin (JB) in the team, and by inviting a group of black educationalists to advise us. This group met regularly about three times a year to discuss and comment on our findings. Whilst they can in no sense be held responsible for what we have done or written, we undoubtedly learnt a lot from our discussions with them.

Given our aim of attempting to understand more about the origin of differences in the educational achievement of children of Afro-Caribbean origin and white children, and of boys and girls, in the context of understanding the factors that affect the school progress of all children, we chose a research design that differs from those of previous studies in a number of important ways.

Firstly, we decided to use a longitudinal design, that is, to follow the children throughout their infant school career. We wanted to find out whether there were ethnic and sex differences in attainment *before* children start school, and if not, at what stage, if at all, during the first three years of school these differences emerge. Almost all previous research has begun when children were aged seven or eight. But if sex and ethnic differences are not present before the children start school, this would constitute strong evidence that parental attitudes and behaviour cannot be the main cause of these differences. The choice of a longitudinal design starting before school entry had two other advantages. Assessing the extent of children's "3R" knowledge before school entry would tell us whether it makes any difference to their later attainment if parents teach their children to read and write at this early stage. And pre-school testing was an essential step in assessing progress during the early years of schooling.

Secondly, once the children had started at school, we decided to compare the strength of home and school influences on progress by studying both these sets of influences at the same points in time. Previous studies had looked at the effect of either home or school factors. In the case of black children, almost all studies have been concerned with home factors only, whilst studies of sex differences in achievement have mainly concentrated on the school.

Thirdly, we decided to control for social disadvantage more effectively than previous studies by selecting children of Afro-Caribbean origin and white children of U.K. origin from the same schools. As discussed earlier, almost all previous studies have either ignored this issue, or tackled it statistically, by equating children on a range of social disadvantage variables. This leaves open the question of whether important factors—for example, to do with the area in which the children are living, or the schools they attend—have been omitted. We hoped to overcome this problem by selecting approximately equal numbers of children of Afro-Caribbean origin and white U.K. children, and girls and boys, from each school in the study, thus ensuring that the black children did not attend "worse" schools and, by implication, live in "worse" areas than the white children.

Fourthly, we decided to study not only the relationship between ethnic group and sex and school attainment, but also the interaction between these variables. Ethnic group, social class and sex are major status groups within our society. But each individual is a member not just of one group, but of all three. A child is not just a girl, but also, say, of Afro-Caribbean origin, and middle-class. Her outlook and experiences may be very different in many respects from those of a working-class boy of Afro-Caribbean origin, even though similar in other ways—notably, both are exposed to the racism in British society. But, as discussed earlier, most educational research has looked at children in terms of only one status group, with an inevitable oversimplification of the issues. In this study we were unable to include social class in our analysis because we had few middle-class, particularly black middle-class, children in the sample. But we were able to compare the progress of four ethnic-sex groups from the same schools—black boys, black girls, white boys and white girls. We hoped, therefore, to be able to discover whether membership of a particular ethnic group has different implications for attainment, and for the way in which parents and teachers behave, for girls and boys.

Finally, we decided to interview the children themselves, a source of information not often used by earlier researchers. We thought it important to get the children's own views on their academic success, and on other aspects of their infant school experience, including the extent to which they articulated experiences of discrimination.

In the next chapter, we will explain our research design in more detail.

2 Our Research

INTRODUCTION

As we explained in the previous chapter, our aim was to study the influences on children's educational attainment and progress during their early school careers. We looked at four groups of influences. The first group consists of background factors about the children and their families. These are either fixed at birth, such as ethnic group and sex, or can be considered fixed for the period of the research, such as the educational qualifications obtained by the mother, and family income. The most important factors in this group were ethnic group and sex, both separately and in combination. The second group consists of "home" process variables concerned with educational practices which vary over time, such as the amount of "teaching" parents do at home, and the contact they have with the school. The third group are the school and teacher variables, such as teacher expectations, and the curriculum experienced by each child. And the fourth group are variables which describe the children themselves, such as how they feel about their achievements at school.

Putting this another way, infant school children of a particular age vary in, say, their reading ability. The reasons for this are complex; certainly one could not accept that variation in reading ability merely reflects variation in general, or innate, intellectual ability. Material circumstances at home, educational practices at home, teacher behaviours at school, educational resources within the school, and so on, are all likely to affect reading ability, albeit in ways which are difficult to understand fully. Nevertheless, it is possible to construct, and work with, a model in the way we have just described, which helps us to organise our ideas and to improve our understanding of the reasons for variation in educational attainment and progress.

OUR RESEARCH DESIGN

At the end of the first chapter, we outlined the main features of the design of our study which, when taken together, make it rather unusual in educational research. First, the design was longitudinal, which means that we collected data from the same children and families over time. Moreover, we collected data on the children's attainment *before* they started their compulsory schooling. Second, we collected data from a number of sources—from our sample children, their parents, their teachers, and their headteachers. Third, we chose black and white boys and girls from the same schools. (By black we mean black British children of Afro-Caribbean origin, by white we mean children of white parents born in the U.K. A small proportion of the black children had one white parent. Further details of the parents' place of birth are given in Chapter 5.) Fourth, the sample of schools was reasonably large when compared with much educational research. Here, we present the design in more detail.

To answer our two main research questions it was crucial to secure and test a sample of children before they entered their first, or reception, year at infant school. Hence we selected children from infant schools with attached nursery classes, for otherwise it would have been difficult to have tested children before they started school. To be included in our sample, schools also had to have at least one representative from each of our four ethnic group-sex combinations going from nursery to reception in September 1982. We did this to try to eliminate the possibility that any ethnic group differences that we might find would be due to black children attending possibly poorer schools in disadvantaged areas, while the white children attended possibly better schools in wealthier areas. A major reason for our choosing schools in inner London, coming under the overall direction of the Inner London Education Authority (I.L.E.A.), was that it gave us a larger pool of such schools to choose from than other, smaller, local education authorities would have done. We restricted our choice of schools to six out of the ten divisions of I.L.E.A. in order to cut down on travelling time for our research team.

We aimed to have 30 schools in our sample, and 3 reserves in case schools chose to leave the study (in fact, none did). We took all the schools from five divisions which fitted our criteria, together with a small number from the sixth division. Only one school refused to participate in the study, but a few others were excluded because they were involved in other research, or were in the middle of major staff changes. We describe the schools in more detail in Chapter 3.

In addition to testing the children in reading, writing, and maths, we collected information from the teachers about the children. This included their academic expectations for the children, their judgements about whether they were a pleasure to teach, whether they had behaviour problems, and whether they were underachieving, as well as information on the range and depth of curriculum coverage in reading, writing, and maths. The classroom teachers and headteachers were also interviewed about their views and practices on parental involvement, multicultural education and anti-racism. The number of teachers involved each year varied; 43 in reception, 65 in middle infants, and 47 in top infants. We also observed in the classroom, using both continuous observations of children's curriculum experiences over one whole day, and time-sampling observations of children's behaviour throughout the day. Finally, the children themselves were interviewed at the end of the top-infant year.

Tested Sample

In the summer of 1982, we tested all the children in each of the 33 schools, who were going from a nursery class into a reception class in the following September, at the beginning of the autumn term. Altogether, we individually tested 343 children then, of whom 171 were white and 106 were black. On average, we tested about 10 children in each school; the minimum was 6 and the maximum was 19. At the end of the reception year (summer 1983), we tested all the children in the project schools who had started the previous September, regardless of whether or not they had been in the nursery class. We also tested those children who had moved to another school in greater London if they had been tested in the nursery class, and if their parents were in the interviewed sample (see following). The same criteria were used for determining the tested samples at the end of middle and top infants in the summers of 1984 and 1985. (Details of the tests we used can be found in Chapter 6.)

Table 2.1 shows how many black and white children were tested at each occasion, and how many were tested on more than one occasion. The first four columns of Table 2.1 give the sample sizes at each occasion testing took place—these are cross-sectional samples. The last three columns show how many of the children who were tested in the nursery were tested again on subsequent occasions—these are longitudinal samples. The numbers in the longitudinal samples decline because some children moved out of London, and also because some children went up into the junior school (and thus were not tested) before completing a full 3 years in infant school; 76% of the black sample and 70% of the white sample were tested on all 4

TABLE 2.1
Numbers of Children Tested Each Year

				Year			
Ethnic Group	1982	1983	1984	1985	1982-1983	1982-1984	1982-1985
Black	106	137	129	111	95	92	82
White	171	234	226	183	152	144	123
% in Original Schools	100	95	91	88	93	86	83

occasions. The final row of Table 2.1 shows the proportion of children tested in their original schools at each occasion; one in six of the children who were tested four times were not always tested in their original school. Further discussion of sample loss can be found in Appendix 5.

Interviewed Sample

Not only did we collect data from the children, but we also interviewed their parents. We did not, however, interview all parents of children tested in the nursery class. We only interviewed parents of black and white children, and also only those who were in our observed sample, and those who were reserves for the observed sample (see below). Thus, the interviewed sample in 1982 had 88 black families and 114 white families. (Ten of the black children had one white parent, in nine cases a white mother. We included these children in the sample, because they are usually seen as black by society.) A maximum of eight families were interviewed from each school.

Table 2.2 shows how the composition of the interviewed sample changed over time. As with the tested sample, families who moved within greater

TABLE 2.2
Numbers of Parents Interviewed Each Year

			Year		
Ethnic Group	1982	1983	1984	1985	1982-1985
Black	88	83	82	68	67
White	114	111	106	91	88

London were followed up, but not those who moved out of London. Parents of children who moved into the junior school before the summer of 1985 were not re-interviewed, and this explains why the sample was smaller in 1985. About three-quarters of the original sample were interviewed on all four occasions. Only 2 out of the target sample of 204 were not interviewed in 1982, because they were persistently out when we visited. There were no refusals then, and subsequent sample loss was almost entirely due to families moving away.

All interviews took place in the children's homes in the summer holidays, usually with the child's mother. The interview schedule contained between 50 and 90 "open" questions each year, and respondents' answers were recorded verbatim and later coded. Some questions were retained from year to year, but others were changed to allow for changing circumstances as children got older. The black parents were interviewed by the same two black women interviewers throughout, the white parents by white women interviewers, six of whom were used during the four years, and one of whom interviewed each year.

Observed Sample

We decided it was important to observe children in their classrooms, but we could not observe all the children we tested because systematic observation is extremely time-consuming. One white boy, one white girl, one black boy, and one black girl who had attended the nursery class were selected for observation in each school (although in many schools there was in fact no choice, and in three schools black or white children moved after being tested but before observation was due to start, and these schools were excluded from the observations). Within sex, an attempt was made to match children on their test scores at the end of nursery school. We also had reserve children within each of the schools who could replace children who moved. Observations were made each year, as shown in Table 2.3. Children who moved out of project schools were not subsequently observed.

It will be clear from this description of our research design that we did not work with a random, or probability, sample of I.L.E.A. schools, and so not with random samples of I.L.E.A. infant school children and their families. Instead, we quite deliberately selected schools with both black and white children going up from nursery class to reception in 1982. Having selected our schools in this way, and having made decisions about how many children we could observe, and because we wanted to link data from different sources on the same children, the composition of the interviewed sample was decided for us. But these choices certainly limit the generalisability, or external validity, of our findings. Our results refer to

TABLE 2.3
Numbers of Children Observed

	1982–83	1983–84	1984–85	Observed all three years
Schools	30	30	27	25
White Boys	28	28	28	16
White Girls	31	29	23	18
Black Boys	29	26	25	20
Black Girls	29	25	22	18
All Children	117	108	98	72

children who attended multi-ethnic nursery classes and infant schools in inner London, and to white and black families of those children. And our interviewed sample contains more black families than would be found in simple random samples of inner-city black and white families. Whether the same pattern of results would be found for schools in other inner-city areas or, indeed, for schools in suburban or rural areas, is something we do not know. But we do not think the restriction of most of our findings to children who were in a nursery class is too severe, given that 63% of I.L.E.A. children at that time attended nursery schools and classes.

Most decisions in research design are taken after weighing the advantages and disadvantages of different approaches. We believe that our sampling scheme gave us the opportunity of more complete answers to our two main questions than the more generalisable alternatives. Equally, we think that the depth of our study, with its many layers of data, more than compensates for the relatively small sample size of children and parents which was all our resources permitted.

There was one area of investigation which we were not, however, able to pursue as far as we would have liked. Although our research took place in 33 I.L.E.A. infant schools, we could not look in detail at differences between schools, or at differences between teachers within schools. If we had set out to do so, we would have needed information about the families of *all* the children in the classes we studied, or on a random sample of each class, in order to control for such factors as social class. But we only had this information on the "interviewed" sample, and in addition, our tested sample was not random, but made up only of the first term's intake. These limitations followed from our decision to select a small number of children in a relatively large number of schools. Having made our decision, we did not collect the kind of information about the schools that would have been necessary to explain school differences. Important as the subject of school and teacher differences at the infant-school level undoubtedly is, our study was simply not set up to study them.

Nearly all the results in this book refer to children's learning experiences in the "3Rs". We focused on what we freely admit is only a partial picture of children's education at these ages, although a very important part. We did this partly because of limited resources, and partly because the concerns of many in the black community are particularly related to their children's progress in these basic subjects. Infant schools have much wider aims than just teaching reading, writing, and maths. Their concerns with their pupils' motivation to learn, love of books, their physical, aesthetic, social, and moral development are important ones. We were not, however, able to include them in our research.

ATTAINMENT AND PROGRESS

Earlier in this chapter, we explained that our research was concerned with the factors and variables associated with educational attainment and progress. The distinction between attainment and progress is an important one, and so we give some space here to describing the differences between these two concepts. A more formal, statistical, definition of progress is given in Appendix 3.

When we talk about attainment in, say, maths, we mean the child's knowledge and understanding of maths as measured by a particular maths test at a *particular point in time*. Attainment is thus a cross-sectional concept. Progress really means change in attainment. And so, when we talk about progress, we mean change over a *specified period of time* rather than attainment at one point in time. Progress is a longitudinal concept. Of course, all children make progress in maths during infant school, because they leave knowing much more maths than when they started, and they learn more maths because they have been at school. However, we are interested in why some children make more progress than others, which we think of as *relative* progress. For example, do boys make relatively more progress in maths than girls? Unfortunately, educational progress is not as easy to measure as physical growth—there is no one educational tape measure, rather a variety of tape measures, some of which are suitable for five-year-olds, some for seven-year-olds, and so on. So we define relative progress as follows: We look at differences in attainments at, say, the end of infants for those children who had the same score on the test at the end of nursery. We use a statistical technique, known as regression analysis, to do this, and it is by use of this technique that we define progress for the infant school period, or for any one school year. We then look at relationships between, say, ethnic group and sex and this measure of progress. Many children doing well at the end of infant school had been doing well at the end of nursery. But there are also children who, at the end of top infants, are doing better than would have been predicted by their attainment at the end of nursery, and others who are doing worse than expected. We wanted to find out why this was, that is, what parents and teachers were doing which helped, or failed to help, children of similar initial attainment. From an educational point of view, we believe that progress is a more useful concept than attainment. Because of this interest in progress, it was crucial to get measures of children's attainments before they started school.

3 The Project Schools: Approaches to Teaching and to Parents

In this chapter, we give a brief description of the project schools, and their staff, the organisation of the schools, their approach to teaching reading, writing and maths, and their policies towards involving parents in the education of their children.

NURSERY EDUCATION

All the children in our sample had attended a nursery class. In this they were not unusual for London children. At the time of our study, 63% of 3- and 4-year-olds within the I.L.E.A. were attending nursery schools or classes, the great majority either in the morning or the afternoon only.

The emphasis in English nursery education has traditionally been on learning through play and direct experience. The aim of nursery educators has been to provide a stimulating environment which promotes the all-round development and motivation of the child, rather than to provide direct teaching of academic skills.

Shortly after the children had entered the infant reception classes, we interviewed the nursery teachers of the classes from which they had graduated (36 teachers in all). We asked them which skills they expected children to acquire before they moved on from the nursery, and how they tried to ensure that they did so.

Table 3.1 shows the proportion of nursery teachers in our sample who said that they expected children to have acquired specific skills by the end of nursery schooling.

TABLE 3.1

The Proportion of Nursery Teachers Who Expected Children
to Acquire Specific Skills by the End of Nursery Schooling

	% Teachers
Writing Skills	
To write own name without a model	56
To copy writing	58
Reading Skills	
To know we read print, not pictures	83
To know we read from left to right	75
To distinguish words, letters, numbers	28
To know any letter names or sounds	36
To read any words	18
Number Skills	
To rote count to no more than 5	33
To rote count to 20	6
To count 10 objects	39
To hand over 7 objects	25
To read at least 3 number symbols	64

These figures show not only that our nursery teachers differed markedly in the emphasis that they gave to the 3Rs (reading, writing, and maths), but also that, overall, their expectations in these areas were limited. In general, they felt that it was important for children to understand that print has a communicative function. However, they were unlikely to expect children to have acquired any reading skills, even at the basic level of recognising a few letters or words. Although some teachers expected children to have learned to copy writing, almost as many did not. And one third of all nursery teachers did not expect children to be able to count beyond five when they graduated from the nursery.

Nursery teachers varied in the methods they employed to encourage early 3R skills. When asked how they encouraged early writing skills, a number of teachers mentioned providing manipulative activities to encourage eye-hand co-ordination (e.g. threading, drawing, painting, cutting, etc.). Some said that they helped children, through demonstration, to hold a pencil properly. In addition, nearly half the nursery teachers mentioned giving children actual writing tasks (such as tracing over or copying under their name or other words), and some even gave handwriting exercises. A few teachers mentioned that they felt they were not supposed to do these things, and some stressed that they never forced children to take part in these activities if they didn't want to. Although teachers were divided over the use of direct writing activities, and many had low expectations concerning the actual skills children should acquire before moving to infant school, by and large writing seemed to be an accepted part of the nursery environment.

Many teachers saw a great variety of nursery activities as mathematical. Some found it hard to articulate exactly how these activities related to maths ("It's unconscious maths"). However, the following explanation of maths in the nursery, provided by one nursery teacher, was fairly typical. She described

> ... number games involving dice, so they need to count and learn to recognise the pattern; finger rhymes; stories linked with number; junk modelling for 3-dimensional understanding; the wooden zoo or village, for sorting activities; sorting trays for objects; manipulative puzzles for fitting shapes—squares, circles, etc.; circle segments which fit together, which we link to cutting up fruit;...

Other teachers mentioned activities such as cooking (for weighing and measuring) and water play (capacity), and many stressed the importance of language in the development of mathematical concepts. Although a number of teachers mentioned teaching counting, 1:1 correspondence (through practical activities such as putting straws in milk bottles), and giving children some understanding of the meaning of numbers ("If they know there's two in the family, or two sons, then they understand 'two', don't they?"), few mentioned introducing children to number symbols. No teachers spontaneously mentioned working with numbers above ten.

INFANT EDUCATION

The term "infant school" goes back at least to 1816, when Robert Owen started the New Lanark Infant School in Scotland. It was called an "infant" school because children were expected to start at the age of two, or as soon as they could walk alone, and to remain until the age of ten, when they started work. Many two-year-olds continued to attend school throughout the nineteenth century (Whitbread, 1972).

Statutory education now begins in England and Wales at five years of age, but local authorities differ in the precise age at which they allow children to enter school. For example, the I.L.E.A. currently accepts children in the term in which they will become five years old, taking in new children three times a year. In contrast, some authorities accept children only once a year, in September, taking in children who have reached the age of four.

Once children have entered infant school, they usually attend school five days a week from approximately 9.00 a.m. until about 3.30 p.m. each day. They remain at infant school until the age of seven. Since seven-year-olds are usually accepted into junior schooling at the beginning of the academic year (that is, in September), children's stay at infant school will vary from a minimum of two to a maximum of three years, depending on their term of entry into infant school.

Many reception classes would appear to an outside observer to be very similar to nursery classes. They would have many of the same play activities—water play, sand play, creative activities with paint and modelling materials, and so on. They would be likely to be laid out in a similar fashion to the nursery, with a carpeted area devoted to bookshelves and quiet reading, a dressing-up corner, display tables, and group activity or work tables, rather than individual desks. Just as in the nursery, most children would be engaged in different activities from each other, rather than all working on the same task or even the same subject area. The teacher would constantly be moving around the classroom, helping and guiding each child with their particular work, and only very rarely standing at the front of the class and teaching the group as a whole.

However, despite these similarities between nursery and infant class-rooms, there are important differences, particularly in the emphasis given to the 3Rs and in the freedom given to children to choose their own activities.

Unlike nursery teachers, infant teachers do see teaching of the 3Rs as an important part of their role. This is reflected in an obvious increase at infant school, compared with nursery schooling, in work on the 3Rs and in work on abstract tasks (e.g. written number work), and an accompanying gradual decrease in learning through direct experience (practical activities). These changes become more obvious as one moves up the infant school, and there is very little free play (e.g. sand or water play) in evidence by the time children are in their third year.

Although teachers vary in the degree to which they organise infant children's time, generally children are expected to complete certain defined tasks each day (such as writing a story, or working on a set of maths problems), and only then are they allowed to select their own activities (known in many schools as "choosing time").

One important feature of infant school education in England, which distinguishes it from many other European countries, is that there is as yet no centrally controlled curriculum, although government proposals to introduce a national curriculum are at present under discussion (Great Britain, 1987). Schools, and individual class teachers, have a great deal of control over the curriculum taught in the classroom. Moreover, the school day generally has no strict work timetable (that is, no set times for individual subjects), although set times are allocated to outside play, usually a short period during each morning and afternoon session, and a longer period at dinner time. Otherwise, timetabling usually only occurs for regular weekly events which require advance organisation (e.g. swimming at the public swimming pool; P.E. in the school hall). Some activities are organised on a whole-school basis, such as school assembly and school plays, and these occasions give children the opportunity to participate as members of the wider school group.

There is no formal "streaming" of children in English infant schools. Children are allocated to classes on the basis of age, not on the basis of ability. Children are rarely kept back to "repeat" a year. The most common forms of class organisation are horizontal grouping (each class made up of children of the same age) and vertical grouping (each class made up of a few children from each age group). Schools vary in the extent to which they follow one or other of these patterns, depending on their particular circumstances.

THE PROJECT INFANT SCHOOLS

The Children's Background

In the 1982 infant reception classes of our project schools the proportion of white children with U.K. parents varied from 17% to 84%. The proportion of children of Afro-Caribbean origin varied from 8% to 66%, and in 12 out of 33 classes, the proportion was greater than 30%. (In most of the schools there were also children from other ethnic groups, most frequently from India and Pakistan.)

The majority of the project schools were in very materially disadvantaged areas. Many of the families lived on large, poorly maintained council estates. Only a few schools were in socially mixed areas, with any significant proportion of private housing.

The proportion of children receiving free school meals varied from 14% to 78% with a mean of 44%, compared with a mean of 34% for all I.L.E.A. infant schools in 1982.

Staffing

The size of the infant schools, or departments, ranged from one school with 2 forms and only 50 pupils, to 11 schools with 6 forms and up to 156 pupils. The average pupil-teacher ratio in the schools was 16 pupils per teacher, with a range from 11 to 21. This ratio includes the head teacher and other teachers who are not class teachers, and hence does not refer to the size of the class. In the second year of the study (middle infants), the study children were in classes which ranged in size from 16 children to 29 children, with a mean of 25. The figures for the third year of the study were very similar.

The school staff were predominantly female and white. At the outset of the study, 24 of the head teachers were women, and 9 were men. The predominance of female teaching staff was similar to that found by the H.M.I. national survey of primary education (1978).

In 1980–1981, the House of Commons Home Affairs Committee urged that efforts should be made to increase the numbers of ethnic minority teachers, and the I.L.E.A. does operate an equal opportunity in employment policy. But despite the fact that most of the schools served a relatively mixed population there was no evidence that these policies had been effective. Only one of the head teachers in the project schools was of Afro-Caribbean origin, and the remainder were of white U.K. origin. Thirteen of the 33 schools had only white teachers, 7 had one teacher of Afro-Caribbean origin, and 15 had at least one south Asian teacher. There were even fewer non-teaching staff who were black. Twenty-nine of the 33 schools had no black "primary helpers" (non-teaching staff appointed to support teachers in their work, either in preparing materials or in helping with children). Twenty-seven had no black dinner supervisors.

Nearly all the class teachers who were interviewed during the study, and who actually taught the project children, were white, and nearly all were women. For example, of the 31 teachers interviewed at the beginning of the reception year, 27 were white U.K. teachers, 1 was Australian and 3 were south Asian. Only one of these teachers was male. At no time were any of the children in our sample taught by a class teacher of Afro-Caribbean origin.

Organisation and Grouping

Two-thirds of the reception classes in the study contained only reception-age children (i.e. were horizontally grouped classes), ten classes were partially vertically grouped, containing both five- and six-year-olds, and one class was vertically grouped, with children from the age of five up to seven.

Although there is no "streaming" in English infant schools, some teachers divide children into groups in the classroom, either on a permanent basis or for particular activities. At any one time, the teacher may allocate different groups of children to work in particular curriculum areas (that is, one group to work on maths, another on writing, and so on). Although one group may be set to work on maths, within that group children may be set slightly different maths tasks. Children are often allowed to choose their own seats in the classroom, so children in the same group may not necessarily sit together, unless they are working on a joint project.

At reception, we found that approximately half the teachers grouped children for teaching purposes, 55% doing so for maths teaching and 48% for language teaching. In the great majority of cases, these groups were formed on the basis of the children's judged ability levels. Slightly more teachers, 61%, used group teaching at top infants than at reception.

However, this was largely because more teachers chose to group children together on the basis of friendship, or because they could work well alongside each other, rather than because of any increase in the use of ability groups.

The Teaching of Reading, Writing and Maths

Curriculum Resources in the Project Schools

Individual primary schools and teachers in Britain can develop or select their own approach to the teaching of each of the 3Rs. Local Education Authorities may issue guidelines related to particular curriculum areas, but these are often general in nature and broad in coverage.

In order to get some idea of the resources that teachers drew on in planning the 3R curriculum, we asked the middle-infant teachers whether they followed published schemes of work, either in whole or in part, and what other materials they used in their teaching.

Reading. Published schemes for the teaching of reading are designed in such a way that, by working their way through books in sequence, children can progress from reading very simple picture books to more complex texts. Most schemes use a controlled introduction of new vocabulary, or of new letter combinations.

We found that only a very small minority of teachers (6%) taught reading by taking children through a single published reading scheme. The great majority (88%) drew reading materials from a variety of such schemes, one teacher using as many as 22 schemes in all. Some teachers used different schemes for different children, or used particular schemes for teaching the first levels of reading, and other schemes at later stages. Others used some system (often a colour-coding system) to group books of the same reading level together, including books from different schemes and non-scheme books, thus broadening the reading materials available to children at each level.

Almost all teachers supplemented whatever scheme(s) they used with materials such as worksheets or reading games, often of their own making. A few teachers specifically mentioned the use of phonic work as a supplement to reading books. Just over half the teachers (59%) said that they used the "Breakthrough to Literacy" scheme which, as well as providing a series of books, allows children to use wordcards to make up their own sentences and stories for later reading practice.

Overall, teachers were flexible in their approach to teaching reading. They seemed to be guided by the perceived needs of individual children, rather than by the necessity to adhere strictly to a set scheme of work. The result was not only that children had access to a wide variety of reading materials, but also that they could follow their own individual sequence of materials or books, at their own pace. These results on the use of reading schemes are similar to those of Bassey (1978), but show teachers choosing from a wider range of books than in the D.E.S. (Great Britain, 1982c) national survey of first schools in England.

The low reliance on single schemes in the project schools may show the influence of the strong movement in primary education towards the use of "real" books in the classroom, rather than "reading primers". Although there may be sound reasons for introducing children to as wide a range of reading material as possible, the absence of a reading scheme may be confusing, and disturbing, to some parents. A number of reception teachers said that it was unnecessary to tell parents which schemes or books they used to teach reading, as this would be obvious from the books sent home (see Chapter 5). But if children bring home a wide variety of books, parents may not understand how reading is being taught. In fact, at the end of the reception year, we found that just under half the parents we interviewed did not know what reading scheme or book was currently being used with their child, and a similar proportion were unable to give any explanation of how reading was taught at the school. Given that the amount of knowledge that parents had about the school and its teaching methods was related to children's progress (see Chapter 7), teachers might well give some thought as to why exactly they have moved away from single reading schemes, and how best to explain their change in approach to parents.

Writing.   We did not ask the teachers directly about the resources they used in the teaching of writing. For many teachers, particularly those using the "Breakthrough to Literacy" scheme or published language workbooks, the teaching of writing is inextricably linked with the teaching of reading, and draws on the same resources. Language workbooks containing puzzles and exercises are used not only to encourage children to read instructions, but also to write appropriate responses. In "Breakthrough", children are encouraged to draw on their own experiences to produce their own writing, and this writing then forms the basis of their initial reading material. Even before they can read or write, the scheme encourages children to produce sentences orally, so that their teachers can write them out for tracing, copying, and reading out loud.

Teachers use a variety of non-scheme stimuli (for example, the children's own experiences—often referred to as "news"—or work on selected topics such as "space", or "animals"), in order to elicit both descriptive and creative writing from infant children. Nowadays, teachers rarely require children to copy much writing from a blackboard.

Maths.   Published maths schemes commonly take the form of graded workbooks, worksheets, or workcards (small cards on which an activity or task will be outlined for the child). In general, a broad range of areas of maths (for example, number, area, weight, capacity, and so on) is covered at each graded level. As with reading, schemes are designed in such a way that, by working their way systematically through the materials provided, children will be taught fundamental mathematical concepts in a logical sequence. Manuals for teachers not only contain some description of the scheme, and guidance over the use of the materials provided, but also discussion of teaching points and suggestions for further related mathematical activities.

We found that nearly all the middle-infant teachers (95%) drew on some published maths schemes to guide or enrich their teaching of maths. Slightly more teachers adhered to just one scheme in maths than had done so in reading—that is, 23% of teachers. A similar proportion based their teaching mainly on one scheme, but found the need to supplement this with other materials, often of their own making. The remainder (just less than half the teachers) drew on more than one maths scheme in their teaching.

We found that teachers who used one element of a scheme (for example, teaching suggestions provided in the manual) did not necessarily use other elements (for example, children's workbooks). Many said that they used schemes as a springboard for other work, rather than as rigid programmes, and found the teaching manuals to be a useful source of inspiration. ("I feel if I run out of ideas I'll use the manual"). Just as with reading, the teachers' use of published schemes was eclectic and flexible.

In all, only eight different schemes were mentioned by teachers, and of these, three were clearly the most popular. The most commonly mentioned scheme (Nuffield Maths) was used, either on its own or in combination with other schemes, by more than three-quarters of the teachers.

The Curriculum Taught

Towards the end of each year of the study, we asked the children's class teachers to tell us which elements of the 3R curriculum they had actually taught in their classes during the year. Interviews were carried out with the help of a 3R curriculum checklist, devised specifically for this purpose. (The teachers were also asked to describe which elements of the 3R curriculum they had taught to each individual child, and the results of this section of the interview are described in Chapter 8; more details of our method can be found in Farquhar, Blatchford, Burke, Plewis, & Tizard, 1987.)

Checklist items varied in number and detail each year, to reflect the changing focus of children's work as they progressed through infant school. The mathematics items in the checklist covered work on early concepts of number; simple written numbers; number operations; measurement; recognition and handling of money; and work on shape. Written language items (that is, items concerned with reading and writing) included items on general reading skills; writing skills; and general book skills, as well as items concerned with the recognition/use of linguistic units at the within-word level, the word level, and the sentence level.

Reading and Writing. In general, the written language curriculum in the project schools moved from an early emphasis on the mechanics of reading and writing (e.g. knowledge of the components of words and of letter formation) through rules for deciphering and producing text (e.g. the use of cues in reading and of spelling conventions in writing), and on to reading for meaning and the production of longer, written texts.

In writing, children progressed from tracing over an adult's writing, to copying writing, and finally to producing their own sentences without any fixed model. (Some teachers have now begun to follow a "developmental" approach to writing, where children are encouraged to write freely and to invent their own spellings, rather than be restricted by their lack of expertise in this area, but at the time of our project this was very uncommon.)

Teachers differed quite considerably in the reading and writing tasks that they gave to children. In three-quarters of the reception classes, teachers had introduced non-repetitive reading books (that is, books which were based on more than simple repetition of a standard sentence, such as "This is a ...") of at least four sentences in length, but books of this nature were not introduced by some teachers until top infants. In writing, a third of the reception teachers had encouraged children to write at least one sentence on their own without copying from a model of some kind (usually the teacher's own writing), but in at least one top-infant class children had not been encouraged to produce as much as three consecutive sentences of writing.

Maths. The pattern that emerged from the yearly checklists for maths was one of movement through the number system from simple manipulation of written numbers at the beginning of infant school to the more complex number operations of multiplication and division by the end of top infants. The results also reflected a movement from almost purely practical work at the early stages, towards an increased focus on formal recording of mathematical operations on paper.

Although it is possible to detect general trends across the project schools as a whole, the results again indicated marked differences between teachers in the items taught. For example, written subtraction had already been introduced during the first year of infant school in one tenth of the reception classes—but there were two teachers who had not yet introduced work in this area, even at top infants. Indeed, there was one top-infant class where written addition work had not yet been introduced. Similarly, with respect to money, there were some classes where children were already being introduced to the concept of "giving change" during their first year at school, whilst there were others where this opportunity did not arise even in the third year. Again, only one third of top-infant teachers had introduced their classes to written division—and yet there was one top-infant class where children were working on complex vertical format division sums with remainders. About a third of top-infant teachers taught multiplication "tables".

These findings show marked differences in the 3R curriculum items taught by different teachers, both in written language (reading and writing) and in maths. Bennett, Desforges, Cockburn, and Wilkinson (1984), and the H.M.I. primary school survey (1978) report similar findings. Debate over the advantages and disadvantages of curriculum diversity, both between and within schools, is not new (see, for example, the selection of writings in Richards, 1985). The issue has taken on greater prominence in the light of current moves towards the introduction of a central core curriculum in Britain (Great Britain, 1987). The debate has hinged on the extent to which teachers, L.E.A.s, or central government should make decisions on curriculum aims and content. There is a conflict between the desire of teachers to preserve their autonomy in the classroom, and the concern of politicians (and of parents) to ensure that some consistency of aims and of coverage is achieved.

As to why teachers taught different curricula, we found that some reception teachers in the project schools believed that certain 3R curriculum items were too difficult for their children, whereas other teachers did not. But there was no difference between the schools in the range of ability of the children entering these classes. These results suggest that the role of teacher expectations in curriculum decision making may be an important one (for a fuller discussion of this point, see Chapter 8). If there is a concern to give equal opportunities to all children, then a clearer understanding of how teachers make curriculum decisions is needed, in order to ensure that their expectations are sufficiently high to prevent children being held back unnecessarily.

Policies on Parental Involvement, Multicultural Education, and Anti-racism

The Plowden Report (1967) advocated greater involvement of parents in their children's education, and subsequent research (eg. Tizard, Schofield, & Hewison, 1982) has suggested that the direct involvement of parents in their children's learning can have a positive influence on children's progress. At the time that we were working in the schools, the I.L.E.A., along with many other authorities, was encouraging greater collaboration between parents and teachers through a variety of projects.

Between the mid-sixties and the mid-seventies, a number of L.E.A.s responded to criticism about the relative failure of black children in their schools by developing policies on "multicultural education". Multicultural education was an attempt to enhance the educational achievements of ethnic minority children by the provision of "positive images" and a more appropriate curriculum. At the same time, it was hoped that all children would learn tolerance and respect towards different cultures through the introduction of elements of these cultures into the schools.

In 1977, the I.L.E.A. produced a policy statement which gave official recognition for the first time to multicultural education. There is no doubt that multicultural education has been interpreted in many different ways. It may be merely a token display of black faces in textbooks, or it may be a celebration of many diverse cultures, or it may be seen as requiring teachers to shape their curriculum so that it reflects the different experiences of their pupils and their different perspectives on the world. However, some black theorists have argued that multicultural education assumes that underachievement is caused by a low black self-image or cultural differences, and that what is required instead is to change the institutionalisation of racism (see Stone, 1981; Troyna & Williams, 1986). According to Carter (1986): "multiculturalism without anti-racism simply tinkered around the edges".

Following riots in the inner cities in the early 1980s, the subsequent enquiry into these disturbances by Lord Scarman (Scarman, 1981), and the report of the Parliamentary Committee on Race Relations in the same year, a number of L.E.A.s produced policy documents which were specifically anti-racist. In 1983, the I.L.E.A. produced five documents, entitled "Race, sex, and class". One of these documents, "Multiethnic Education in Schools" (I.L.E.A., 1983), picked out "anti-racist teaching" as the first of four priorities (the others being increased black representation, the development of bilingual teaching, and further strategies for overcoming underachievement). At the same time, the I.L.E.A.'s perspective on equality stated that: "It is necessary to remove those practices and procedures which discriminate against black pupils/students and their families.

These include courses, syllabuses, schemes of work, topics, textbooks, materials and methods which ignore or deny the validity of black experience, perspective and culture." A second document, entitled "Anti-racist statement and guidelines" (I.L.E.A., 1983), outlined the elements which the I.L.E.A. believed should be found in every school's written policy on anti-racism, and stated that these should include not only methods for dealing with specific racist incidents, but also a statement of practices in the school which would help to foster a cohesive and diverse school community. These documents represented an attempt to "confront and dismantle all forms of racism" and to tackle issues at a more fundamental level than through the simple introduction of a multicultural curriculum.

Given our concern in this study with the role of parents in children's attainment and progress, and with the attainment of black and white children, we were interested in the schools' policies on parental involvement, and in the extent to which the initiatives launched by the I.L.E.A. concerning multicultural education and anti-racism were reflected in the schools themselves. We interviewed the head teachers in 1982, just prior to the launch of the I.L.E.A. equal opportunities policy, and in 1985 we looked at the response of class teachers to the I.L.E.A. initiatives on multicultural education and anti-racism through interviews with the top infant teachers.

Parental Involvement

The 33 head teachers described a number of ways in which they created opportunities for informal social contact with parents. All but one of the schools invited parents to school plays, and all but three held fetes or fairs in collaboration with parents. Two-thirds of the schools provided other social events, such as coffee mornings or discos. Just over a third of the schools provided a parents' room, and just under a third had a parent-teacher association. None of the schools had a general policy of visiting the parents in their own homes.

The schools also made opportunities for contact with parents about the curriculum and about teaching methods. Three-quarters of the heads said that they held parents' evenings on academic topics (for example, to explain the maths curriculum to parents). Two-thirds said that they had some parental help in some of the classrooms, and a similar number invited parents into school to watch school assemblies. However, only six schools said that they ever invited parents in to watch occasional lessons.

All the heads made some positive comments about the benefits of parental involvement, some stressing benefits to the child or the parents, and others stressing benefits for the teachers or the schools. When asked about possible disadvantages, eight of the heads said that there were none, and nine said that any problems that involvement might arouse could be overcome. Sixteen heads felt that there were definite problems associated with parental involvement, mainly concerned with parents helping in schools, the most frequently mentioned anxieties being that children "play up" when their parents are present in school, and parents "tend to interfere" or "want to take over".

By assigning schools one point for each of 20 different forms of, or attitudes towards, parental contact that we inquired about, we found that the "top" school received a score of 15, and the lowest a score of 3. The latter school saw only problems in parent involvement, and its only contacts with parents were in showing new parents round the school, inviting them to the school play, and organising a jumble sale with them. In contrast, the top school invited parents into school on a wide variety of occasions, including watching lessons and helping with academic work in the classrooms. They provided a room for parents within the school and saw the involvement of parents as a definite asset.

Parental involvement in education is discussed in greater detail in Chapter 5, and we will only comment briefly here on the schools' policies in this area. A national survey of primary schools carried out just before our study began (Clift, 1981) suggested that schools had "progressed cautiously towards a greater involvement of parents over the decade since Plowden". As in our study, the survey found that most schools invited parents to talk to teachers, and provided open days, but few sent written information concerning children's work home to parents, particularly at the infant level. The D.E.S. survey of first schools (schools for children from five to nine years of age) (Great Britain, 1982c) reported similar findings.

Despite this general increase in parental involvement, some of the project schools were clearly less committed to such involvement than others. Clift (1981) found that involvement was greater for schools in less disadvantaged areas. But our study shows that schools serving comparable areas in terms of social class differed in the extent to which they encouraged the involvement of parents. At the same time, there was no evidence that schools with higher proportions of either black or white children had different parental involvement practices.

Thus the overall policies of schools towards parents were apparently not influenced by the populations they served, in terms of either social class or ethnic group. But some of our findings do suggest that teachers did interact differently with parents of black and white children. Although we found no evidence that black parents made less contact with school than white parents, fewer black than white parents had been given feedback by teachers about how their child was progressing at school relative to other children, and in Chapter 5 we describe how three-quarters of the reception teachers had negative comments to make about black parents.

Communication can either be encouraged or discouraged by the context in which it takes place. Some of the activities that the schools provided, such as open evenings, may have been less attractive, or even intimidating, to parents of different cultures, particularly if these parents were aware of some of the teachers' negative attitudes towards them. Teachers need to take a critical look at their attitudes and their practices if parental involvement policies are to lead to real communication with all parents. At the same time, an increase in the numbers of ethnic minority teachers in infant schools might foster greater understanding between home and school.

Multicultural Education

Nearly half of the heads had been on in-service training courses on multicultural education, and the proportion of class teachers who had done so was slightly higher. In one school all the class teachers, and in 17 schools some of the class teachers, had attended courses. In addition, school-based multicultural or anti-racism courses had been held in 4 schools.

Despite a relatively high attendance on courses, many head teachers in the project schools had yet to be convinced that a policy on multicultural education was important or necessary. Ten of the 33 heads said that they had a definite policy on multicultural education, which they had discussed with their staff, and in 3 cases this was a written policy. A further 5 heads said that they were currently considering whether to have a policy in this area. But 9 heads said that they definitely did not have a policy, whilst the remaining 8 said that they had no policy as such, but that the issues were discussed with the staff. In no school had the issues involved in multicultural education been discussed with the parents.

Fourteen of the 33 head teachers (those who had no policy, and some of those who were currently considering one) were opposed to the idea of multicultural education. Of these, 5 heads said that all children should be treated as individuals; 6 said that they tried to treat all the children the same; one didn't want to be "pushed around" (by the Authority); one said that all the children had been born here and were British; whilst one felt that all London children had similar interests, and the minority communities were the best people to preserve their own culture.

Despite these views, we found evidence that many schools were endeavouring to teach a more multicultural curriculum than previously, as witnessed by their efforts to obtain multicultural materials, to promote positive images of children of different colours and ethnic backgrounds in the schools, and to celebrate festivals from different faiths and cultures. At least some of these changes were being introduced in schools where the head voiced some opposition to "multicultural education". Twenty-four of the 33 heads (again including some who voiced some opposition to multicultural education) said that they thought that it was important, or very important, for children of different colours to have positive images in the school to identify with. Of the 33 heads, 32 not only felt multicultural books and pictures were important, but had specifically ordered as many books as possible which reflected the multicultural nature of society, and which presented black people in positive roles. Twenty-seven heads felt there was a multicultural input into their music. A similar number provided black dolls as part of their policy. Twenty-two schools celebrated various different festivals, such as Diwali and Eid and Chinese New Year, as well as the Jewish and Christian festivals.

At the end of the reception year we sought the parents' views about multicultural education. We asked: "I expect you know that there are children from different backgrounds in the schools, including Caribbean, Asian and Irish. Do you think that their stories, songs and history, for example, should be taught at school?" Many more black than white parents—82% compared with 44%—answered "Yes" without any qualification. But only 17% of white mothers and 2% of black mothers definitely opposed the idea.

We asked how many heads knew about, or had contact with, any of the Saturday or supplementary schools run by the Caribbean and other minority communities. Any contact that existed could, we felt, be taken as indicative of the heads' willingness to acknowledge and respect the children's educational experiences outside school. Twenty-five of the heads knew that some of their children attended these schools, but the rest were uncertain. In spite of such knowledge, only five heads had been in contact with these schools. Contact varied from the head being invited to an opening ceremony, or a head of a supplementary school wanting to discuss the school's maths methods, to one school head who said: "They did my notices for the video film and we always invite them to what's going on."

We assigned a "multicultural" score to each school, by awarding a point for the presence of each different form of multicultural practice that we had inquired about. Out of a possible score of 16, one school scored 15, whilst one school scored only one (for the provision of multicultural books). The "top" school displayed a wide variety of multicultural materials and practices (evident in their choice of books, dolls, topics for discussion at assembly, provision of alternative meals, etc.), and promoted and valued positive images of minority cultures in the school.

The Relationship Between Parental Involvement and Multicultural Practices in the Schools

There was no overall tendency for schools with a wide range of parental involvement practices to display a wide range of multicultural practices, or vice versa (rank correlation = 0.01).

Anti-racism

There is a strong belief within the black community, endorsed by the Swann Committee, that racism is one of the major underlying causes of the underachievement of ethnic minority children in our schools. However, in 1982 (prior to the I.L.E.A.'s official anti-racist statement), only eight project schools had formulated an anti-racist policy. These policies had focused on ways of dealing with the more obvious features of racism, such as name calling, but had not attempted to tackle institutional racism (for example, by employing more black staff). In all schools that had a policy, the heads had discussed this policy with the staff, but not with the parents, and no school had a written policy.

The I.L.E.A. policy on anti-racism subsequently resulted in a number of booklets and courses for teachers. In the summer of 1985, two years after the official adoption of the I.L.E.A. equal opportunities policy and anti-racist statement, we asked the top-infant teachers if they had found this support helpful in any way. Of 32 class teachers, 23 (72%) said they had found it helpful, particularly as it had made them more aware of the issues involved, through discussion as well as action. Thirteen teachers specifically mentioned books and teaching resources as being most helpful. A few teachers, although generally positive, were concerned about the "insensitive" way the initiative was introduced—as though all teachers were racist. They also thought that although the initiative had been designed to encourage teachers to tackle the issue of racism in schools, it had resulted in some teachers no longer having any confidence in their own expertise.

There were nine teachers who had not found the initiative helpful. One did not know what it was; two felt that the children were the same and should be treated as such; three that it was creating more problems; and two felt that not only had they not been helped, but that things had been made more political and therefore difficult to deal with.

Prior to the I.L.E.A. initiative, in 1982, we asked reception teachers whether they felt that black children were likely to meet with any discrimination from teachers at school, and just over half stated that this would definitely not happen. Some teachers (16%) agreed that cases of overt discrimination might occur, but fewer (13%) mentioned the possibility of unconscious discrimination. The majority of teachers were clearly reluctant to see that teachers might discriminate, either consciously or unconsciously, against children. But until teachers are able at least to admit to the possibility of racism in schools, current practices will remain unchallenged. The negative response of some class teachers to the I.L.E.A.'s initiative on anti-racism highlights the difficulties involved in changing attitudes and practices in schools. Where teachers feel that their views and expertise are being undervalued, and that change is being imposed from above, they may use their resentment as an excuse to avoid looking at their own

attitudes and positions, and may become more, rather than less, resistant
to change.

SUMMARY

Many of the project schools were in materially disadvantaged areas of
inner London, and served a relatively poor population. More than a third
of the schools took at least 30% of their intake from the Afro-Caribbean
community, but none of our children were taught by an Afro-Caribbean
class teacher, and there was only one Afro-Caribbean head teacher.

The nursery teachers differed in the degree to which they taught any
reading, writing, and maths skills, but in general had limited expectations
for children in these areas. In the infant school, teachers differed markedly
in the 3R curriculum items that they chose to cover each year. In general
infant teachers were eclectic in their approach to 3R teaching, drawing on a
wide variety of schemes and materials.

The schools differed markedly in their attitudes towards parental
involvement, the introduction of a multicultural curriculum, and anti-
racism. Most schools provided a variety of opportunities for parents to
come into schools, but these were rarely backed up with communication to
parents who were unable to attend. Although some head teachers were not
in favour of a multicultural curriculum, nearly all the schools had made
efforts to provide some multicultural books and materials. But in 1982 few
schools had yet attempted to tackle the issue of racism.

4 The Project Schools: Observation of the Children

In this chapter we describe the results of systematic observations in the project schools. In the course of the project, we carried out two different types of observation, one describing how the children spent their school day (that is, the proportion of time spent in different activities), and one describing the children's classroom behaviour.

THE TOP-INFANT SCHOOL DAY

Observations were made of 90 top-infant children (48 boys and 42 girls). The observed group of children consisted of our core sample of four children per school (ideally one boy and one girl whose parents were of white U.K. origin, and one boy and one girl whose parents were of Afro-Caribbean origin). In cases where core children had left the study schools, these children were replaced, where possible, with children from our reserve pool in the same schools. (Full details of the sample are given in Chapter 2.) Observations were only carried out in schools with at least 3 core or reserve children remaining by the third year of the study, that is, 26 schools in all. Teachers knew the research was concerned with the September entrants but were not informed that particular children had been chosen for observation.

Observations were carried out in the spring term of 1985, when all the study children were in their eighth term of infant school. The observations therefore provide a picture of what school life was like for these children towards the end of their infant schooling.

Each class was observed by one of three observers for one full day. Continuous observations were made throughout the day (with the exception of playtimes). The observer scanned all the target children in the class, noting the activities they were engaged in, and the time at which they changed from one activity to another. Although the observation is described as "continuous", from the observer's point of view recording took place in concentrated bursts. These bursts occurred when children were engaged in frequent changes of activity, and they were interspersed with quieter periods when relatively little, or no, recording was necessary. These quieter periods arose because certain periods of the day at infant school are devoted to class activities (e.g. school assembly, P.E.,"story time", and so on).

Observations were carried out on days selected by the class teacher as being both predominantly classroom based (i.e. preferably not days when the children went on outings, or swimming), and days on which children were likely to be observed in at least some reading, writing, or maths. This procedure was followed in order not to underestimate the proportion of time devoted to the 3Rs. (However, this selection procedure may have led to an overestimate of class-based time.)

Observations commenced for each child from the moment they arrived at school at the beginning of the day, and continued until the children were dismissed by the class teacher at the end of the day. Observations focused on the nature of all activities or tasks that the child engaged in (except fleeting activities of less than 15secs duration), and on the setting up and rounding off of these activities. Children's activities were recorded in as much detail as possible, so that they could be accurately categorised (for example, as maths work in the area of number) at a later date.

Time Spent in Different Activities

The proportion of time that children were observed to spend in each major activity is given in Table 4.1. Proportions are given for the whole school day, and also for the proportion of all working time spent in the classroom. By "working time" we mean those times in the classroom when the child was expected to be engaged in some purposeful, learning activity, either of their own or of the teacher's choosing, and not those times in the classroom which were devoted to administrative or organisational matters (e.g. tidying up, answering the register, drinking milk, and so on). Of course, as can be seen from Table 4.1, working time in the classroom did not amount to children's total working time, as a number of learning activities took place outside the classroom.

At top infants, somewhat less than half the school day (46%) was devoted to learning activities in the classroom. The rest of the children's

TABLE 4.1
The Proportion of Time Children Were Observed in Different
Activities (Continuous Observations of 90 Children)

	% Working Time in Class	% School Day
Working Time in Class		
Art/craft/construction, etc.	21	10
Writing	20	9
Maths	17	8
Oral language	23	10
Reading	4	2
Being allocated activities	4	2
Permitted "free" play	3	1
Not assigned/wandering/other	4	2
Procedure (e.g. fetching books)	2	1
Uncodeable	2	1
Total	100	46
Other Time		
Work Activities		
Music/PE/Rehearsals etc.		4
Assembly		3
TV/Tape recorders		1
Other school work, out of class		2
Total		11
Non-work activities		
Outside play/dinner time		28
Lining up/tidying up, etc.		5
Toilet visits, etc.		4
Register/dinner money/milk, etc.		3
Uncodeable		3
Total		43

day was spent largely in non-work activities. That is, almost half the school day (43%) was taken up by dinner time, school breaks, lining up, tidying up, register time, and so on. The most common learning activities which were not classroom based were physical exercise, music, and assembly.

In his earlier study of primary teachers, Bassey (1978) relied on Nottinghamshire teachers' estimates of how time was spent, and found that, of an estimated 25-hour week, children typically were thought to spend just over half their time in "activity time" in class and a somewhat lower 18% in play time and "administration". The discrepancy between this study and ours in the amount of time spent in play time appears to be due to the apparent failure of the Nottinghamshire study to take account of dinner-time play. Parents might be surprised to learn that children spend a quarter of their time at dinner and in the playground. Perhaps alternative methods of organising the division between "work" and outside "play" need to be examined, not only in order to maximise learning time, but also because play time is sometimes a disturbing experience for children (see Chapter 9).

Classroom Working Time Devoted to the 3Rs

Overall, 64% of classroom working time was spent in 3R activities. Table 4.1 shows that children spent 17% of classroom working time in maths, 20% in writing, and 27% in language activities, such as reading, discussion and story times. Only a small proportion of time (4%) was spent in reading. (These figures are almost identical to estimates obtained through our time-sampling observation techniques [discussed later], these estimates being 67% of classroom working time in the 3Rs, 20% in maths, 20% in writing, and 27% in other language activities.)

Evidence from other studies has focused on the amount of time devoted to different activities across a period of a week. Bennett, Andreae, Hegarty, and Wade (1980), using direct observation in open-plan infant classes in England, found that on average 37% of class time was spent in all language activities (47% in our study), 16% in maths, and 22% in administration and transition times.

The marked emphasis on language work in infant classrooms suggested by these findings is in contrast to the small amount of time actually devoted to reading (4% of class work time). The fact that so little time is spent in reading surprises and disturbs classroom teachers with whom we have spoken, many of whom feel that they spend a great deal of time teaching this area of the curriculum. This is not surprising, given that a class teacher who endeavoured to listen to each of 25 children read for 5 minutes during the day would spend 2 hours in this activity (or two-thirds of working time in the classroom), compared with the 5 minutes spent by any given child. (Our observations focused on the child, not the teacher.) The small amount of time devoted to reading is also in marked contrast to studies of primary teachers' aims (e.g. Ashton, 1978), which have shown that teachers place great importance on children learning to read. This suggests that the organisation of the teaching of reading may need to be re-examined, if it is to be given the emphasis that teachers believe it deserves (see Chapter 11).

The Type of Work Observed in the Areas of Maths, Reading and Writing

We describe the children's work in terms of the tasks they engaged in in the classroom. The word "task" is used here to refer to any unit of work allocated to or undertaken by a child. Unlike Bennett et al. (1984), we made no attempt to differentiate between the cognitive demands of different types of tasks. In general, tasks were defined by the teacher (e.g. "go and write a story"). Teachers tended to allocate tasks in page or work card units, rather than in numbers of problems or sentences. For this reason, where task definition was unclear (e.g. "get on with some maths"), the observer defined one page of a work book, or one side of a work card as equivalent to one task.

Maths

During our observation of top infants, we observed the target children working on a total of 164 maths tasks. Table 4.2 shows how these tasks were divided between the different mathematical areas.

Clearly, the great majority of children's maths tasks at top infants were in the area of number, usually concentrating either on underlying number concepts or on the formal operations of addition, subtraction, multiplication, or division. Other areas of maths, with the exception of time, weight, and length, were rarely observed, and no children were seen working on volume or capacity.

Reading

We observed children working on a total of 171 reading tasks. These tasks are described in Table 4.3. (Although we observed more reading tasks than either maths or writing tasks, many of these were of very brief duration.)

TABLE 4.2
Maths Tasks Observed in Top-infant Classrooms

Maths Tasks	% of Maths Tasks (n=164)
Number work	62
Time	14
Weight/length	12
Area/shape/symmetry	4
Money/shopping	4
Board games	3
Computer maths	2

TABLE 4.3
Reading Tasks Observed
in Top-infant Classrooms

Reading Tasks	% Reading Tasks (n=171)
Silent reading alone	32
Flipping through books	23
Reading to teacher (books, flashcards, etc.)	22
Reading to/with another child	10
Reading own writing to teacher	5
Reading task instructions to teacher	4
Reading games	4

More than half of the reading tasks involved a child looking at a book on her own, either actually reading the text, or simply flipping through the book and looking at the pictures. Children rarely read their own writing to the teacher.

Writing

We observed a total of 108 writing tasks, and these are described in Table 4.4.

The three most common forms of writing observed were writing related to language workcards or workbooks (that is, children responding in writing to questions set out on individual cards or in printed exercise books); descriptive writing (that is, writing to describe either a topic or a

TABLE 4.4
Writing Tasks Observed
in Top-infant Classrooms

Writing Tasks	% Writing Tasks (n=108)
Workcards/workbooks	24
Descriptive writing	23
Story writing	19
"News" writing	11
Handwriting practice	10
Greeting cards	7
Labelling pictures	3
Writing poems/plays	2

picture); and creative writing without a visual stimulus (most commonly, story writing). "News" writing (that is, writing about what children had been doing, mainly out of school) was also quite common, as was simple letter formation practice.

The Balance Between Practical and Written Work in the 3Rs

Modern primary theory places great importance on the provision of practical activities for the development of children's conceptual understanding and learning. On the other hand, assessments of children's progress are frequently based on formal paper-and-pencil tasks. We were interested to examine the relative emphasis given to these two types of activity in top-infant classrooms.

As would be expected, the balance of practical and written work was different for different areas of the curriculum.

Maths

The most common form of top-infant maths work was written work in number. Perhaps surprisingly, written number work was more often observed being carried out without, as opposed to with, practical aids such as counters, or unifix cubes.

A large proportion of maths work was based around discussion, and this was particularly true for areas of maths other than number (for example, listening to the teacher explaining how to tell the time). Only a small proportion of maths work was purely practical, or practical work followed by some form of recording, and the proportion of such work was again higher for areas of maths other than number.

Infant teachers themselves might argue that many play activities in the infant classroom are mathematical. It may be true that children are building up mathematical concepts through, for example, constructional and creative activities, even though these activities are not set up specifically as mathematics learning tasks. However, we saw very little free play of the type that teachers most often argue to be mathematical, that is, activities such as cooking, sand play, or water play (see Table 4.6).

The Cockcroft Report (1982) stated that practical work is fundamental to the development of mathematics at the primary stage, and that a broad maths curriculum is desirable. But we found a marked emphasis in our top-infant classrooms on number work, relative to other areas of the maths curriculum, and the majority of number work was written, rather than practical. Moreover, as we have pointed out, other practical activities were notably absent from these classrooms. Although the teachers' choice of activities may in some way have been influenced by the presence of an outside observer, one would expect any initial influence to have been greatly reduced by the third year of the project, when these observations took place.

The emphasis on written work that we report here is greater than that found by Bennett et al. (1984). The difference between the two sets of findings cannot be explained by the fact that the majority of teachers in our study made use of workbooks from published maths schemes. Bennett et al. (1984) reported that in four out of five maths tasks, children worked from textbooks or workcards, but that nevertheless almost half the tasks they observed required practical work of some kind. It is possible that, by asking teachers to select days for observation when children would be likely to be involved in class-based activities, we oversampled work in the 3Rs. But it is difficult to see how these selection criteria could have affected the type of work being carried out in these areas. It appears that, for some reason, teachers in our project schools found the organisation of practical work in maths either difficult or unimportant.

Writing

The writing tasks given to children vary in the extent to which they derive from, or draw on, practical activities in the classroom. The great majority of the writing that we observed at top infants was unrelated to practical work (for example, language worksheets and workbooks, or unillustrated prose writing), and these tasks were carried out without the aid of associated materials such as library books or flash cards. The most common form of writing that was related to any form of practical activity was illustrated prose writing (most commonly, drawing a picture and then writing about it).

Other Classroom Activities

Topic Work and Science

We did not detail the extent to which teachers used topic work (that is, work on different themes, such as "trees", or "our school") in their teaching. Most work on topics involved either writing, reading, or discussion, and was therefore coded under whichever of these categories was appropriate. Practical topic or science work (e.g. tasting a variety of foods for a topic on "food"; testing water absorption for different materials) was coded separately, but was rarely observed. Any such observations have been included within the category "other" in Table 4.1.

Oral language

There were 279 activities observed in the classrooms which were categorised as "oral" language activities (see Table 4.5). As can be seen, the commonest of these activities was discussion (for example, discussion about a story which had been read, or a topic being studied). Listening to stories being read by an adult, or reciting rhymes or poems, was quite a frequent activity. Direct teaching of language, either through teaching of letter sounds or of vocabulary, was less common.

Art, Craft and Construction

Of 195 constructional or creative activities, about half involved drawing, crayoning or tracing (see Table 4.6). Many other creative activities which are a feature of nursery schooling, such as painting or clay modelling, were only seen relatively infrequently at top infants. Hardly any children were seen doing puzzles.

"Free" Play

"Free" play was extremely rare at top infants (i.e. 1% of the school day, see Table 4.1). Most of the 28 activities which we observed in this category were imaginative in nature; either imaginative role play or doll play of one form or another (see Table 4.7). Sand play occurred infrequently, and water play was non-existent.

TABLE 4.5
Oral Language Work Observed
in Top-infant Classrooms

Oral Language	% Oral Language Tasks (n=279)
Discussion	38
Listening to story	20
Reciting poems, rhymes	15
Letter-sounds (I-spy, spelling games, etc.)	7
Vocabulary, points of language	7
Drama	5
News	5
Days of week, seasons, etc.	3

TABLE 4.6
Constructional/Creative Activities Observed
in Top-infant Classrooms

Constructional/Creative Activities	% Constructional/Creative Activities (n=195)
Drawing/crayoning/tracing	51
Construction sets	14
Collage/sticking/cutting out	14
Painting	7
Junk modelling/ woodwork	5
Clay/plasticine/dough	3
Puzzles	3
Sewing	2
Non-fitting blocks	1

TABLE 4.7
Free Play Activities Observed in Top-infant Classrooms

Free Play Activities	% of Free Play Activities (n=28)
Role play (home/hospital/shop, etc.)	46
Small figure play (doll/farm/fort/cars, etc.)	21
Sand play	14
Board games	11
Uncodeable	7

Differences in the Classroom Experiences of Boys and Girls, and of Black and White Children

We found only one consistent difference in the experiences of our four groups of children (that is, only one difference which was replicated in observations, not reported here, of a second group of children over two full days), namely that white boys spent a greater proportion of the school day than other groups in maths. In general, we found that the great majority of maths tasks (78%) were allocated to the children by their teachers, not spontaneously chosen by the children themselves, or negotiated between teacher and child. This finding was as true for white boys as for other groups, indicating that the greater proportion of time spent in maths by this group was not because they themselves chose this curriculum area more often than others, but rather that they were allocated to it more often by their teachers.

TIME SAMPLING OBSERVATIONS OF CLASSROOM LEARNING TIME

In this section we look at results from observing children's classroom learning time for each of the three years, using a time sampling method. These observations were only conducted during the parts of the school day when children were in their own classrooms. Whereas the whole-day observations described earlier produced a record of the curriculum activities engaged in, the time sampling study recorded children's social interactions and behaviour within work activities. The aim was to provide, for the children observed, a numerical count of the prevalence of pre-selected categories of behaviour, so that we could compare boys and girls, and black and white children, and also look for associations with children's educational progress.

We observed during classroom learning times. This meant we did not observe during parts of the day when children were either out of the classroom, for example in assembly, swimming, or music and movement, or times when children were not expected to be working, for example, at register time or waiting to go out. Some activities—drinking milk—for example, are usually non-work activities, but they may accompany story time or provide the basis for a maths teaching situation. The basic principle was to observe children's behaviour when engaged in learning activities, including permitted play, in their classrooms.

Method of Observation

We used a systematic observation schedule to provide a description of time spent by children in five ways:

1. in different "settings" (individual work, group work, play etc.);
2. in different "subjects" (maths, language etc.);
3. when in contact with teachers;
4. when in contact with other children; and
5. when not interacting.

Within each of these last three "social modes", behaviour was coded in terms of whether it was related to work or permitted play (i.e. "on-task"), "procedural" (e.g. sharpening pencils), social (e.g. discussing T.V. programmes), or "task avoidant" (e.g. disruptive, disengaged, or aggressive behaviour). The schedule was "systematic" in the sense that the categories of behaviour were worked out in advance. Categories chosen were those that earlier research suggested might be related to attainment and which might differ between boys and girls, and black and white children. This kind of research technique has a long history in education and psychology (Croll, 1986), and is one way of providing a statistical account of classroom behaviour.

The schedule was child based, in the sense that one child at a time was observed, and teachers and other children were observed only if they came into contact with that child. A sub-sample of children in each class was observed, ideally one white boy, one white girl, one black boy, and one black girl (see Chapter 2).

Each child was observed for six 5-minute periods each day, these periods being divided into 30 consecutive 10sec time intervals. Within time intervals, choices between sets of mutually exclusive behaviours ("setting", subject, etc.) were made on the basis of which occurred for the longest time (so-called "predominant activity sampling"). These five-minute sessions were repeated throughout the days chosen for observation. In the first year we observed on three separate days in the autumn term and two separate days in the summer term. In the second year observations took place on three days in the spring term, and the third year observations took place on two days in the spring term. This resulted in a large number of observations—93,990 10sec intervals in the first year, and 55,680 and 46,740 in the second and third years.

Full details of the systematic schedule and how it was used can be found in Blatchford, Burke, Farquhar, Plewis, and Tizard (1987a).

Setting

Children could be coded in one of five settings: individual work, group work, permitted play (e.g. sand and water play, dressing up), situations involving the teacher (e.g. story time, talk about numbers and letters), and transitions between activities. Table 4.8 shows in which of these settings we were most likely to observe children. Most time was spent in individual work, and this tended to increase over the three years of infant school. Group work, where children worked co-operatively on a task or activity, for example to solve a problem or produce a joint product, occurred rarely, as others have found in junior schools (Galton et al., 1980). Permitted play decreased over the three years, virtually disappearing by the top infants. Only the proportion of settings involving the teacher remained constant over the three years— occurring in about a quarter of all observations every year.

Subject

We were interested in finding out how much time was spent in the different subject areas because research (e.g. Stallings, 1975) has shown this to be

TABLE 4.8
Setting and Subject of Children's Behaviour

| Variable | Category | % of All Observations Standard Errors in Brackets | | | Linear[b] Trend (P Values) |
		First Year	Second Year	Third Year	
Setting	Individual taskwork	49 (2.4)	61 (2.2)	66 (3.1)	.001
	Group work	3 (0.5)	3 (1.0)	7 (2.0)	(.15)
	Permitted play	14 (1.0)	11 (2.0)	2 (1.0)	.001
	Teacher-led situations		26[a] (1.5)		
	Transitions	5 (1.0)	3 (0.4)	1 (0.3)	.001
Subject	Maths	11 (1.1)	19 (2.8)	21 (2.1)	.001
	Language	37 (1.7)	41 (2.7)	48 (2.9)	.01
	Other task work		24[a] (1.3)		
	Any other activity	21 (1.5)	14 (1.7)	·4 (1.2)	.001

[a] These variables showed no evidence of differing between years and so percentages and standard errors are given for the combined data for three years.
[b] For full description of statistical analyses see Blatchford et al. (1987a).

associated with attainment in those subjects. There were four main subject categories: *maths* (as well as number work, weighing, sorting, measuring, worksheets etc., this also included games and apparatus with a clear mathematical focus); *language* (including all reading activities, e.g. reading to teacher, flashcard work, writing, copy writing, listening to stories, discussion of points of language, e.g. letter sounds, spelling checks); and *other task work* that resulted in an end product (e.g. construction materials, paintings) or had clearly defined procedures (e.g. instructional card games). Topic, science, geography, and history work are included here too, although any reading or writing work within these areas would have been categorised as language. The fourth category was *any other activity*, which included mostly play, but also transitions, etc.

Results for observations on these subject areas are shown in Table 4.8. Most time was spent in language work, and this increased over the three years. This was followed by time spent in "other task work" (i.e. construction, painting, etc.) This category took up a quarter of observations of learning time. Although we did not subdivide the categories during observations, it was the observers' impression that more time was spent in painting and construction work than in topic or science work. Maths occurred in about only one in ten observations in the reception year, and, though it had virtually doubled by the top-infant year, still did not exceed one in five observations. Taken together, maths and language increased steadily over the three years. In the top-infant year, we found that two-fifths of all the language work (or 20% of all observations) was devoted to writing—about the same amount of time as to maths.

Social Interaction

A number of research projects have found children's educational achievement to be related to types of interaction in the classroom, for example, teachers' instruction about tasks (e.g. Dunkin and Biddle, 1974; Rosenshine, 1977). In our observations, interactions could be of three kinds—interacting with the teacher, with other children, and not interacting.

Teacher-child Contact

The kinds of contact that children had with their teachers remained fairly stable over the three years, so we combined results for the three years.

The Plowden Report (1967, Vol.1, p.273) was a major source of encouragement to schools to move towards individual work and instruction for children. "Schools . . . have increasingly realised how much children of the same age differ in their powers of perception and imagery, in their interests, and in the span of their attention. The more obvious this becomes, the less satisfactory class instruction seems." It was argued that children should often be taught individually for reading and maths. But teaching children in groups, and co-operative work in groups, were also seen to be valuable for children and a practical way of using teachers' hard-pressed time.

In most contacts with their teachers, children were one of a class (65% of all teacher-child contacts), listening to the teacher address either the whole class or another child. In only one in five teacher-child contacts was the observed child the main focus of the teacher's attention (whether in a class, group or individual setting). One-to-one contacts between teacher and child only occurred in 17% of contacts between them, and teaching to a group occurred in 19% of all contacts.

It is important, though, not to exaggerate the amount of class teaching throughout the infant school day. A sizeable proportion of the time children spent in a class situation was listening to stories read or told by the teachers (often at the end of the school day).

These results extend into the infant school those found in the ORACLE study on English Junior schools (Galton et al., 1980). They lead to an important conclusion: From the child's point of view, though individual *work* is common in the infant school, individual *teaching* is not. This is not to apportion blame to teachers. As Galton et al. argue, given the size of classes in British primary schools, the time teachers can spend with individual children is inevitably limited. However, as we have said, teaching to groups—a setting recommended by Plowden and others as a way of overcoming this problem—was also not common.

Not only group teaching, but also co-operative work in groups—where children work to solve problems together, make models, etc.—has been recommended by educationalists as a valuable learning environment for children. In principle, such group work should have strong practical advantages for teachers trying to manage a large class. However, as we have seen, this also occurred rarely. Bennett et al. (1984) and Galton et al. (1980) have both queried the quality of learning experiences in group settings and Bennett et al. found that talk between children in groups was generally of a relatively low level, for example, arguing about who should have the unifix cubes. These results suggest the need to re-evaluate the circumstances in which group work for young children is feasible and desirable. Part of the problem, as Galton et al. (1980) point out, is that although group work is valued, for example, by the Plowden (1967) and the Bullock (1975) Reports, there is very little specific advice available to teachers about how to organise group work.

The most common type of teacher behaviour toward children was what we called "task teach". That is, 69% of all teacher-child contacts were directly concerned with communicating facts, ideas, or concepts whether by explaining, informing, demonstrating, questioning, or suggesting. Reading or telling stories to the children were also included here. If times when teachers were organising and preparing children for task work were included, this figure rose to 80%. Clearly, then, infant classrooms are businesslike places where much of the contact between teachers and children is concerned with the tasks in hand. Indeed, social and personal contacts between teachers and children, for example, about life outside the classroom, children's health and appearance, were observed in less than 1% of all observations (though these contacts may have occurred more often outside classroom learning times, e.g. on entry into school, and during registration). We also found that more emotionally charged behaviours, like praise and disapproval/criticism of children—which North American research has shown to be important in children's educational achievement (e.g. Rosenshine, 1977)—occurred rarely. Praise occurred in less than 1% of teacher-child contacts, disapproval/criticism in 3%.

We coded whether children initiated, responded, or simply attended to their teachers when in contact with them. In 67% of observations of teacher-child contacts children were listening to the teacher speak, even though this was rigorously defined as having to occur for the whole 10sec time interval. We added up the amount of responses and initiations to the teacher to produce what might be viewed as a measure of the child's *active* contribution to contact with their teachers. This figure decreased over the 3 years—from 9% of all observations in the reception year to 7% and 6% in the middle and top infant years ($P<0.001$). The children's role in contact with their teachers became, therefore, a more *passive* one. Such contact about social matters as we did observe in the reception year was four times more likely to be initiated by the child than by the teacher. Disruptive comments to the teachers were uncommon (less than 1% of all observations). Children did not attend to teachers when it was expected of them in 11% of all contacts with their teachers.

Child-child contact

Contacts between children were relatively less concerned with task work—about one half of all child-child contacts. Contacts about social matters, as one would expect, were more common than in teacher-child contact, though still only coded in about one in every five observations. "Fooling around" between children (e.g. throwing pencils and erasers, playing with sponges during a session on water absorption) occurred in only 4% of all child-child observations and aggression between children in less than 1% of all observations.

Our results therefore showed that overtly disruptive and aggressive behaviour was rare. This finding seems to conflict with reports from teachers in this study, reported in Chapter 8, about children's behaviour problems in school. We report there that over the 3 years together, 17% of the children were seen as having mild problems and 16% definite problems (e.g. distractability, aggression, disobedience, withdrawal, etc.) that interfered with their learning. These results also appear to conflict with the conclusions of a recent report, organised by one of the teachers' unions, and based on questionnaires sent to infant, first, and primary schools (report of a survey to A.M.M.A.'s Primary Education Committee, 1984). This claimed that there has been a worrying increase in children's disruptive behaviour, and inability to concentrate or attend to teachers, even on activities they enjoyed.

It is difficult to reconcile the discrepancy between our observations and teachers' reports. Disruptive behaviour—some very severe—occurred whilst we were present in the schools, but was often not picked up by our observations (because we only observed a few children, one at a time, at different times during the day). It is true that even rare occurrences of disruptive behaviour can be very disturbing to teachers and other pupils. It seems likely, too, that disruptive behaviour occurred more often at times not observed, perhaps particularly at tidying-up times, and in the playground. It is also possible that teachers may have based their judgements on behaviour in children that might not have been coded by our observation method as "task avoidant" because the child was also working, e.g. tapping pencils, fidgeting, and "jigging around" whilst working. Teachers' judgements also covered a wider range of behaviours than the observations, though, as we shall see in Chapter 8, for the most part there was overlap between judgement and observation categories. But our results do suggest that alarmist reports of school behaviour should be treated with caution.

Not Interacting

When the child was neither in contact with the teacher nor with other children the most prevalent behaviour, once again, was involvement in the task in hand—64% of all "not interacting" observations. Children were "task avoidant" in 10% of all not interacting observations. This could either be active, e.g. the child was engaged in an activity other than the task in hand, or passive disengagement from the task, e.g. wandering around or daydreaming.

Combined Variables

Many studies have looked at children's "time-on-task" as a factor in their educational achievements (see, e.g., Stallings, 1975). In order to get an overall picture of the amount of time children spent "on-task" we added up all the different "on-task" behaviours (that is, task behaviour in the three social modes). To get a picture of non-task-related behaviour, we also added up all observations within which "task-avoidant" behaviours were coded (that is, disruptive comments to teacher and not attending when expected; child-child "fooling around" and aggression; active and passive task-avoidant behaviour when not interacting). We also calculated the total amount of social contacts, and the total amount of procedure behaviour (that is, behaviour concerned with classroom management and routine—clearing up, fetching materials, pencils, etc.).

Results for these combined variables are shown in Table 4.9. It can be seen that in the bulk of all observations, across the three social modes, children are engaged in the work at hand. In only 9% of all observations are they "task avoidant", whether by being disobedient, aggressive, or disengaged from their work.

Evidence from our time-sampling observations of children's classroom behaviour therefore shows that, for the majority of their time, children were busy and involved in their work. And, as we have seen, they were mostly not playing, but working individually on the "basic" subjects of language (including reading and writing) and mathematics. It has often been shown by British educational researchers (Galton et al., 1980; H.M.I., 1978), but in the light of continuing press reports and political rhetoric it is perhaps worth repeating: Children, even at this young age, spend the bulk of their time in classrooms working on the 3Rs.

SEX AND ETHNIC DIFFERENCES IN CLASSROOM BEHAVIOUR AND INTERACTION

We found no evidence of differences in the total amount of task inter-action teachers had with boys or girls, or black and white children. The absence of a difference between boys and girls in the total amount of teacher-pupil interaction tends to contrast with what has been found in other research. For example, Kelly (in press), in her meta-analysis of 81 studies, found that girls were involved in only 44% of total interactions with teachers. But Galton et al. (1980), in a major British study of junior schools, did not find statistically significant differences in the overall total of girls' and boys' interactions with teachers.

Our results showed, however, the importance of considering sex and

TABLE 4.9
Combined Variables

	% of All Observations Over Three Years[a] (Standard Errors)	
Total "on-task"	61	(0.8)
Total "procedure"	13	(0.3)
Total "social"	5	(0.3)
Total "task avoidance"	9	(0.6)

[a] This column does not equal 100% because other behaviours are not included in this table (e.g. "unclear").

ethnic group together. We found statistically significant differences ($P<0.05$) between the four sex and ethnic groups in the total amount of contacts about tasks they had with their teachers. Mean percentages were 23 for white boys, 21 for white girls, 20.5 for black boys and 22 for black girls. These group means were based on the percentage for all those 145 children who were observed in any of the 3 years. White boys therefore had the most contact with teachers, black boys least.[1] Our results show that white boys initiated more contacts than the other groups with their teachers, and this may account for some of the difference. In addition, the teachers may have initiated more contacts with them, but since we did not code teacher initiations we cannot be sure about this.

In line with previous research, boys received more disapproval/criticism (boys 55%, girls 45%) and more praise (boys 56%, girls 44%) from their teachers than girls. Black boys received the most disapproval/criticism of the four groups. The white girls received the least disapproval/criticism and also the least praise. However, data for individual children were too sparse for us to assess the statistical significance of these differences.

It could be argued that the greater amount of disapproval/criticism directed at black boys is explained by the greater tendency of black boys to "fool around" with other children when the expectation was they would be working ($P<0.05$; percentage of all observations was: white boys 0.7%, white girls 0.8%, black boys 1.8%, and black girls 0.9%). The results also suggested that they more often behaved inappropriately towards teachers (e.g. making silly or disruptive comments) and were more aggressive towards other children, although these last two behaviours were infrequent, and differences were not statistically significant. One would expect such behaviour to arouse negative comments from teachers. However, the question remains as to *why* black boys more often engaged in these "task–avoidant" behaviours, and our data do not allow us to answer this question. But whatever the explanations and processes at work it is important not to lose sight of the fact that "task–avoidant" behaviour and teacher disapproval/criticism were relatively infrequent and that there were no differences between the four groups in the amount of the much more common "on-task" behaviour.

As for other aspects of children's behaviour, there was a tendency ($P<0.06$) for boys to engage in more permitted play activities than girls,

---

[1] In order to be regarded as statistically significant, differences between the four groups had to satisfy two criteria: firstly the same pattern had to occur for each of the three years, and secondly, they had to be statistically significant on Friedman's non-parametric test, for those nine schools which maintained an ethnic group and sex balance of one white boy, one white girl, one black boy, and one black girl throughout the three years. The restricted sample was used only for tests of ethnic and sex differences in time–sampling observations. Percentages in text are for the full observation sample.

for example, sand and water play, and play in the home corner (boys 13%, girls 10% of all observations over the 3 years). As we have seen, there was very little play in the top-infant year. Girls more than boys failed to attend to the teacher when it was expected of them, e.g. when being read a story, or being given instruction ($P<0.05$; boys 3.0%, girls 3.3%). As well as a tendency for white boys to have more contacts with their teachers about work, they also had fewer social contacts with other children ($P<0.05$; white boys 3.6%, white girls 4.9%, black boys 5.5%, black girls 5.7%); their interactions, in other words, were more work oriented. Lastly, the white girls spent more time than other children on procedural matters, like getting materials, sharpening pencils, etc., when on their own ($P<0.05$; white boys 5.8%, white girls 7.9%, black boys 5.9%, black girls 6.3%).

Finally, we recognise fully that systematic observation of this kind does not give a complete picture of life in the classroom. It does not, for example, tell us about the quality or effects of individual behaviours—all of us can probably remember from our own school experiences how crushed we felt by just one criticism from a teacher, or how encouraged we were by a word of praise. Although in most observations the children were "on-task", the results cannot inform us about the quality of the work children do or the quality of their involvement in their work. What they can provide is a reliable account of the prevalence of certain categories of behaviour and hence a picture of how the children spent their time in infant classrooms.

SUMMARY

Continuous full-day observations carried out when children were in their third year at infant school showed that somewhat less than half the school day was devoted to learning activities in the classroom. Only 4% of the day was spent in reading. A large amount of time (43% of the day) was taken up by dinner time, school breaks, lining up, tidying up, register time, and so on.

The most common form of maths work observed at top infants was written work in number. Only a small proportion of maths work was purely practical. The majority of creative work involved drawing, crayoning, or tracing. Painting and modelling were relatively rare, as were most free-play activities, particularly sand or water play. The most common form of free-play activity observed was imaginative role play. Only one difference was found in the classroom experience of different groups of children (that is, of white boys, white girls, black boys, and black girls), namely that white boys spent a greater proportion of the school day than other groups in maths.

Time-sampling observations, conducted during all three years of children's time in infant school, provided a description of children's behaviour during classroom learning time. We found that children were mostly busy and involved in their work. They were mostly not playing, but working individually on the "basic" subjects of language (including reading and writing) and mathematics. However, although individual working was common, individual teaching was not. Most of the children's contact with a teacher was listening to her address the whole class about work. One-to-one contacts between teacher and child, and interactions between a group of children and their teacher were not common. From a child's point of view, they were the focus of a teacher's attention (whether in a class, group, or individual setting) in only one in five observations. Children's active contribution to contact with their teachers declined over the three years of infant school.

Co-operative work, where children worked together to solve problems, make models, and so on, was rare, as were disruptive and aggressive behaviour, and teacher disapproval/criticism and praise.

In contrast to previous research, we did not find a difference between boys and girls in the total amount of interaction with their teachers. But we found an interaction between sex and ethnic group, such that white boys had most and black boys had least total contacts with teachers. Overall, boys received more teacher disapproval/criticism than the other groups, and white girls less disapproval/criticism and praise. Black boys were more likely to "fool around" with other children. However, there were no differences between the four groups in the much more common "on-task" behaviour.

5 The Parents' Role in Infant Schooling

THE PARENT SAMPLE

In order to gain some insight into the role of parents in infant schooling, a sample of parents was interviewed every summer from 1982 to 1985, that is, from the time when their children were about to enter the infant school reception class until these children had completed three years of schooling. (A description of the size of the sample, and of how the parents were selected, can be found in Chapter 2.) The results are presented for the total sample of parents, except where statistically significant differences existed between the black and white parents.

Parents' Place of Birth

Although we had attempted to confine the white sample to children of white parents born in the U.K., in the event, 6 of the original 114 white children proved to have either one or both parents from Eire. Two white children had Australian mothers, and 2 had European fathers, but these fathers had little or no contact with their children. Ten (of the original 88) black children had one white parent, in 9 cases a white mother. The black parents came from 9 different Caribbean islands, and from Guyana. The largest number were from Jamaica.

Two-thirds of the white parents had been brought up close to where they were now living, some in the same block of flats. Some had themselves been to the same school that their child was now attending. In contrast, few of the black parents were living close to where they had been brought up. Of the 79 black mothers of the black children, only 11% had been born in the U.K. (The 1981 census shows that this proportion is in line with national figures on the place of birth of Caribbeans aged 30–35 living in Britain. In contrast, 92% of the generation aged 15–19 in 1981 were born in the U.K.) Although 39% of the black mothers had received either all their education, or all their junior and secondary education in Britain, 34% had been fully educated in the Caribbean.

The black families in our sample were by no means a homogeneous group, either in cultural or in educational terms. Those mothers brought up in differing parts of the Caribbean may have had very different early cultural experiences from each other, and no personal experience of the English education system. In contrast, many other black mothers in our sample had grown up in London. These mothers were in no sense immigrants, and had come through the English school system, often from an early age.

Age and Education of Mothers

At the time of the first interview, more than half the mothers (57%) were between the ages of 22 and 30. The black mothers varied more widely in age than the white mothers ($P<0.001$). Two were aged 21 or less, whilst 12 were aged 40 or more.

Fifty-six per cent of the white mothers and 51% of the white fathers had no educational qualifications, compared with the national figure of 48% of women and 38% of men aged 25–39 (Great Britain, 1982d). The black mothers, on the other hand, were significantly better qualified than the white mothers (Table 5.1, $P<0.001$) and than the national average. (Our sample of black fathers was very small.) The superior achievement of the black mothers was mainly due to the large proportion who had at least one CSE or O-level, although few had received high grades. The black mothers had often obtained these qualifications because they chose to stay on at school longer than the white mothers. Whilst 61% of white mothers had left school as soon as they reached the minimum age of 16, before the end of the school year and therefore before sitting formal examinations, only 8% of the black mothers had done so. And 20% of the black mothers had gone on to complete one or 2 years post-16 education, compared with only 7% of the white mothers. Maughan and Rutter (1986) had similar findings.

Family Structure

We asked the mothers whether they were a single- or a two-parent family, rather than whether or not they were married. In all except three cases the single mothers lived in their own flat, rather than in an extended family

TABLE 5.1
Mothers' Educational Level

	Black	White
Degree, A-levels, H.N.C., nursing, etc.	11 (12%)	16 (14%)
O-levels, C.S.E.s	34 (39%)	15 (13%)
Other, e.g. secretarial, City and Guilds	18 (21%)	18 (16%)
None	21 (24%)	64 (56%)
No information	4 (5%)	1 (1%)

unit, but they often lived very near to their own mothers. There was a higher proportion of black compared with white single parent families in the sample (43% vs. 13%, $P<0.001$).

Although the overall proportion of single–parent families remained approximately the same throughout the study, and well above the national average of 11% for families with dependent children (O.P.C.S., 1982), the situation of many individual families changed during this period. Thirty–seven percent of the sample (50% of the black families and 27% of the white families) were single-parent families at some point in the study, but only 16% (30% of the black families, and 6% of the white) remained so throughout.

The average family size for the sample was above the national average (O.P.C.S., 1980). The most common number of children under the age of sixteen living in the sample households was 2. Single-child families and families with four or more children were relatively rare (18% and 12% of families respectively).

Housing, Employment, and Income

Compared with national figures (O.P.C.S., 1983), a relatively low proportion of the interviewed families (16%) were owner-occupiers, and a relatively high proportion (66%) were council tenants.

Thirty-nine percent of the male heads of households were (or had previously been) employed in semi-skilled and unskilled occupations, a much larger proportion than in a national sample of families with school-age children (O.P.C.S., 1978). There was a higher proportion of professional and managerial workers (social class I) amongst the white compared with the black husbands or cohabitees (19% vs. 6%, $P<0.05$).

The majority of mothers (61%) were not employed outside the home. Only a small proportion of mothers worked full-time (15%), but this proportion was higher among the black than the white mothers (22% vs. 11%, $P<0.05$). Few mothers worked overtime or did shift work (13%). The average income of the families was low, and this was particularly true of the black families (with a mean weekly income in 1983 of £86 vs. £147 for the white families, $P<0.001$), partly because of the large group of black single mothers, most of whom were on Supplementary Benefit, and no doubt partly because of the discrimination that blacks encounter in the British labour market (see Chapter 1).

THE INVOLVEMENT OF PARENTS IN THEIR CHILDREN'S SCHOOLING

Within the I.L.E.A. there have been a number of initiatives in recent years which have been aimed at encouraging greater collaboration between schools and parents. Parents have been given greater representation in the education system (for example, on the governing bodies of schools) and they have actively been encouraged to come into the schools. But changes often filter slowly through the education system, and the overall policy of the school may not be reflected in the practice of individual class teachers.

To obtain a picture of the extent to which individual teachers in the study schools actively encouraged parental involvement in their children's education, we interviewed the children's class teachers each year. In schools where the sample children were not all in the same class, the interview was carried out with the teacher who taught the greatest number of these children. We present results from these interviews alongside the information obtained from parents, so that the parents' views may be seen in the context of the practice of the schools.

We present the parents' responses to a number of individual interview questions from each of our annual interviews. The information from parents has been grouped under three headings:

1. The children's experiences of reading, writing and maths at home.
2. The parents' educational beliefs and attitudes.
3. Parent-school relationships.

Within these headings, certain questions were clearly inter-related, and we grouped these related questions together to form a total of nine parental variables (see Appendix 1). In order to provide a picture of parental practices and attitudes over the infant school period as a whole, some results are presented using combined data from the three interviews carried out from 1983 to 1985.

Before presenting the results, we should point out that our information was collected from teachers and parents retrospectively, at the end of each school year. Certain caveats must always apply to interview data of this nature. In this case, reliability was clearly dependent on the accuracy and objectivity of teacher and parent report. Estimates of the frequency with which teachers or parents engaged in activities over the year as a whole (for example, sending books home with children, or listening to children read) undoubtedly masked some variability occurring in these activities during the year. Moreover, some teachers and parents may, consciously or unconsciously, have exaggerated their involvement in certain activities, particularly those which they felt would be approved.

THE CHILDREN'S EXPERIENCES OF READING, WRITING, AND MATHS AT HOME

Help with the 3Rs

Reading

Teachers.   At the beginning of the study, one in four of the reception teachers said that they disapproved of parents teaching any reading, writing or number to children under the age of five (that is, before statutory school age), and the majority of those who said they approved, nevertheless expressed reservations. Teachers were concerned that parents should only teach their pre-school children if teaching was made enjoyable, and was not forced on children, and if nothing was taught that would be incompatible with teaching in the school (for example, parents should teach lower case letters, not capitals). Similar fears have been reported amongst teachers elsewhere (see, for example, Hannon & Cuckle, 1984).

Once children had actually started at school, however, we found evidence of widespread encouragement of parental help with reading, and there was a tendency for encouragement to become more common as the children became older. Virtually all reception, middle-infant and top-infant teachers said that they had sent reading material home with at least some of their children so that parents could listen to their children read at home. Whereas at reception more than a quarter of teachers had only sent reading home for certain children (for example, those who asked, or whom the teacher felt would benefit from it), most top infant teachers (88%) had sent reading home for all children as a matter of policy. Indeed, at least half the teachers at middle and top infants said that they had encouraged children to have school reading books at home every night.

Most teachers said that they had explained to at least some parents how to help their children with reading; for example, what to do if the child made a mistake (see Table 5.2). A small minority of teachers had made a point of explaining this to all parents. Roughly a quarter of teachers each year said that they had given information of this kind to parents at parents' meetings or workshops. But only a small number of teachers had provided parents with written handouts on how to help their child with reading.

Teachers were generally not very optimistic that parents would provide

TABLE 5.2
How Teachers had Explained to Parents about Helping
Their Child to Read (Multiple Responses)

	Reception %	Middle %	Top %
Individual chat with parents who asked	55	33	22
Individual chat with all parents (teacher-initiated)	24	12	19
At a parents evening/ workshop on 3Rs	21	27	28
At a general meeting on several topics	18	6	3
Individual chat to some parents (teacher selects)	12	30	16
By written handout	9	6	13
Parents pick up methods at open evenings	–	3	–
Not at all	9	12	13

adequate support for their children's learning at home. About a third thought that the majority of parents would provide the support they felt was necessary, but almost as many (29%) thought that few, or none, of the parents would.

Within the I.L.E.A., schemes such as P.A.C.T. (Parents and Children and Teachers) have attempted to encourage communication between teachers and parents about children's reading. In this scheme, special cards accompany children's reading books home and carry messages and comments between teacher and parent. (For a description of P.A.C.T. and other similar schemes see Bloom, 1987.)

Some of the project schools operated a formal P.A.C.T. scheme and others, though not formally involved in P.A.C.T., had home reading schemes, sometimes involving the use of cards. But at least a third of both middle- and top-infant teachers said they sent reading books home without any accompanying information for parents. Some teachers sent information cards home with the children's reading material, usually giving information on the pages to be read, or on any problems the child was experiencing with a particular book or words. One fifth of middle-infant teachers, and one third of top-infant teachers, had sent home cards or booklets in which parents could also write comments on the child's progress at home.

Communication about children's reading at home was not restricted to the exchange of written comments. Some face-to-face discussions were also held between teachers and individual parents on how their children were progressing with reading at home, more often with middle-infant than with top-infant teachers. All middle-infant teachers had held such discussions with some parents, but more than a third of top-infant teachers had had no discussions of this nature. (It is possible that opportunities for parent-teacher discussion about reading were affected by industrial action in the schools.)

Parents.   Virtually all families said they gave some help to their children with reading (see Table 5.3).

More black than white parents said they had started to teach their children to read before they started school (69% vs. 50%, $P<0.01$). At this stage, parents said that they helped their children with reading by pointing out words and letters in a variety of situations (on household products, television, shops etc.), and in some cases (28% of parents) by using flashcards or reading books. Although almost two-thirds of the parents said they had helped their young children in some of these ways, generally they had not done so either frequently or regularly. Of the parents who did help, only 23% did so every week, whilst a smaller percentage (17%) did so most days. (Examples of the variety of contexts in which parents teach pre-school children can be found in Tizard & Hughes, 1984.)

Once the children were attending infant school, help with reading greatly increased (see Table 5.3).

Maths

Teachers.   Whereas teachers said they were happy for parents to hear their children read, they were far less enthusiastic about parents teaching "maths" at home, not only at the pre-school level, but also throughout the infant school period. None of the teachers had actively encouraged all the parents to help.

TABLE 5.3
Proportion of Families Giving Their Child Help at Home with Reading

	Pre-school	1st year	2nd year	3rd year
Some "teaching" (even if only occasional)	63%	97%	94%	95%
Listens to child 5–7 days a week	17%	48%	40%	37%

When teachers had encouraged some parents to help with maths, they had often suggested the same kind of activities to parents at each level of the infant school, despite the changing age of the children. The most favoured activities were counting, mentioned by a third of both reception and top-infant teachers, practical activities such as cooking, mentioned by a quarter of reception and a third of top-infant teachers, and games such as snakes and ladders, cards, and so on.

Parents. In contrast to the teachers' relative lack of enthusiasm for involving parents in maths, we found that many parents were in fact not only enthusiastic, but actively involved in helping their children in this area.

At our first interview, we found that 94% of the parents said they were teaching their children to count. By the end of the reception year, nearly all parents said they were not only helping with counting (95%), but were also helping children to recognise numbers (97%), and to learn the number series (91%). A smaller number (69%) were teaching adding, and some (43%) had already started teaching subtraction.

By the end of the middle-infant year, 90% of parents said they were helping their children to learn to handle money, either by teaching them to recognise coins, or to make up amounts of money with different coins or to work out change. Many parents (65%) had also started to try and teach their child how to tell the time.

At the end of the top-infant year, we found that many parents were teaching addition and subtraction, and some were also teaching multiplication and division (see Table 5.4). In some cases, parents were giving children quite difficult "carrying" sums (for example, 45% of parents were giving such sums for addition, and 20% for subtraction). More than half the parents said that they had taught their children multiplication tables. Black parents were more likely to have taught tables than white parents (74% vs. 48%, P<0.01), but were less likely to have involved their children in weighing or measuring than white parents (29% vs. 55%, P<0.01). Eighty-three per cent of all parents said they had helped their child to tell the time using a conventional clock, and many had also pointed out the time to children on digital watches or clocks.

Teachers were unlikely to encourage mathematical activities at home, and when they did, they were unlikely to encourage number work. Parents, on the other hand, were actively involved in helping their children with all aspects of maths, sometimes to quite complex levels, though this willingness and ability to help their children was neither expected nor acknowledged by the schools.

The difference in attitude between parents and teachers over maths is well illustrated by the teaching of "tables" and handling of money. Only 9% of top-infant teachers said that they had encouraged any parents to teach

TABLE 5.4
Percentage of Parents Who Said They Taught Different Number
Operations During the Top-infant Year

	Any Teaching	Written "Sums"
Addition	94	76
Subtraction	82	67
Multiplication	45	36
Division	28	18

tables during the year, but 59% of parents had done so. Indeed, only just over a quarter of children were introduced to tables at school during top infants. Similarly, only 6% of middle-infant teachers had encouraged any parents to help their children understand and use money, but 90% of the parents said that they had done so.

Whatever teachers' misgivings may have been about parental involvement in children's mathematical learning, they were clearly not effective in stopping parents from being involved. Rather than resisting parental involvement, teachers might do better to acknowledge the help that parents are already giving children with maths, and seek to work with, rather than against, parents.

Writing

Teachers. Very few teachers (a maximum of 15% in any year) had, as a matter of policy, asked parents to encourage their children to write at home. In fact, most teachers said they had not attempted to involve parents in this area of the curriculum at all. At top infants, where encouragement was slightly more evident, teachers had most often directed their encouragement only towards parents of specific children (possibly those children experiencing difficulties).

Parents. At the end of the nursery, despite the lack of encouragement from teachers, we found that the great majority of parents (about 90%) said they were helping their children to write their name. Girls had been taught to write other words as well as their name more frequently than boys (57% vs. 47%, $P<0.05$). Some parents, more white parents than black (30% vs. 13%, $P<0.001$), said that they had also encouraged their children to draw.[1]

---

[1] For a comparison of the views of parents and reception teachers, see Farquhar, Blatchford, Burke, Plewis, and Tizard, 1985.

As the children grew older and their own writing skills increased, we found that direct teaching was replaced by children writing spontaneously on their own, often without any participation on the part of the parent.

At the end of top infants, parents reported that 82% of children were copying writing at home, 91% were writing sentences (for example, under pictures that they had drawn), and 81% had written stories or letters, perhaps asking members of the family for help in spelling difficult words. Some children were engaging in quite difficult writing without any assistance. Half of them had written short stories or letters completely on their own, and about a quarter had written complete, longer stories. The proportion of children who were reported by their parents to write at home at least five times a week remained steady across the infant school period at about 45%. Using combined data over the three years, we found that black children were reported as doing more writing at home than white children (a difference of about half a standard deviation, $P<0.01$), and girls were reported as doing more writing than boys (a difference of about three quarters of a standard deviation, $P<0.001$).

Home Computer Use

Teachers.   We did not ask teachers whether they were aware of, or encouraged, any computer use by children at home.

Parents.   At the end of the children's third year at infant school, a quarter of the parents (more white than black parents, 35% vs. 12%, $P<0.01$) owned home computers. Possibly the white families, who had higher incomes, were more able to afford to purchase such expensive items. A further 14% of parents reported that, though they themselves did not own computers, their children had had access during the year to a home computer elsewhere, normally through friends or relations. In all but three cases, parents with computers said that their child had gained some experience of reading or maths or both through using the computer, either by playing games which involved having to read or use numbers, or by using programs specifically designed to teach.

Total Help with the 3Rs

Using a combined measure of parental teaching, which incorporated the teaching of reading, writing, and maths over the three-year infant school period (see Appendix 1, variables 2–4), we found that black parents gave their children significantly more help with school work than white parents (a difference of 0.4 S.D., $P<0.05$).

The Child's Experience of Books at Home

Teachers. We did not ask teachers directly whether they encouraged parents to read to their children at home. However, at the beginning of the study, we did ask the reception teachers what kind of things they hoped that parents might have done with their children to prepare them for school. More than two-thirds of them spontaneously mentioned that they liked parents to have read to their children, and to have told them stories.

Parents. In our pre-school interview we asked the parents to show us how many books (excluding comics) they had for reading to the children, or for the children to look at themselves. About a quarter of the parents (20% of white parents, 34% of black parents, $P<0.001$) had ten or less books. Eighteen percent (29% of white parents, 3% of black parents) had 50 or more.

Before the children started school, we found that 81% of the parents said that they (or somebody else, such as a grandparent or older sibling) read to the child at home. Thirty-nine percent said that they did so once a day or more.

Most parents continued to read to their children during their first year at school, and only 18% of parents said that they never, or hardly ever, read to their child. Forty-one percent said they had read every day, 15% 3 to 4 times a week, and 26% once or twice a week. Overall, a third of the parents borrowed children's books from a school or public library at least once a month, and 15% did so once a week. When we asked the parents at the end of the reception year *why* they read aloud to their children, 47% of the white parents, compared with 21% of the black parents, said that it was mainly because the child or they themselves enjoyed it, whilst 47% of the black parents, compared with 25% of the white parents, said it was because the child learned from books ($P<0.001$).

At the end of the middle-infant year, the majority of parents said that they still read aloud to their children. However, there had been some decrease in frequency, with only just under a quarter of parents still reading to their children every day. By the end of the top-infant year, some parents (18%) said that it was no longer necessary to read to their child as they could read fluently on their own, and only 16% said that they still read to their child almost every day. And at this age, just over a third of the children were reported to read to themselves at home almost every day.

Using our combined measure of children's experiences of books over the three-year period, taking into account the number of books in the home, as well as the frequency and manner in which children were read to by their parents (see Appendix 1), we found that girls were given significantly greater experience of books than boys ($P<0.05$).

THE PARENTS' EDUCATIONAL BELIEFS
AND ATTITUDES

Beliefs about Educational Success

At the outset of the study we asked the parents (and the reception teachers) to tell us what their own personal theories were concerning children's success at school.

As Table 5.5 shows, although many parents (especially black parents—70% vs. 59%, $P<0.01$) believed that a child's success in education is largely attributable to the school, teachers were more likely to attribute success to the family or the child's home background. Interestingly, none of the teachers, and few of the parents, spontaneously mentioned home-school collaboration as being of paramount importance to a child's success.

Table 5.6 shows the family attributes that parents and teachers felt were most important in determining whether children would be successful at school.

About a quarter of parents believed that success is bound up with social class, or with the level of education or occupation of parents, and this was true much more often of white than of black parents (40% vs. 12%, $P<0.001$). These parents believed that children from middle-class families would do better than children from lower-class families. Almost a third of parents saw parental interest and encouragement as an important factor in children's success.

There were a number of parents who did not feel that there were any

TABLE 5.5

The Main Influences on Educational Success, as Viewed
by Parents and Reception Teachers

	Parents (n=202) %	Teachers (n=31) %
Mainly school/teachers	29	10
Mainly family/parents	18	48
School and family equally or working together	13	–
Mainly child	12	16
School and child equally or together	4	–
Family and child equally or together	3	10
All three equally	19	13
Don't know	3	3

TABLE 5.6
Family Attributes Seen by Parents and Reception Teachers
as Determining Children's Educational Success

Relevant Family Attributes	Parents (n=202) %	Teachers (n=31) %
Parental interest/encouragement/time spent with child	30	58
Class/education/occupation of parents	26	10
Ethnic background	5	–
Loving, caring parents	5	6
Parents supportive of school	–	19
Other/don't know	11	6
No special type of family/depends on the child	25	–

family characteristics which were of particular importance to success at school. Not so the teachers; not only did they all feel that some families are indeed more likely to have successful children than others, but they were in quite strong agreement over which families these would be—that is, families where the parents were interested in their children, spent time with them, and encouraged them. Some teachers also felt that children were helped by having parents who were supportive of the school.

Attitudes to Helping Children at Home

We found that the overwhelming majority of parents (roughly 90% each year) felt that help at home was a necessary part of their children's education. Enthusiasm for help at home stemmed not so much from any serious doubts that the parents had about the schools, but rather because they were interested in their children's education, saw helping as part of their role as parents, or felt it would help their children to get on. Over the three year infant period as a whole, black parents were more positive about helping their children at home than were white parents ($P<0.001$). Less often did they see helping either as a burden, or as something that it was difficult to find time for, and they had fewer worries about whether they might confuse their child.

Parental Hopes and Aspirations for Their Children

At the pre-school interview, we asked parents whether they thought their child was a bright child compared with others of her age, and half answered that their child was definitely bright, while 39% said that they expected her to be an above average pupil at school. Only one parent thought their child would be below average.

Although some researchers might have described many of the children as "deprived", this is certainly not how their mothers saw them. To the question: "Do you feel your life has allowed you to give your child a reasonably good start, or do you think she has missed out in any way?", the great majority of mothers (87% of black mothers and 77% of white, $P<0.01$) answered that their child had been given a reasonably good start. Only a few mothers thought that their child had missed out because she was in a single-parent family, or because of poverty, or poor housing, or because of the area they lived in. It was, indeed, clear that in the most important ways the children were by no means deprived. Our interviews suggested that most of the children were given a great deal of love, support, and encouragement by their families.

The great majority of the parents, particularly the black parents (94% vs. 62%, $P<0.001$), felt that it was extremely important to pass exams, and, overall, only 17% expressed a view that "exams are not everything", or were not important for their child.

At the end of the reception year we asked all the parents how long they would like their child to stay in full-time education. About half said they would like their child to go to a university or polytechnic, and less than 10% of parents wanted their child to leave before the age of 18. Thus virtually all the mothers wanted their children to have a better education than they had received themselves.

Almost half of the parents (44%) said that it was too soon to say at the beginning of their child's schooling what kind of job they hoped their child would acquire, or that it was really up to the child. About a fifth of parents (again, more black than white parents: 36% vs. 9%, $P<0.001$) stated that they hoped their child would acquire a professional job, and a further 8% hoped that they would acquire a skilled job of some kind. Most parents were less specific in their aspirations, hoping, for example, for a satisfying job (10% of parents), a better job than they themselves had acquired (5%), or a well-paid job (3%).

PARENT-SCHOOL RELATIONSHIPS

During the period in which the study took place, a number of the teacher unions were involved in a dispute with the Government over pay and conditions. The resultant teacher action seriously curtailed teachers' involvement in activities held outside normal school hours. Our discussion of parent-school relationships must be seen in this context.

Parents' Contact with the Schools

Meetings with parents

Teachers.[2]   All reception, middle- and top-infant teachers stated that they were available to talk to parents either before or after school, or in some cases at any time during the school day. However, very few teachers had actually made a point of arranging individual appointments with *all* their parents (12% of reception teachers had done so, and 3% of top infant teachers), and to this extent contact seemed to have been dependent on the extent to which *parents* had been able to seek out teachers at school.

In fact, all reception teachers said that they had had individual discussions with at least half of the parents of their class, but in subsequent years there was decreasing contact with parents.

Parents.   The number of parents who reported that they had had some contact with the school, or with class teachers, was higher than the proportion reported by the teachers for the class as a whole. It is possible that participation in the project, even though this involved only one interview a year, somehow encouraged our parents to make greater contact with the schools than other parents. But it is also possible that some of the non-project parents were restricted in their contacts with schools because of limited use of English.

In the reception year, 81% of the interviewed parents had been to at least one meeting during the year, and 88% had had some kind of individual discussion with the teacher. In the top-infant year the comparable proportions were 84% and 69%. There was some evidence that contact was more frequent between teachers and white than black parents. At the end of the top-infant year, for example, a higher proportion of white than black parents (36% vs. 9%, $P<0.01$) had had individual discussions with their child's class teacher more than once a term. A similar finding was reported in the I.L.E.A. Junior School Study (I.L.E.A., 1985a).

Parental Help in Schools

Teachers.   Some teachers, particularly reception teachers, expressed doubts about the parents' ability or willingness to help in school, and therefore had not asked for help. But others had asked for and received some form of help from parents (see Table 5.7). Most help had been

---

[2] Our interviews with teachers concerned their relationships with parents of all the children in the class, rather than only with the sample of parents that we interviewed.

TABLE 5.7
Help Received from Parents During the Year (Multiple Responses)

	Reception % (n=33)	Middle % (n=33)	Top % (n=32)
Help with children out of class (e.g. outings, swimming)	36	21	47
Non-academic work (eg.cooking, sewing)	30	27	34
Academic work (e.g. hearing children read)	21	21	28
General assistance, not with children (e.g. preparing materials)	12	12	16
Topic work (e.g. parents talking about their jobs)	6	3	0
No help received/asked for	63	45	28

received in non-academic areas, either outside the classroom (e.g. on outings), or with activities such as cooking or sewing.

Parents.   Only about half of the parents interviewed (for example, 44% in 1984) said that they had actually been asked to help in school. Twenty seven per cent had helped at school over the year, mainly in a non-teaching capacity, such as on outings, and 29% said they had been asked but had not helped. (The figures for 1985 were very similar.)

Parents' Knowledge of the Schools

The School Day

Parents' knowledge about the school day varied. Most knew that there was no rigid timetable, and at the end of the first and second years about half of them could give some account of how the day was organised, or could say on which days of the week fixed events, such as swimming or television programmes, took place.

Teaching Methods: Reading (Reception and Middle Infants)

Teachers.   All but one reception teacher and two–thirds of middle-infant teachers had made an attempt to explain how they taught reading to at least one parent. But generally information would only have reached those parents who asked, or who had been able to attend some kind of meeting in school. Very few teachers had taken steps to get information across to all parents, either by providing a written handout (6% of reception teachers and 3% of middle-infant teachers), or by having a policy of individual explanations to all parents (12% of teachers in both years).

About a third of reception teachers and nearly half the middle-infant teachers said that they had not told parents which reading scheme or reading books they used in school. However, many of these teachers, particularly at middle infants, felt that there was no need to tell parents, as they would be able to see for themselves from the books that were sent home with the children.

Parents. At the end of the reception and middle-infant years, 52% of the parents were able to describe in one way or another how they believed reading had been taught to their child that year. Some of the answers (for example, those of 24% of parents at the end of the reception year) were fairly simple, such as "they teach sounds", whilst others (28% in the same year) were more detailed, for example, "they give them look-and-say words, but also teach letters". However, very few parents (only 18% in the reception year) said that the teachers had actually explained reading methods to them during the year.

Teaching Methods: Writing (Reception and Middle Infants)

Teachers. Even fewer teachers had explained how they taught writing, compared with reading, to parents. About one–fifth of all reception teachers, and nearly half of all middle-infant teachers, said that they had given no explanations at all of methods of teaching writing to any parents. As with reading, any information which had been given was most likely to have been given to parents who attended meetings, or open days, or who had specifically asked for details from teachers. Again, there was evidence that fewer teachers had given parents information at middle infants than at reception.

Parents. We did not ask the parents to explain how they thought writing was taught to their children.

Teaching Methods: Maths (All Three Years)

Teachers. At reception, fewer teachers had explained how they taught maths than had explained how they taught reading. However, whereas explanations of reading were given by fewer teachers in middle infants compared with reception, those concerning maths were given by equal numbers of teachers in each of the first two years (70% of teachers), and by more teachers (88%) at top infants. (It is important to bear in mind that we do not know how many of these teachers had restricted their explanations to only a small proportion of parents.)

Parents.   At the end of the reception and the middle-infant years, just under three-quarters of the parents could say something about the teaching of maths. (This means that more parents knew something about how their child was being taught maths than had known how their child was being taught to read.) However, few parents (30% in the reception year) were able to give a relatively full account of the actual teaching methods used in maths, or of the areas of maths which were being covered. Whereas these parents gave answers such as "they teach 'more than' and 'less than', and they do a lot of practical work, and sets", as many might simply mention the name of a maths scheme—"they do Fletcher maths", or say that "they do counting with a sheet of numbers".

At the end of the top-infant year, just over three-quarters of the parents could say something about the maths that had been taught during the year. However, as was the case with reading, only a small proportion of parents said that the maths work being covered had been explained to them by the teachers, either individually or at a parents' meeting or evening. Many parents said that most of their knowledge came from looking at children's work, either in the school or when it was sent home completed. In many cases, therefore, their knowledge was only acquired after the work had been covered, rather than before or at the time that it was introduced to the children.

Computer Use (Top Infants)

Teachers.   At the end of the top-infant year, more than three-quarters of the top-infant teachers told us that their school had a computer, but only just over half said that they had actually used one with the children. Of the 18 teachers who had used the computer, 14 had used it for maths, six for reading, and four for spelling and creative writing. We did not ask the teachers whether they had specifically informed the parents about computer work in the classroom.

Parents.   Forty percent of parents were uncertain whether their child had used a computer at school during their top-infant year, or even whether the school owned a computer. Only 8% said that they knew for certain that their child had used a school computer for maths or language work, or both. In contrast, as we have described, many of the parents were providing maths and language experience for their children on home computers.

Overall, despite industrial action, which restricted teachers' activities outside school hours, teachers and parents had met together quite frequently, both at open days and meetings, and informally before or after school. But there had been little written information sent home to parents, and many parents were relatively uninformed about the schools' curriculum and teaching methods. These omissions cannot reasonably be attributed to industrial action. But studies have shown that even written information does not guarantee that parents become well informed about what actually happens in classrooms (Pugh & De'Ath, 1984). The fact that much of what parents in our study knew had been gleaned from looking at children's work, rather than from teachers, suggests that the meetings with teachers had focused on matters other than the curriculum and how it was taught. This may have been because teachers did not feel it was important to explain their teaching to parents, or felt unable to do so. But it may also be true that it is only possible to explain a teaching framework which has been worked out and discussed thoroughly. Few schools held regular, or frequent, curriculum policy meetings (sometimes because of industrial action), and they were not therefore in a strong position to explain curriculum policy to parents.

Our results clearly show that contact between home and school is not sufficient for communication to occur. Given the association that we found between the level of contact and knowledge that parents had about schools and the progress made by their children (see Chapter 7), failure to communicate effectively has serious implications. Perhaps the essential ingredients for successful communication are first, agreement on the importance of sharing information (for example, agreement on the importance of informing parents of teaching plans); second, a clear outline of the information to be shared (for example, a clear curriculum policy or teaching plan); third, a concern to communicate this information to *all* parents (for example, by sending information in written form, if not to all parents, then at least to those who are unable to come into school); and fourth, skill and confidence in communication (perhaps developed through in-service training).

Parental Satisfaction

Parents' Satisfaction with the Schools

Instead of asking parents whether they were satisfied with the school, we asked which aspects of the school they were satisfied and dissatisfied with, and whether there were any things that they would like to see altered or improved. We found that parental satisfaction with the schools was generally high. For example, at the end of top infants, 91% of parents were able to mention at least one thing they were satisfied with, and 34% said that they were satisfied with "everything or most things about the school". Some parents were more specific. For example, 17% mentioned "the head" or "the teachers", and 15% mentioned "the good atmosphere", "caring atmosphere", or "good discipline". At the end of the reception year 88% of parents said that their child was either happy or very happy at school. In the subsequent two years this proportion decreased to 77%.

Despite this high level of general satisfaction with the schools, each year between 30% and 50% of parents did express views on things that they were dissatisfied with, or would have liked to have seen altered or improved. For example, some felt that school cleanliness (particularly of toilets) could be improved, and others would have liked more supervision in the playground. Nineteen percent of parents said that they were dissatisfied with some aspect of the school's teaching methods, but only 9% were dissatisfied with discipline in the school. The I.L.E.A. Junior Schools Study, carried out at the same time, showed that roughly two-thirds of the interviewed parents were satisfied with the schools (I.L.E.A., 1985a).

White parents seemed somewhat more ready to make comments about the schools than the black parents. Not only did more white than black parents pick out aspects of the schools they were satisfied with (96% vs. 82%, $P<0.05$), but they were also more likely to express specific dissatis-factions (54% vs. 35%, $P<0.05$). This may be because, although there was no difference over the three-year period in an overall measure of both the contact and knowledge that black and white parents had of schools (see Appendix 1), white parents did tend to meet teachers more frequently and to be given more feedback about their children (see following). They were therefore possibly in a better position to make judgements, either good or bad, about the school's performance.

Parents' Satisfaction with and Knowledge about Their Child's Progress

At the primary level, it is unusual for parents to be given a report written specifically for them on their child's work at school. Children are not given grades or marks in each subject, nor are they ranked in order of merit. Under the 1981 Education Act, parents have legal access to all records on their children's educational progress. Parents in the I.L.E.A. are given access to a copy of the final summary page of the teachers' own record sheet for their child, but during the time of the study, teacher record-keeping was affected by industrial action in many schools. In order to know what basis parents had for making judgements about their children's work, we asked teachers what information was made available to parents about children's progress. Each year, we asked parents what information they had received concerning their child's relative progress, and how satisfied they were with the progress that they felt that their child had made.

Teachers.   Although teachers said that they were available to discuss children's progress in general terms with parents, the majority of reception and middle-infant teachers did not give parents any information, either verbally or in written form, about the child's relative position in the class (that is, whether the child was average or above or below average). Teachers said that they avoided giving information of this kind, most often because they did not like to label or compare children.

Parents.   Overall, the majority of parents had received no information on their child's relative progress and fewer black than white parents had been given feedback by the teachers. At the end of the reception year, 41% of the white parents said that they had been told how their child's reading compared with that of other children, whilst only 16% of black parents had been told ($P<0.001$). In the middle-infant year a similar situation was found—44% of white parents had been given this information, compared with 23% of black parents ($P<0.05$). In the top-infant year almost half the parents had been given a written record concerning their children's work, but this did not always give an indication of the child's relative standing in the class. Again, fewer black than white parents were told of their children's relative standing, but in this year the difference was not statistically significant.

The teachers' apparent reluctance to give feedback to black parents may have been related to the teachers' stereotypic views of these parents. When we asked our reception class teachers "What has been your experience of West Indian parents?", only 13% said that they could not generalise about them. Seventy per cent mentioned negative attributes, mainly that they were "over-concerned with their children's education", "had too high expectations", "lacked understanding of British education", "were too authoritarian at home", and "were aggressive, they have a chip on their shoulders". Thirty-four percent of the teachers, including some of those who also made critical remarks, mentioned positive attributes. These often referred to the same characteristics viewed in a positive way, for example, that black parents were "keen on education".

Teachers were more likely to have told parents that their child was doing well than that she was not. In fact, only 20% of all the parents had been given any indication that their child had any difficulties with school work, although our testing suggested that a much larger proportion of children than this were not doing well.

The same reluctance to give feedback was evident in relation to behaviour problems. At the end of the reception year, only 12% of parents had been told their child was, for example, aggressive, quarrelsome, unruly, or showed poor concentration, whilst the teachers had told us that, overall, 26% had problems of this kind. At the end of the top-infant year 22% parents had been told their child had behaviour problems at school, yet a month before this, the teachers had told us that, overall, 34% had problems that interfered with their learning (see Chapter 8).

Despite relatively little information from teachers, at the end of the reception year 70% of the parents said that they were pleased with their child's general progress that year, and this level of parental satisfaction was maintained throughout the infant school period. However, even though many parents said they were pleased with their child's progress, quite a number (for example, 42% in the middle-infant year) also thought that their child had not actually done as well during the year as she was capable of. But parents blamed the school and the child equally for this "under-achievement", rather than just the school or the teacher and her methods. At the end of the top-infant year, only 9% of the parents said that they were definitely worried about how their child had progressed that year.

At the end of the top-infant year, we asked parents to look back at their children's progress in reading and in maths or "number work" over the whole three-year period, and to tell us how satisfied they felt with this progress. The proportion of parents who were either satisfied or very satisfied—namely, two-thirds of parents—was identical for both areas of the curriculum. There were nevertheless a few parents who were dissatisfied, particularly concerning children's progress in reading (16% of parents).

When we asked parents if they had any anxieties about their child's imminent move to junior school, black parents were less often concerned about the move than white parents—that is, 84% were not worried, compared with 65% of white parents ($P<0.05$).

The current impression, created by both politicians and the media, is one of falling standards in state schools, and of parental dissatisfaction with the education system, despite evidence that, in terms of success at public examinations, standards are improving. But our interviews showed that most parents were satisfied with the project schools, and with their children's progress. Given parents' relative lack of knowledge about what went on in the schools, and about their children's progress, it is difficult to know whether the parents were right to be satisfied, or whether theirs was a satisfaction based on ignorance. On standardised tests of reading and of maths, the children were in fact performing overall at a level which was *below* average for their age, a finding which most parents would presumably think was unsatisfactory.

We have already pointed out that, if parents did want to know more about what went on in school, they had to take the initiative in finding out. Asking questions may be difficult for many parents. They may not wish to appear ignorant, or pushy, or to be classed as "over-anxious". In fact, about 80% of parents said that they *felt* that they could approach the head teacher if they had worries about how or what their child was being taught at school, and about one in five parents said that they had actually done so. At the end of the top-infant year, more white parents than black parents said that they had worries that they had *not* approached the school about (10% vs. 2%, $P<0.05$). These worries may possibly have been based on the more specific feedback that white, compared with black, parents had received from teachers about their children's progress. In the absence of feedback, black parents may have believed there was no cause for concern. Tomlinson (1984) has suggested that white parents are less willing than black parents to accept what teachers tell them about the school and their children's progress, and may build up concerns, even though teachers tell them that everything is fine.

The most frequently mentioned worry (mentioned by 13% of parents) which had resulted in them actually approaching the schools was general worry about the teaching of reading. Of those who received a response only about half had been satisfied with the explanation or action that had been taken. Of course, it is unrealistic to expect all parents to be fully satisfied with what teachers tell them. But if we are going to create true partnership between teachers and parents, rather than a situation where "parents feel the teachers only want them to help—not to share" (Wikeley, 1986), then an atmosphere needs to be created, firstly where parents feel that they have open access to information about the schools, and secondly where parents feel that their opinions about their children's education are not only welcomed, but are also genuinely respected and taken into account.

SUMMARY

A high proportion of the male heads of households were (or had been) in semi-skilled or unskilled occupations, and a high proportion of mothers, particularly black mothers, were living as single parents. The majority of the mothers were not in paid employment, and almost half had no formal educational qualifications.

Fewer of the black than the white men were in professional or managerial positions, and the black families were on lower levels of income than the white families. More black than white mothers worked full-time, and more of the black than the white mothers possessed educational qualifications.

There were marked differences in the educational attitudes and beliefs of parents and teachers. The great majority of parents were not only keen to help their children academically at home, but were actively involved in doing so. The level of help being given at home was much higher than had been anticipated by the reception teachers. The help given by parents extended not only to reading (which was encouraged by most class teachers), but also to maths (which was clearly not encouraged by at least one third of teachers each year). By the end of the top-infant year, some of the help given by parents in maths involved quite complex "sums".

We found that the black parents gave their children significantly more help with school work than did the white parents. The black parents were also more positive than the white parents about helping their children in this way.

As well as helping children to learn to read, many parents (or other family members) frequently read stories to their children. This was particularly true during the reception year, when less than one in five parents said that they rarely or never read to their child. Nearly all children wrote spontaneously at home, and by the end of the top-infant year, half of them had written short stories or letters completely on their own. Black children did significantly more writing at home than white children.

When asked to theorise about influences on educational attainment, parents (particularly black parents) were likely to attribute success at school to the teachers or the school itself, but reception teachers were apt to attribute it to the family, or the child's home background. More than three-quarters of the parents, and more black than white parents, hoped that their children would eventually achieve public examination success, but at least a quarter felt that success at school was more likely to come to children from middle- rather than from lower-class backgrounds. Almost none of the reception teachers mentioned any relationship between social class and educational attainment, but many mentioned the importance of parental interest and encouragement.

The proportion of parents who had contact with teachers each year was high, but contact was more frequent between teachers and white, rather than black, parents. We found that the onus had been very much on the parents to find out what was happening in the schools, by looking at children's work, and attending meetings. Very few teachers had made a point of informing all parents about their child or about the curriculum, either by making individual appointments or by keeping parents informed in writing where necessary. Few parents were able to explain in much detail how their children were being taught to read or do maths. About a quarter of the parents had helped in some capacity in the schools each year.

In general, although many parents could think of aspects of the schools that they would have liked improved, many could also mention aspects with which they were satisfied. At least three-quarters of the parents said each year that their child was happy or very happy at school. White parents were more ready than black parents to make comments about the school, whether negative or positive. Parents expressed high levels of satisfaction with their children's progress, despite having been given relatively little information on this matter. Black parents in particular had rarely been told how their children's work compared with that of other children.

6

School Attainment and Progress: Ethnic Group, Sex, and School Effects

In this chapter, we give our results on attainment and progress. First we look at attainment before the sample started compulsory schooling (the nursery results). We then move on to the progress they made during each of the three years of infant school, and over the whole three-year period. Readers will need to bear in mind the distinction we draw between attainment and progress in Chapter 2. We concentrate on the associations between attainment and progress on the one hand, and ethnic group and sex on the other. We also give our results on school differences, and we present correlations between tests, both over time and at any one time.

END OF NURSERY

Tests Used

At the end of nursery, we gave our sample children the vocabulary subtest of the Wechsler Preschool and Primary Scale of Intelligence (W.P.P.S.I.) (Wechsler, 1967), which tests children's ability to define words such as "bicycle". There were no standardised tests of reading, writing and maths which adequately covered the skills in which we were interested, and which were suitable for children of that age (about $4^3/_4$ years). Consequently, we had to construct our own tests of these skills, drawing on items from existing tests.

We tested four different early reading skills. The first was word matching, which involved selecting one out of four possible matches for a target word. The second was an adaptation of Clay's "concepts about print" test (Clay, 1979), which required children to know that one reads print and not pictures, to know that print goes from left to right and from one line to the next, and to know the difference between letters and words. The third was letter identification, where children were shown letters (in upper or lower case) and asked either to name or sound them. Finally, we presented children with ten common words to see if they could read any of them.

To test their writing, children were asked to write their first name without a model, and to copy a phrase ("on the ground").

For maths, we tested five different skills: reading numbers, rote counting, placing and giving (counting out bricks to match the number on a card), one-to-one matching (synchronised counting and pointing), and a test of mathematical concepts. This was adapted from Boehm's Test of Mathematical Concepts (Boehm, 1971), and required children to answer questions such as: "show me the *second* animal", "show me the *widest* door" by pointing to the correct picture on a card.

All the tests were individually administered, and the whole test battery took about 20 minutes to complete. As part of our pilot work, we tested 19 children twice in order to estimate test-retest reliabilities. We obtained values of 0.88 for reading, 0.86 for writing, 0.97 for maths, and 0.89 for W.P.P.S.I. vocabulary, all of which are satisfactory. Certainly, there is no evidence from our study to support the hypothesis that it is not possible to get reliable test scores for such young children. The scores for reading, writing and maths were obtained simply by adding, or giving equal weight to, the relevant subtest scores. Other weighting schemes are possible, however, and some are discussed in Appendix 4.

Attainment

The basic results for each of the subtests are given in Appendix 2. Briefly, we found that at the end of nursery, the average child in our sample could recognise three numbers and name five letters, but less than 3% could read any of the words in our test, and less than half knew that one reads print rather than pictures. About one quarter of the children could write their first name correctly. The average child could count at least a little beyond ten, and could correctly define five of the mathematical concepts. The mean score on the W.P.P.S.I. vocabulary test was slightly below the national norm. For all these subtests, however, there was a wide range of scores.

We found very few differences between black and white children, and between boys and girls, at the end of nursery. The statistically significant differences were that, on average, girls wrote better than boys (the means were 5.2 and 3.9; $P<0.001$), and black children were a little behind white children on two of the maths subtests—placing and giving (5.3 vs. 6.2; $P<0.05$), and mathematical concepts (5.4 vs. 6.3; $P<0.01$)—although there was no difference between the ethnic groups for the maths test as a whole. There were no group differences for reading or for the vocabulary subtests. Also, we found no evidence of any ethnic group sex interactions at this stage. In other words, we did not find that any one of the four groups (white boys, black boys, white girls, black girls) was ahead of or behind the other three, nor that, say, boys were ahead of girls in one ethnic group and behind them in the other. The means and standard deviations for reading, writing, maths and vocabulary for the four groups can be found in Appendix 2 (Table A2.2).

The paucity of differences between the four ethnic group sex combinations in attainments at the end of nursery is one of the most important findings of the project. It means that if any differences between the four groups emerged during infant school, the reasons for these differences could not plausibly be attributed to differences in academic skills before the children started school. Apart from the girls' advantage in writing, the four groups started school with similar reading, writing and maths attainments. But not all children started from the same position, and findings on the home variables associated with children's attainments at nursery are given in Chapter 7. Further discussion of the associations between ethnic group, sex and home factors, and attainment at the end of nursery can be found in Blatchford, Burke, Farquhar, Plewis, and Tizard (1985).

We also found no statistically significant differences between schools in the mean nursery test scores (treating school as a "random" effect—see Aitkin, Bennett, & Hesketh, 1981). However, it must be remembered that we knew nothing about the attainments of children going into reception who had not been in the nursery class, and so there could still have been differences in mean attainment between the 33 schools in the sample at the beginning of the 1982 autumn term.

INFANT SCHOOL

Tests Used

We chose tests which seemed to relate well to the curriculum of inner London infant schools. We also used tests which were known to be reliable (in the sense that if the test were given twice in a short period of time to the same child, the two scores would be close).

The reading test at the end of the reception year consisted of the concepts about print and letter identification subtests used the year before, together with a list of the 30 most common words found in reading schemes used in I.L.E.A., to test word reading. Writing was tested by children copying two phrases which were scored on measures of transcription skills such as letter formation, spacing, and horizontal alignment. The reading and writing scores were an equally weighted sum of the subtests. For maths, we used the Basic Number Skills subtest from the British Ability Scales, which includes both conceptual and arithmetic items. The reception test, like the nursery test, was individually administered. Test-retest reliabilities calculated on a pilot sample of 17 children were 0.98 for reading, 0.64 for writing, and 0.92 for maths.

Reading at the end of middle infants and the end of top infants was assessed with a group test, the Young's Reading Test (Young, 1980). This test is divided into two sections—matching words to pictures and completing sentences, which involves reading for meaning. Maths was assessed with the Young's Group Maths Test (Young, 1978), which consisted of questions such as choosing from five pictures of jars the one which was three-quarters full (which were presented orally), and written addition and subtractions sums. We did not, at any stage, test practical maths skills such as weighing and measuring. The reliabilities given in the manuals for the Young's Reading and Maths tests are 0.95 and 0.94 respectively.

We did not test writing at the end of middle infants because it is difficult to devise a suitable group test for children of that age. But at the end of top infants, the children were given a specially devised writing test in small groups. The test consisted of two separate tasks. In the first, the teacher showed the children a picture and told them an unfinished story about it. The children's task was to write an account of the story as told by the teacher, and then finish it in any way they liked. The stories were scored for independent vocabulary (the number of different words used by the child minus those given to the child by the teacher), quality (e.g. cohesion, complexity and creativity), and transcription and grammar skills. In the second writing test, the children were asked to write a sentence describing each of three pictures. These were scored in terms of grammar, spelling, and appropriateness to the picture. The children were given about an hour to complete the writing tasks, which was usually sufficient.

The development of the writing test required extensive pilot work. As part of the piloting, 28 children were assessed twice, and the following test-retest reliabilities were obtained: 0.83 for independent vocabulary, 0.65 for quality, 0.89 for transcription and grammar, and 0.79 for the sentence test. The test-retest reliability for the writing test as a whole, which again was an equally weighted sum of the separate scores, was 0.88. Inter-rater reliabilities were also calculated for 31 children: these ranged from 0.80 for transcription and grammar to 0.99 for independent vocabulary.

The detailed descriptive results for these tests can be found in Appendix 2. At the end of reception, the average child could name 14 letters and read 11 of the 30 common words. By then, about 90% of the sample knew that one reads print rather than pictures. The mean standard score for reading at the end of middle infants was 89 and at the end of top infants it was 95, compared with the national average of 100 (although, as pointed out in Levy & Goldstein [1984], there must be some doubt about the sampling method used to select the national standardisation sample). For maths, the mean standard scores were 92 at the end of middle infants, and 93 at the end of top infants.

Results for the top infants' story task showed a wide range of skill in writing. Some stories were short, incoherent, and lacked inventiveness, punctuation and neat transcription. Others, on the other hand, were impressive in their breadth of vocabulary, the creativeness and coherence of ideas, and in their correct use of punctuation. The number of words used in the stories varied from 0 to 320, with a mean of 80 words. The number of different words ranged from 0 to 123, with a mean of 45. Just under a quarter of words were "nonsense", in the sense of not being visually or phonetically recognisable, or making sense in context. On average, children asked for 11 words to be written out for them—about one in 4 of all different words used in the story. Stories were mostly easy to read, with words adequately spaced apart, but there was very little use of either capital letters or, more especially, punctuation.

Progress

Reading Progress. It will be remembered that, at the end of nursery, there were no differences between the four groups of black and white boys and girls in reading. During reception and middle infants, the four groups made about the same amount of progress, so they were still at approximately the same level by the end of middle infants. But during top infants, girls made slightly more progress than boys ($P<0.05$).

A more sharply focused picture came from looking at progress over all three years of infant school—in other words, looking at reading attainment at the end of infant school for fixed scores at the end of nursery for those children (n=205) tested on both occasions, and ignoring their reception and middle infants' scores. We then found a statistically significant interaction between ethnic group and sex ($P<0.05$); black girls made more, and black boys made less, progress than the two white groups. (The method we used is explained in Appendix 3; note that all the group differences given in this chapter have allowed for differences between schools.) Figure 6.1 presents the differences between the groups in standard deviation (S.D.) units, with the mean for the groups as a whole set at zero. We see that black girls made 0.4 S.D. units (or the equivalent of 6 points for standardised tests with S.D.s of 15) more progress than black boys, but that white boys made, if anything, slightly more progress than white girls.

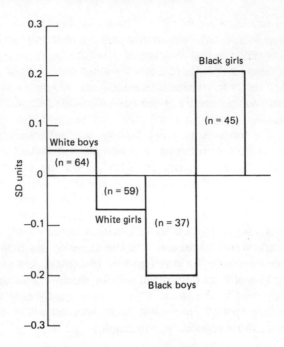

FIG. 6.1   Reading progress: three years of infant school.

A similar pattern of results is obtained if we look just at attainment at the end of top infants. The sample then includes children who were not in the nursery, and is thus larger (n=294). But again we found black girls ahead and black boys behind ($P<0.05$), with the difference between them greater, if anything, than it was for the longitudinal sample.

Writing Progress.   Girls were 0.4 S.D. units ahead of boys in writing at the end of nursery. The four groups made about the same amount of progress during the reception year. As writing was not tested at the end of middle infants, it was not possible to look at progress for the individual years after reception. But we were able to measure relative progress for the whole infant school period and we found, just as for reading, a statistically significant ethnic group sex interaction ($P<0.05$), as shown in Fig. 6.2. Black girls made 0.5 S.D. units more progress than black boys, whereas white boys made slightly more progress than white girls.

The attainment data at the end of top infants (n=253) show black girls 0.8 S.D. units ahead of black boys ($P<0.01$), a difference which is greater than the difference in progress because black girls were ahead of black boys at the end of nursery. The gap between white boys and white girls is,

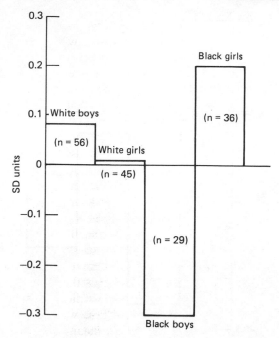

FIG. 6.2   Writing progress: three years of infant school.

however, smaller at the end of top infants than it was at the end of nursery.

In this chapter, we present results for reading and writing separately. In later chapters, however, we combine these, partly because they are obviously related skills (and strongly correlated, as we show later), partly because the pattern of results for reading and writing are similar, and partly so that we can give our results in a more concise form.

Maths progress. The results for maths are more equivocal than the results for reading and writing. During reception, boys made more progress than girls, and white children more progress than black children, the difference being about 0.25 S.D. (and $P<0.05$) in each case. Again, during top infants, boys made 0.2 S.D. more progress than girls ($P<0.01$). There were no statistically significant ethnic group and sex differences for middle infants, and no ethnic group difference for top infants.

Turning to the three years of infant school, we found boys made 0.33 S.D. more progress than girls ($P<0.001$). However, there is some evidence that the difference between white boys and black boys is important, although the interaction is not statistically significant at conventional levels ($P<0.13$). The differences are shown in Fig. 6.3. The possibility that the

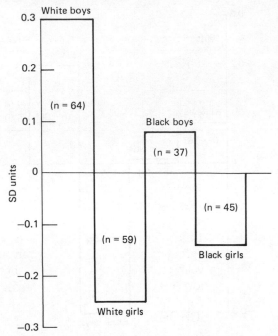

FIG. 6.3   Maths progress: three years of infant school.

ethnic group sex interaction is important for maths, as well as for reading and writing, is reinforced by the attainment data at top infants, which showed black boys, black girls, and white girls all at the same level, and about 0.4 S.D. units behind white boys. But the interaction for attainment is only significant at the 0.10 level.

ATTAINMENTS AT THE END OF THE FIRST YEAR OF JUNIOR SCHOOL

Our study was essentially limited to the infant school years. However. we did test our sample children again at the end of their first year in junior school. We used the Young's reading test again and the N.F.E.R. Basic Mathematics Test B (N.F.E.R., 1971). We tested 160 white children and 102 black children, that is, 89% of the sample tested at the end of infant school (see Table 2.1). Table 6.1 gives the means and standard deviations for our four groups for the reading tests at the end of top infants and the end of first-year juniors.

The pattern of results for the two years is almost identical, with the difference between girls and boys much more marked in the black group,

TABLE 6.1
Reading Attainments (Raw Scores), Top Infants and First-year Juniors

	White Boys	White Girls	Black Boys	Black Girls
Top Infants	21.8 (10.4)	22.6 (8.4)	20.8 (9.9)	26.3 (9.1)
First-year Juniors	27.6 (11.0)	28.9 (8.9)	27.2 (9.6)	32.4 (9.4)

although the interaction between ethnic group and sex is only significant at the 0.12 level for the first-year juniors.

Table 6.2 gives the results for maths for the two years. Again, the pattern of results shows little variation over the two tests, with white boys ahead of the other three groups and with the interaction significant at the 0.07 level for the first-year juniors. The correlations between the top-infants and first-year juniors tests were high (see Table 6.5).

SCHOOL DIFFERENCES

We pointed out in Chapter 2 that we did not set out to study school differences in a systematic way in this project, and so our study of infant schools was not like the I.L.E.A. Junior School Project (I.L.E.A., 1986), or the earlier study of 12 London secondary schools (Rutter et al., 1979). Nevertheless, for the technical reasons explained in Appendix 3, we allowed for differences between schools in our analyses.

When we talk about school differences in progress, we mean that children's progress in reading, writing, and maths was associated with the school they attended. In other words, there were statistically significant differences between schools in the mean amount of progress made by the children in them. Or, putting it another way, the progress of two randomly selected children of the same age within a school was, on average, more similar than the progress of two children attending different schools. Just how large

TABLE 6.2
Maths Attainments (Raw Scores), Top Infants and First-year Juniors

	White Boys	White Girls	Black Boys	Black Girls
Top Infants	32.5 (11.8)	29.0 (10.8)	28.2 (12.6)	28.1 (10.3)
First-year Juniors	22.3 (7.6)	19.7 (7.9)	19.2 (8.2)	19.7 (7.5)

Note: The scores for the first-year juniors are lower because a different test was used then.

these differences were forms the material of this section, but we urge readers to bear in mind the following caveats.

The first caveat is that we did not obtain information on all children in a class or in a school year, nor could we claim that the children we did test were a random sample of their classes. Our sampling strategy will have had unknown consequences for our estimates of school differences. Secondly, we were unable to distinguish between school differences and teacher differences with our data; a more complete analysis would have estimated both differences between teachers within schools and differences between schools, but we did not have enough data to do this. We refer to our results as school differences, but a sizeable proportion of these differences is likely to be attributable to differences between teachers. For these reasons, and particularly because our data on the schools' intakes were limited, the results given here should be read merely as descriptive measures of differences between schools. The fact that children made more progress in some schools than in others does not necessarily mean that those schools were more effective than others (in the sense of "causing" their children to make more progress than children in other schools). We are not in a position to explain the differences between schools that we found; more research is needed before we are able to make statements about what makes an effective infant school teacher and an effective infant school. But, despite all these reservations, we do believe that our results are worth presenting, particularly as there is a dearth of published data on infant school differences.

We concentrate on school differences in progress, rather than on differences in attainment, and we present results for reading, writing and maths separately. As before, we give results for each year separately, and for the whole three-year period. The differences are expressed in two ways. First, we use an intra-class correlation coefficient which measures the similarity of children within a school. This coefficient is rather like the usual Pearson correlation coefficient in that the higher it is the greater the similarity of children's progress within schools, and the greater the differences in progress between schools. If the intra-class correlation were one, then all children within a school would have made the same amount of progress, so that all variation in progress was between schools; if zero, then there is no variation between schools. Results are also presented as the range, in standard deviation units, between the school for which progress was greatest and the school for which progress was least. And, because the range is vulnerable to one or two extreme values, results are also given as standard deviation unit differences for the middle 80% of schools. A more formal description of our measures of school differences is given in Appendix 3.

Reading. We found statistically significant school differences for reading for each of the three years, although the sizes of these differences declined as the children got older; the intra-class correlation coefficients ($\hat{\rho}$) were 0.30 ($P<0.001$) for reception, 0.15 ($P<0.001$) for middle infants, and 0.10 ($P<0.01$) for top infants. Moreover, for the three year period, $\hat{\rho}$ was only 0.09, which was statistically significant only at the 0.06 level. There were no statistically significant differences between schools for the first-year junior test. Table 6.3 presents the differences in S.D. units, and also shows how the differences narrowed over the period; if we omit the three schools at either end of the distribution, then the difference for the whole period (0.3 S.D. units) was quite small.

Writing. For writing, we only have results for the reception year and for the whole period. The school differences for both these periods were substantial, the estimated values of $\hat{\rho}$ being 0.15 ($P<0.001$) and 0.23 ($P<0.001$) respectively. The difference between the two extreme schools was 0.9 S.D. units for reception and 1.3 S.D. units for the three years; the corresponding figures for the middle 80% were 0.65 S.D. units and 0.75 S.D. units. So, for the reception year, school differences for writing progress were smaller than they were for reading but, for the whole period, they were larger.

Maths. Turning to maths, we found no school differences for reception. For middle infants, $\hat{\rho}$ was 0.13 ($P<0.001$), for top infants $\hat{\rho}$ was 0.22 ($P<0.001$), and for the infant school period, $\hat{\rho}$ was 0.11 ($P<0.06$). Table 6.4 gives the difference as S.D. units. For the first-year juniors, $\hat{\rho}$ was 0.14 ($P<0.01$).

Our evidence tends to suggest that differences between schools for any one year are greater than they are for the infant school period as a whole. This is at least consistent with the hypothesis that differences between teachers within schools are greater than the constant differences between schools, and that these teacher differences tend to cancel each other out over the three years. Our finding that there are no differences between schools for maths progress in the reception year is not entirely surprising,

TABLE 6.3
School Differences, Reading (S.D. Units)

	Reception	Middle	Top	All 3 Years
Range	1.5	0.75	0.5	0.6
Middle 80%	0.75	0.5	0.3	0.3

Table 6.4
School Differences, Maths (S.D. units)

	Middle	Top	All 3 Years
Range	0.9	1.0	0.75
Middle 80%	0.6	0.5	0.3

given that we observed little maths teaching during that year (see Chapter 4). However, for reading, the reception year school differences are marked, and suggest that more thought should be given to how reading is taught then.

CORRELATIONS BETWEEN TESTS

For each of the four years of testing, the reading, writing and maths tests were all quite strongly associated with each other. The correlations varied between 0.6 and 0.7 at the end of nursery, and between 0.5 and 0.6 at the end of reception. The correlations between reading and maths at the end of middle and top infants were both about 0.6. The correlation between reading and writing at the end of top infants was 0.77. That is, there was a tendency for children doing well or not so well on one test to do well or not so well on another test. But the correlations are not so high as to preclude children having high scores on one test, and not such high scores on another.

The correlations across time for each of the tests are given in Table 6.5. They are for the black and white sample, but very similar values were obtained for the complete sample. We see the same pattern of correlations for reading and maths: The year-by-year correlations get bigger as the children get older, so that test scores at the end of middle infants are very good predictors of scores at the end of top infants, suggesting that children's attainments relative to their peers become more and more fixed. Also, for all three tests, the correlations between the nursery and reception scores are essentially the same as the correlations between nursery and top infants. Clearly, children who start school with the kinds of skills measured by our nursery tests are likely to be, but will not necessarily be, doing relatively well by the end of infant school. Although it is possible for children lacking those skills on entry to catch up, it is more likely that they will still be behind three years later. But it should be remembered that these correlations tell us only about children's attainments relative to one another, and not about their absolute levels of attainment, or what they learned during their three years of infant school. (The estimated correlations in Table 6.5 are probably on the low side as no corrections have been made for measurement error; this issue is discussed in more depth in Appendix 4.)

TABLE 6.5
Correlations Across Time for Reading, Writing, and Maths

	Nursery and Reception (n=247)	Reception and Middle (n=346)	Middle and Top (n=288)	Top and First-year Juniors (n=256)	Nursery and Top (n=205)
Reading	0.57	0.78	0.85	0.89	0.56
Writing	0.50	n.a.	n.a.	n.a.	0.49[a]
Maths	0.63	0.69	0.81	0.84	0.66

[a] n=166

When we looked at the associations between the oral vocabulary test and our attainment tests at the end of nursery, the correlations were all about 0.45, and thus lower than the correlations between the attainment tests. Vocabulary was also associated with the reading test (correlation, $r = 0.36$), the writing test ($r = 0.34$), and the maths test ($r = 0.40$), at the end of infant school, and again these are lower than the correlations between the tests themselves over time.

Looking in more detail at the correlation between oral vocabulary and the writing test at the end of infants, we found that there were associations with independent vocabulary ($r = 0.34$), with the quality of the stories ($r = 0.32$), and with the ability to write sentences ($r = 0.23$), but not with the measure of transcription and grammar.

We were also interested in which of the separate tests of early reading skills predicted later reading attainment. We discovered that letter identification was a stronger predictor ($r = 0.61$) of reading at the end of top infants than either concepts about print ($r = 0.27$) or word matching ($r=0.31$). We also found that neither concepts about print and letter identification, nor word matching and letter identification, predicted reading at seven any better than letter identification on its own. More details of this work can be found in Blatchford et al. (1987b), and some of its implications are raised in our last chapter.

SUMMARY

The results in this chapter have provided further evidence on sex and ethnic differences in educational attainments, to set alongside the data described in the opening chapter. We have shown that, in inner London infant schools with a multi-ethnic intake from their nursery classes, black and white children started from essentially the same academic position, and that boys and girls started from the same position in reading and maths, but girls had an advantage in writing. There was still no overall ethnic difference at the end of infant school. However, within the black group, we found a considerable divergence of the sexes for reading and writing; black girls were doing relatively well (although even their average reading attainment was below the national average), and black boys relatively poorly. For maths, the pattern was rather different, with an overall sex difference which was, if anything, less marked in the black group than in the white group, and which was at least consistent with the possibility that black boys were falling behind white boys.

Our findings clearly demonstrate that ethnic and sex differences in attainment should not be looked at separately, as we have found evidence for an interaction between them. However, the social class spread of our sample was too small relative to its size to allow us to see whether, and how, ethnic group, sex and social class all interact in their associations with attainment.

We found some evidence that there are differences between infant schools and classes in the amount of progress made. We also found that attainments on entry to infant school are highly predictive of attainments at the end of infant school.

7

Factors at Home Associated with Children's Pre-school Skills and Their Later School Progress

In Chapter 5, we described the parents' role in infant schooling from interviews with the parents. In this chapter, we look at the relationship between information about the children's homes, taken from the pre-school interview, and their reading, writing and maths skills at the end of nursery. We then combine information from the three subsequent interviews to look at the relationship between aspects of the home during the infant school period and the children's progress at infant school. The way in which we constructed variables from the interview responses is outlined in Appendix 1. These variables were of two kinds: "background variables", referring to information about the families and their circumstances, and "process variables", referring to information about the families' educational practices and attitudes.

FACTORS AT HOME RELATED TO CHILDREN'S PRE-SCHOOL SKILLS

Table 7.1 shows the associations between the children's skills at the end of nursery and each of the pre-school home variables (both background variables and process variables). Associations are presented for reading and writing together, and for maths.

TABLE 7.1
Associations Between Home Variables and Children's
Pre-school Skills in Maths, Reading and Writing

	Range of Effect (S.D. Units)			
	Maths	P Value	Reading and Writing	P Value
Background Variables				
Mother's education	0.9	0.001	0.9	0.001
Income	0.7	0.01	0.7	0.05
Single-parent status	–	n.s.	–	n.s.
Process Variables				
1. *Educational experience at home*				
Home teaching	–	n.s.	1.2	0.001
Experience of books	n.a.	n.a.	1.1	0.001
2. *Parent-school relations*				
Contact/knowledge	0.6	0.05	0.5	0.08
3. *Parental attitudes/ beliefs*				
Attitudes to home teaching	0.7	0.01	0.9	0.01
"Theories of educational success"	0.5	0.01	0.3	0.05

Notes: P values for "range of effect" come from a one-way analysis of variance or simple regression. "Range of effect" means the difference that on average was found between the test scores of children at opposite ends of a particular scale. For example, the first entry in the table shows that the differences in maths score between a child whose mother had the lowest possible score for education (i.e. had no formal qualifications) and a child whose mother obtained a maximum score (i.e. had A-levels or above) was 0.9 S.D. units for the maths test.

Background Variables

Because of the large proportion of single-parent families, we did not use a measure of social class. We found that mother's education and family income were both associated with children's early reading, writing, and maths skills (see Table 7.1), so that children of mothers with higher qualifications and children from families with higher incomes had higher scores on entry to school than other children. We found no relationship between single-parent status and children's reading, writing, and maths skills at the end of nursery. That is, children in single- and in two-parent families had comparable levels of skills.

When we looked at the independence of relationships between background variables and children's reading, writing, and maths skills at the end of nursery, we found that mother's education and family income were not only individually, but also independently, related to children's scores. This meant that the relationship between these variables and children's scores could not be explained by the fact that mothers with higher educational achievements tended to have higher family incomes. The two variables together accounted statistically for 8% of the variation in children's reading and writing scores, and 8% of the variation in their maths scores.

Process Variables

Each of the five process variables in Table 7.1 was individually related to children's early skills in reading and writing. That is, children whose parents reported that they had more often tried to teach their child to read; had provided them with more experience of books (by reading to them more frequently, reading right through books, rather than just talking about the pictures, and providing more books); and who had a more positive attitude to helping their children at home, scored higher than other children. Children whose parents believed that educational success was most influenced by the characteristics of the child, rather than of the family or the school, had lower scores than other children. And there was a tendency for children whose parents reported that they had had greater contact with and knowledge of the nursery class to have higher scores than other children.

Only three of these process variables were independently related to children's attainment—the amount that parents said they had taught their children at home, the amount they had given them experience of books, and their theories of educational success. Once these variables had been taken into account, parents' contact with and knowledge of the nursery and parents' attitudes to helping their children at home did not help to explain any variation in children's reading and writing skills.[1] The three independently related process variables together accounted statistically for 16% of the variation in children's scores in reading and writing.

In the case of maths, parents' contact with and knowledge of the nursery, their attitudes to helping their children at home, and their theories of educational success were each related to children's test scores, and each

---

[1] Here and elsewhere in this chapter we use the word "explain" purely in the statistical sense, and do not mean to imply that there is necessarily a causal link between any of the home variables we measured and children's attainment or progress. Such links could best be established through experimental intervention.

was independently related to attainment. Together they accounted for 7% of the variation in maths scores. Parent teaching was not significantly related to children's maths skills. This was perhaps because at the nursery level it was assessed by the parents' response to only one question, whether they taught their child to count, which was answered "yes" by 87% of our sample.

The Relative Contribution of Home Background and Process Variables to Pre-school Attainment

Three variables were significantly and independently related to children's reading and writing skills, and together they accounted for 22% of the variation in scores. These variables were mother's education, the amount that parents taught their children to read and write at home, and the experience that children had of books at home. Once these three variables had been taken into account, family income and parental theories about educational success were no longer important in explaining any variation in children's test scores. Table 7.2 also includes the range of effect for a measure of the children's language skills, the vocabulary subtest from the Wechsler Preschool and Primary Scale of Intelligence (W.P.P.S.I.), which was also highly significant. When this measure was added to the three parent variables discussed earlier, the four variables together explained 37% of the variation in reading and writing scores.

In the case of maths, we found that only mother's education, parents' contact with and knowledge of the nursery, and parental theories of educational success were independently related to children's early maths skills. Together these three variables explained 11% of the variation in children's scores. Once these variables had been taken into account, family income and parents' attitudes to helping their children at home were no longer important in explaining differences between children's scores. Just as for reading and writing, mother's education was a more significant factor in children's early number skills than family income.

TABLE 7.2
Independent Associations Between Home Variables
and Children's Reading and Writing Skills Expressed in
Terms of Range of Effect (S.D. Units)

Home Variable	Range of Effect (S.D. Units)
Mother's education	0.4
Home teaching	1.1
Experience of books	0.6
(W.P.P.S.I. vocabulary score)	(2.3)

Table 7.3
Independent Associations Between Home Variables
and Children's Maths Skills Expressed in
Terms of Range of Effect (S.D. Units)

Home Variable	Range of Effect (S.D. Units)
Mother's education	0.6
Knowledge and contact with school	0.5
(W.P.P.S.I. vocabulary score)	(1.9)

When children's W.P.P.S.I. vocabulary scores were added into the analysis, the proportion of the variation in maths scores explained rose to 22%, and parental theories of educational success were no longer important in explaining differences between children (Table 7.3). Although the relationship between children's W.P.P.S.I. vocabulary scores and maths skills was not quite as strong as the relationship with reading and writing skills (see Table 7.2), it was nevertheless substantial.

Thus the most consistent predictors of the children's pre-school attainments across both reading and maths were the level of the mother's education, and the child's score on the W.P.P.S.I. vocabulary test. This test assesses more than the extent of the child's vocabulary, since the task is to define words (beginning with "What is an apple?"), and the score given depends on the abstractness of the definition ("It's a fruit" is marked higher than "You eat it"). The significance of this test score can be interpreted in several ways. It may be seen simply as a measure of the child's language ability, or as "standing for" more general intellectual abilities, since the correlation between this test and the full W.P.P.S.I. score is 0.6. On the other hand, it may be seen as reflecting the influence of a particular kind of family environment, where stress is laid on understanding the meaning of words. At any rate, the predictive power and independence of this variable is a reminder that it is not only parental support for literacy that is strongly related to attainment, but also the child's own characteristics.

Mother's education was found to be strongly related to attainment at the pre-school stage, and was related to children's skills independently not only of other background variables, but also of all process variables. In other words, families with more highly educated mothers differed in some way that was not measured either by other background variables or by any of the process variables (such as parental teaching) that we selected for study—and this difference was positively related to children's attainments.

The Relationship Between Social Background and Parents' Practices

Up to now we have discussed the relationship between various aspects of the children's homes and their pre-school attainments. We now raise a different issue, that is, the extent to which social background and parental educational practices were related. Did parents with higher incomes, for example, have different educational practices from those with lower incomes? We found that children in families with high incomes had more experience of books than other children ($P<0.001$), but they did not have parents who helped them more with reading, writing, and number at home, nor who had more positive attitudes to helping them in these ways. Higher-income parents were also more likely than other parents to have greater contact with and knowledge of the school ($P<0.01$), and to believe that success at school was due to family influences, rather than to the school or the child ($P<0.05$).

Mothers with higher educational qualifications were more likely to have positive attitudes towards helping their children with reading, writing, and number than other parents ($P<0.01$), but they had not actually given their children significantly more help. Like mothers on higher incomes, they were more likely than less-educated mothers to attribute a child's school success to the family, rather than the school or the child ($P<0.01$), to have read to them more often, and provided them with more books ($P<0.001$), but they had not had significantly greater contact with and knowledge of the school. In contrast, there were no differences in the educational practices of single- and two-parent families, though mothers in two-parent families had significantly greater contact with and knowledge of the school ($P<0.05$).

Two other recent studies have looked at the question of whether parents from different backgrounds provide different educational experiences for their children. Wells (1985) found strong associations between family background (parents' occupation and education) and a number of activities concerned with children's literacy in the pre-school period. These variables included the number of books provided for the child, and the parents' and children's interest in literacy, results which are in many ways similar to our own.

In a study of older children, a research team working in I.L.E.A. junior schools found little difference between families of 8–9-year-old children from different social class backgrounds (measured in terms of either mother's or father's occupation, whichever was "highest") in their involvement in reading activities with their children, in the extent to which they talked with their children about school or in their attitudes towards education. But they did find a significant social class difference in the ownership of different types of books and in the extent to which families took their children on outings and trips of educational value (e.g. visits to exhibitions or museums), and to the library (I.L.E.A., 1985a).

FACTORS AT HOME RELATED TO CHILDREN'S PROGRESS THROUGH INFANT SCHOOL

The majority of research in this area has concentrated on the relationship between factors at home and children's attainment at a particular point in time. In the present study, we analysed the relationship between home factors and children's attainments on entry to school, in order to understand why some children started school with much higher levels of literacy and numeracy skills than other children. But once the children had started at school, we thought that the crucial question was why children with the same skills at entry made different amounts of progress at school.

Progress in Reading and Writing

Our year-by-year analyses are based on progress in reading and writing together in the reception year, and on progress in reading alone for each of the subsequent years. Our analyses of progress over the full three-year period are based on combined results for reading and writing.

The most striking finding was that very few home variables were related to children's progress in reading and writing over the three years of infant school. Commonly used measures of social disadvantage, such as family income or single parent status, were not significantly related to children's progress, either in any individual year or over the three-year period. Mother's education, though significantly related to progress in reading in the middle-infant year, was not related to children's progress over the three-year period as a whole. Nor was there evidence that the parents' satisfaction with the school or their attitudes to helping their children at home were related to progress in these areas, although the extent to which parents were satisfied with their child's progress was related to the progress the child had actually made (range of effect = 1.1 S.D., $P<0.01$).

One factor that was significantly related to children's progress was the level of contact that parents had with the school (range of effect = 0.7 S.D., $P<0.05$). Children of parents who reported more frequent contact with the school, and who expressed greater knowledge of the school's timetable and teaching methods, made greater progress in reading and writing than other children. This relationship was particularly significant in the reception year.

Turning to the children's educational experiences at home, we found that children who wrote more frequently and to a more complex level at home made greater progress in reading and writing than other children (range of effect = 1.7 S.D., $P<0.001$). There was also a tendency for children who had more experience of books (that is, who were read to more frequently, and who had more books—and more complex books—at their disposal at home), to make greater progress (range of effect = 0.7 S.D., $P<0.08$). But we found that children whose parents had listened to them read more frequently at home did not make any greater progress in reading and writing than other children.

It is difficult to know why some children wrote more frequently and to a higher standard at home than other children. It may be that these children found it easier because their writing abilities were greater, or that they were more highly motivated than other children. Or it may be that the parents of children who wrote more were somehow more supportive and encouraging in this area than other parents. Unfortunately, we do not know whether this was the case, but it does seem likely that not only parental behaviour, but also the children's own ability and motivation affected their progress. In line with this, we found that the W.P.P.S.I. vocabulary test was related to progress in reading and writing (range of effect = 0.8 S.D., $P<0.05$).

The fact that we did not find a relationship between the family background factors that we studied and children's *progress* in reading and writing does not mean that background did not play an important role in the children's educational *attainment*. Children from particular types of homes started school with more advanced skills, and, even though they did not make faster progress than other children, they were likely still to be ahead at the end of top infants (Chapter 5).

Our failure to find a relationship between progress and social background may be due to the relatively homogeneous social class background of our sample. The I.L.E.A. Junior School Study, in a more diverse parent sample, found a significant relationship between reading progress in the first two years of junior school and social class (parent's occupation) and home ownership (I.L.E.A., 1985b). Evidence from national cohort studies (see Fogelman & Goldstein, 1976) also shows that working class children make less progress than middle-class children in their junior and secondary school years. Thus, not only did socially disadvantaged children start at a disadvantage, but this educational disadvantage increased during their time at school.

Parent Involvement and Reading Progress

One important, though negative, finding from our study was the absence of any significant relationship between the frequency of parental help at home and children's progress in reading and writing. This finding is disappointing, and puzzling, because it conflicts with other evidence that parental help can be effective in improving reading skills. This evidence is of two kinds. Studies of children attending schools where parents had *not* been encouraged to help their children read have found that children who received most parental help had significantly higher reading scores in the top-infant year than those who received less help (e.g. Hewison & Tizard, 1980; Wells, 1985). The second kind of evidence comes from intervention studies, both in this country and in the U.S.A., where all parents have been asked to hear their children read at home several times a week. In a widely reported London study, carried out in 4 Haringey schools, at the end of 2 years of intervention 66% of the children were reading at or above the national average, compared with 29% in parallel "control" classes in the same schools. And only 6% of the children who had received increased help were very poor readers, with scores of 84 or less, compared with 17% in the control classes (Tizard et al., 1982). A number of other smaller-scale interventions have been equally successful.

However, not all interventions of this kind have been so successful. Hannon and Cuckle (1984) introduced a carefully organised parent involvement scheme in one Lancashire primary school, in which parents were encouraged to hear their children read daily over a period of three years. Since there were no control classes, comparisons could only be made with the reading scores of earlier cohorts of children in the same school. These comparisons suggested that the effects of increased parental involvement on the children's scores were marginal. Similar non-significant results have been reported by Ashton (1978).

One explanation for our own findings could be that because so many of the parents in our study were helping their children, it was not statistically possible to show that parental help improved progress. In fact, 71% of parents in our sample said that they heard their children read at least three times a week in the top-infant year, or had done so in the past, but had stopped because their children were now fluent readers. And 92% of the parents in our sample had heard their children read three times a week or more in at least one of the infant-school years.

However, if this explanation were correct, the general level of reading in our sample schools should have been at least average, as in the Haringey intervention. But the mean reading score of 95 for our sample at the end of the top-infant year was below the standardised average, and very similar to that of other surveys in working-class areas before parental involvement was common. Further, the proportion of poor readers in our sample (25%) was unusually high. Table 7.4 shows that two-thirds of the poor readers were being helped by their parents at least three times a week.

It may be, therefore, that parental involvement is only effective if extra staff are available to support both parent and teacher. In the Haringey project, for example, the researchers worked with the teachers and visited

TABLE 7.4
Reading Scores (Young's Group Reading Test) and Frequency
of Parental Help, Top-infant Year

Reading Score	% of Sample	*Frequency of Help*			Total	
		Occasional or none (n=19)	*1–2 × Per Week (n=27)*	*3+ × per week + Fluent Readers (n=113)*	*%*	*n*
<84	25	23	15	63	100	40
85–99	40	2	27	72	100	64
100+	35	16	7	76	100	55

parents at home twice a term to observe home reading and offer help and encouragement. This may have increased the motivation of teachers, parents, and children, and altered the way in which parents helped their children, and even the books they bought. In our study, we found that few teachers had given demonstrations of how to help with reading, or had sent written information to parents about helping their child with reading. It may be for this reason that we found that parental contact with and knowledge of the infant school was of relatively greater importance for children's reading progress than the frequency with which parents listened to their child read. Parents who have access to more information about teaching in the school may use this to inform, and adapt, their own practices at home with their children. It is also possible that when parent involvement is not part of a carefully planned reading approach some teachers not only fail to inform and support parents adequately, but also devote less time than before to reading, believing that the job can largely be left to parents. Certainly, as we showed in Chapter 3, we found that very little of the children's time in school was spent reading.

Whilst it would be wrong to conclude from our study that parents cannot help to improve reading, our findings do suggest a need to look more closely at what is going on in both successful and less successful parent involvement schemes. This may help to identify the essential features required for parental help with reading to be effective.

Progress in Maths

None of the home background or process variables that we studied were significantly related to children's progress in maths over the three-year period as a whole, although there was a tendency for children who had been given more help with maths at home to have made greater progress in maths than other children (range of effect = 0.4, $P<0.09$). Yearly analyses of progress showed that this relationship was statistically significant only in the reception year ($P<0.001$). Possibly this was because relatively little time was devoted to maths in the reception classrooms (see Chapter 4), so that help at home was all the more influential during this period.

There was no evidence that measures of family background, such as mother's education, family income and single- or two-parent status, were significantly related to children's progress in maths over the three year period as a whole. As was the case with reading, the I.L.E.A. Junior School Study differed from ours in finding that both mother's education and home ownership were significantly related to progress in maths over the first two years of junior school (I.L.E.A., 1985b). We suggested a possible reason for this difference earlier.

We found no evidence to suggest that the amount of knowledge of and contact with the school that parents had, or the degree to which they were satisfied with the school, were significantly related to children's progress in maths. But as with reading and writing, the extent to which parents were satisfied with their child's progress in maths was related to the child's actual progress (range of effect = 0.8 S.D., $P<0.01$).

The findings that we have described for children's progress in maths are in some ways opposite to our findings for reading. That is, we found a tendency for parental help at home to be related to children's progress in maths, though not in reading, whereas we found that the extent of parents' contact with and knowledge of the school was related to children's progress in reading, though not in maths. The W.P.P.S.I. vocabulary test was not related to progress in maths.

As we showed in Chapter 5, teachers in the project schools did not encourage parents to help their children with maths at home. Parents who did help their children did so because they chose to, and not because they had been asked to. The current situation with regard to parental involvement in maths might therefore be described as comparable to the situation that existed in reading before the encouragement of parental help with reading became widespread. At that time, a significant relationship was found between parental help with reading and reading attainment. It seems possible that parents who spontaneously engage in teaching at home do so in a different (and apparently more effective) way than parents who are told they should teach their children, particularly if no guidance is given to these parents as to how to set about such teaching.

SUMMARY

A small number of home variables were found to be statistically (though not necessarily causally) related to children's attainment and progress.

Taking both background and process variables into account, only mother's education, parental teaching of reading and writing at home, and children's experience of books were independently related to children's skills in reading and writing on entry to school.

Turning to children's numeracy skills, only mother's education, the extent to which parents had been in contact with, and knew about, the nursery class that their child had attended, and parents' educational theories (that is, whether or not they believed that success at school could be influenced by factors outside the child) were independently related to children's skills on entry to school.

We found that parents' contact with and knowledge of schools was significantly related to children's progress in reading and writing over the three-year infant school period. Children with higher W.P.P.S.I. vocabulary scores, and those who wrote more extensively at home, also made significantly greater progress than other children.

We found no relationship between the frequency with which parents had listened to their children read at home and children's progress in reading. Our failure to find a significant relationship between parental help with reading and either reading attainment at seven or reading progress over the infant-school period is in contrast to results from previous studies, and we discuss some of the possible explanations for this difference.

Finally, when we looked at progress in maths, we failed to find a significant relationship between any of our home variables and children's maths progress over the three-year infant-school period, although parental teaching was strongly related to progress in maths during the reception year.

8 Factors at School Affecting Progress and Attainment

Our discussion in this chapter is based on information we collected about the children during their three years in the infant school. This information covered two main areas. The first was *teacher judgements*, that is teachers' academic expectations of children, and their judgement about whether children had behaviour problems, were underachieving, and were a "pleasure to teach". The second area was *curriculum coverage*, that is, the range and depth of curriculum coverage in reading, writing, and maths.

We address four issues:

1. Whether teachers' judgements about children, for example their expectations of them, were affected by such factors as the child's sex and ethnic group.
2. The prevalence and nature of children's behaviour problems in school, as perceived by their teachers, and whether these differed between girls and boys, and black and white children.
3. How coverage of the 3R curriculum varied from child to child within the same class.
4. The association between school factors and children's attainment and progress.

TEACHERS' JUDGEMENTS ABOUT CHILDREN

Teachers' Expectations

The Relationship Between Teachers' Expectations and Children's Sex and Ethnic Group

Shortly after the beginning of each school year we asked the teachers of our tested sample whether they considered the children's potential to be above average, average, or below average relative to other children in the class. For the reception year we asked the question of academic work in general. For the middle and top infant years we asked the question separately for maths and reading.

We analysed our results in terms of the mismatch between expectation and actual attainment. There will always be some degree of mismatch, of course, but it is a different matter if the mismatch is systematically related to a child's ethnic group or sex. If this is the case, then it would suggest that teachers are influenced by these factors over and above being influenced by the children's attainment at the beginning of the year.

We defined mismatch in the following way. Each child who was both rated by their teacher and tested was given two scores: the first was the teacher's expectation (above average, average, below average), the second was a three-point rating from their test score. The second score was obtained by ranking the children from high to low by their test score and then grouping them into above average, average, and below average so that the size of these three groups was the same as the size of the three teacher expectation groups.[1] A mismatch, or misclassification, occurred if the teacher expectation rating was not the same as the test rating. We found that about 40% of children were misclassified, a figure which varied little from year to year, or between reading and maths. But only about 5% of children were seriously misclassified in the sense that they were rated below average by their teachers and had an above average test score, or vice versa.

For reading, there was no evidence that misclassification was systematically related to ethnic group or sex. For maths, however, there were systematic relationships. As Table 8.1 shows, teacher expectations for black boys were high relative to their test scores, i.e. more were put in the top group by teachers than would have been expected by their test results and fewer than expected in the bottom group. On the other hand, expectations for white girls were low, in the sense that more were put into the

---

[1] Given the small size of sample in some classes it would have been difficult to divide test scores within classes. Although not ideal, division of test scores was therefore done for the whole sample.

TABLE 8.1
Mismatch Between Teacher Expectations and Test Results for
Maths, by Ethnic Group and Sex (Top Infants)

Teacher Expectations	White Boys (n=95)		White Girls (n=82)		Black Boys (n=50)		Black Girls (n=49)	
	Expect. %	Test %	Expect. %	Test %	Expect. %	Test %	Expect. %	Test %
Above Average	38	39	24	38	46	26	39	33
Average	39	42	56	39	30	44	43	51
Below Average	23	19	20	23	23	30	18	16

Note: To determine whether there was statistically significant variation in mismatch by ethnic group and sex, a test of marginal homogeneity was used (see Koch, Landis, Freeman, Freeman, & Lehnen, 1977). There was a statistically significant ethnic group sex interaction for middle infants ($P<0.01$) and a significant ethnic group effect for top infants ($P<0.01$). However, the pattern of results for middle and top infants was similar. Note that if there is mismatch for one group, there will be a compensating mismatch for at least one other group because, by definition, there is no mismatch for the sample as a whole.

average group, when from their test results we would have expected them to have been in the top group.

These results portray a complicated picture and interpretation can only be speculative. In view of the widely-held concern that teachers' academic expectations for black children are too low, the most puzzling of these results to explain is why expectations for black boys were high, relative to their measured attainment in maths. The finding appears to make no sense, since neither the children's own attainment, nor the teachers' past experience of black children, nor any research findings would seem to warrant such expectations. One possible explanation is that teachers may have been affected by recent I.L.E.A. initiatives on anti-racism, and government reports about the negative effect of low expectations of black children, and did not want to appear biased in their expectations. Results for the white children suggest what one might expect in the light of some previous research (see Chapter 1); that is, the teachers seem to underestimate the maths potential of white girls. The expectations and test results for black girls are fairly well matched, and, if it is true that in general teachers tend to underestimate girls' potential in maths, this could mean that, again, teachers are over-compensating because these girls are black. The effect seems most evident with black boys, indicating a combined effect of higher expectations because they are boys and over-compensation because they are black. A problem with this explanation is that it applies to maths, but not to reading. Teachers' expectations for black boys for reading were not too high relative to their attainments.

A further reason for doubting whether teachers generally believed in the high academic potential of the black boys is that there was no sign that these expectations were translated into action. For example, the black boys had less contacts with their teachers about work, and received more criticism from them than did other groups (see Chapter 4).

The Relationship Between Teachers' Expectations and Other Characteristics of the Children

There are factors other than ethnic group and sex on which teacher expectations might be based. There is evidence that teachers tend to have lower expectations of children with nonstandard English and lower verbal skills (Brophy & Good, 1970; Rist, 1970). It has also been found that expectations are affected by children's social class background (e.g. see Baron, Tom, & Cooper, 1985; Dusek & Joseph, 1985). Douglas (1964), in a British study, found that placement of children in ability groups at the age of eight years was affected by children's socio-economic status (S.E.S.) and personality characteristics. In general, high S.E.S. pupils were misplaced upwards, whilst low S.E.S. pupils were misplaced downwards. Barker Lunn (1970) found similar results. Further, Brophy (1983) argues that teachers are likely to have lower academic expectations of children with problem behaviour, in particular that which threatens a teacher's control of a class. Another important feature has been shown to be the attractiveness of children to teachers. Crano and Mellon (1978) found that teachers had higher expectations of children they thought were a pleasure to have in the class.

On the basis of these studies, we looked to see if the mismatch between teacher expectations and tested performance was related to four factors:

1. children's verbal skills, as measured by W.P.P.S.I. vocabulary subtest scores, assessed at the end of nursery;
2. parental income (a measure of home circumstances)[1]
3. whether children were seen by teachers as having a behaviour problem that interfered with their learning; and
4. whether children were seen by teachers as a pleasure to teach.

Of these four factors, we found evidence in support of two. Children who were misclassified upwards (expectations were higher than test results) tended to have higher verbal skills and to be seen by teachers as "a pleasure to teach". Children misclassified down (expectations too low for

---

[1] It was not possible to use fathers' occupation as a measure of social class because of the relatively large number of single-parent families in the sample (see Chapter 5, p. 73).

tested attainment) tended to have worse verbal skills and not to be seen as "a pleasure to teach". These results suggest that the personal relationship between teacher and child can affect judgements of children's potential attainment. Crano and Mellon (1978) found that teachers' academic expectations were in fact affected more consistently by children's social than academic performance. However, as we shall see later in this chapter, we found that the reasons why teachers found children attractive to teach were most often to do with the children's motivation and inventiveness rather than their physical attractiveness, or even their ability.

There was no evidence that teachers' academic expectations were different for children with behaviour problems or from lower-income families. However, information on income was only available on the smaller, interviewed sample (see Chapter 2), and there were therefore fewer possible instances of "mismatch" between expectations and attainment.

Teachers' Views on Underachievement

If groups of children have similar average test scores, but one particular group (for example, boys, or white children) are more often said to be underachieving, this suggests that the teachers had higher expectations of this group than of the other children. At the end of each school year we asked the teachers to say whether they considered each of the children in our sample to be doing as well as they were capable of, and if not, why this might be the case.

Characteristics of Children Seen as Underachieving

The proportion of children said to be underachieving increased from 24% in the reception class to 38% in the top infants. Children who were seen as "underachieving" had lower test scores than other children not considered underachieving (p<0.01). Only about half of the children with very low test scores in reading and maths were considered to be underachieving, compared with a third of the children with higher scores. The judgement of underachievement was more likely to be made (correlation = 0.38, P<0.001) if, in a separate judgement, the teacher also considered that the child had behaviour problems (see later).

When asked why they thought individual children were underachieving, the teachers most often mentioned emotional and behavioural problems (e.g. "lack of confidence", "he's got to be in the right mood", "easily frustrated", "loses his temper") and failure to concentrate. Other causes, including absence from school, laziness and adverse home circumstances, were less frequently mentioned.

Table 8.2 shows the percentage of children in each of the four groups—

TABLE 8.2
Children Seen by Teachers as Underachieving: Ethnic Group and Sex Differences

	White Boys (n=86)	White Girls (n=75)	Black Boys (n=44)	Black Girls (n=45)
3 points in time	3%	1%	11%	2%
2 points in time	23%	9%	30%	11%
1 point in time	35%	36%	30%	42%
0 point in time	38%	53%	30%	44%

Girls seen as underachieving less than boys, $P<0.001$. Ethnic differences and ethnic x sex interaction n.s.

Note: This table was analysed using a log-linear model with the response (underachievement) treated as an ordered linear scale.

white boys, white girls, black boys and black girls—who were seen by teachers as underachieving. This ranged from those seen as underachieving every year ("3 points in time"—scored 3) to those never seen as underachieving ("0 points in time"—scored 0). It can be seen that boys were much more likely than girls to be seen by teachers as underachieving. As we saw in Chapter 6, whilst black (though not white) girls were ahead of boys in reading over the three years, boys were slightly ahead of girls in maths. These sex differences in attainment seem too small to account for such a large difference in teacher judgements about underachievement, and suggest that teachers expected a higher level of attainment from boys.

One limitation of the underachievement ratings was that they were for children's overall achievement in relation to their perceived potential; we have not got separate results for maths and reading that would directly be comparable with the expectation results. The expectation results suggest that it is only in maths that the mismatch with test results occurs. It is possible that had we obtained underachievement judgements for maths separately, we would have produced a similar finding.

Parents' Assessment of Underachievement

In order to find out how much agreement there was between teachers and parents in their judgement about whether individual children were underachieving, and to compare parents' and teachers' reasons for why children were underachieving, we asked parents at the end of the middle and top infant years the same question as teachers (see Chapter 5), that is, "Do you think he/she is doing as well as he/she is capable of?"

Many more parents than teachers thought their children were underachieving—55% did so in the top infant year, compared with 38% of children picked out by teachers. Presumably, therefore, parents had higher expectations of their children than the teachers did. There was not very good agreement between teachers and parents as to which children were underachieving—for example, in the top-infant year, in about 50% of cases where the mothers thought the children were underachieving, the teachers did not, and in a third of cases where teachers thought children were underachieving, the parents did not. Unlike teachers, parents did not think that boys were underachieving more than girls. And black parents were no more likely to think their children were underachieving than white parents.

Like the teachers, the parents most often gave as the reason for underachievement the child's own characteristics, e.g. poor concentration, laziness, lack of confidence, but over a third of the parents thought that the teachers were to blame, because they did not stretch the child enough, had too low standards, or used the wrong methods. No teachers mentioned such factors as a cause of children's underachievement.

Pleasure to Teach

Overall there was a rise, from middle to top infants, in the numbers of children seen to be a pleasure to teach. In middle infants there were 29%, in top infants 39%, with 17% of the sample so rated on both occasions.

We also asked teachers to say for what reason they found children a pleasure to teach. In both years the most common reason given was that the children were highly motivated (e.g. child was "keen to learn", "a trier", "enthusiastic"). The next most frequently given reason in both years was that these children were inquisitive, creative, etc.—what one might call having a "lively mind". Other qualities mentioned were the child's personality (e.g. "just a nice, pleasing child"), being receptive and quick to respond, and being helpful. Teachers felt particularly warm towards children who they saw as having a lively and motivated approach to classroom activities, but they rarely mentioned ability as a reason for finding them a pleasure to teach. Later, we discuss whether those children seen to be a pleasure to teach did in fact have higher attainments in reading, writing, and maths.

There was no evidence that teachers were more inclined to say that either girls or boys were a pleasure to teach, or black or white children.

CHILDREN'S BEHAVIOUR PROBLEMS AT INFANT SCHOOL

Research has shown that distractability or aggressiveness in children is associated with poor school performance, at least in reading (see Chapter 1). At the end of each of the children's three years we asked the teachers whether they thought, for each child, that they had a definite behaviour problem, a mild problem, or no real problem. We told teachers that by behaviour problems we meant behaviour—aggressiveness, distractability, withdrawal, etc.—that concerned them because it interfered with academic or social learning. We then asked, for those children considered to have problems, what type of problem or problems they had.

Prevalence of Behaviour Problems

Taking a mean for the 3 years, 67% of the children were seen as having no behaviour problems, 17% were considered to have mild behaviour problems, and 16% definite behaviour problems. There was a marked increase from the reception to the middle infant year in the number of children considered to have a behaviour problem (26% to 39% for the 392 children asked about on both occasions; $P<0.01$). One explanation for this may be that during the reception year children were still finding their feet, whereas by the middle infants they may feel freer in the classroom and less inhibited, and thus more likely to show the kind of behaviours seen by teachers as a problem. Or the increase may be due to the greater demands placed on children in the middle infants. Only 17% of children were seen as a problem on both occasions, perhaps because of a lack of persistence in the problem behaviour, or because most children had different teachers each year and may have been perceived rather differently by them. There was no change in the prevalence of behaviour problems from the middle to the top infant year.

It is difficult to assess how much teachers were disturbed by children's behaviour problems. According to the teachers only 7% of children at the end of the top infants were difficult to control, but it is possible that teachers were reluctant to make this admission.

Types of Behaviour Problems

The problems described by teachers were aggressiveness, shyness or nervousness, withdrawn behaviour, tearfulness, disobedience, distractability, overactive behaviour, immaturity, laziness, slyness or teasing, and children being overdemanding for attention, having social difficulties with peers, and having tempers and emotional problems (e.g. "screams and has tantrums", "terrible moods"). We combined these individual behaviours into three groups: (1) aggressive/disobedient (aggressive, disobedient, demanding, social difficulties with peers, sly, or teasing); (2) distractible (distractible, overactive), and (3) anxious (shy or nervous, withdrawn, tearful). Taking a mean for the 3 years, aggressive/disobedient and distractable behaviours were equally prevalent (15% and 16% respectively of all children). Anxious behaviour was less common (about 8% of all children).

Ethnic and Sex Differences in Behaviour Problems

Ethnic and sex differences are shown in Table 8.3 for the three years together. A definite problem in one year was given a score of 2, a mild problem a score of 1, and no problem a score of 0. These scores were summed for the three years to produce a score that could be seen as representing the severity of children's behaviour problems.

We found that there were statistically significant differences between the sexes and ethnic groups. That is, boys were seen as having more problems than girls and black children were seen as having more problems than white children. This meant that black boys were particularly likely to be described as having behaviour problems, especially definite problems. For example, 14% of black boys were said to have definite problems every year, and only 20% were said never to have a problem.

By adding up the number of problems over the three years (to produce a scale from 0—no problems any year—to 3—the same specific problem every year), and using the statistical analysis described in Table 8.2, we found that black boys were said to have more problems to do with aggression and disobedience than the other three groups ($P<0.05$). Black children and boys were seen as having more problems of distractability than white children and girls ($P<0.01$). Black children were also seen as more anxious than white children ($P<0.05$), though, as we have said, problems of this kind were not often reported.

It must be remembered that our data on children's behaviour problems are based on teachers' judgements. To what extent are the judgements

TABLE 8.3
Behaviour Problems (Teachers' Views)—Ethnic Group
and Sex Differences: All Three Years

Score	White Boys (n=79) %	White Girls (n=70) %	Black Boys (n=44) %	Black Girls (n=46) %
6	4	3	14	2
5	1	4	9	0
4	5	3	11	13
3	1	3	14	11
2	22	13	16	17
1	25	14	16	20
0	42	60	20	37

Scoring: Definite Problems = 2, Mild Problems = 1, None = 0.

For details of statistical analysis see note to Table 8.2. Ethnic group and sex differences both $P<0.001$

valid? Do they reflect a bias or prejudice against black boys? Or do they reflect teaching problems with children?

Another source of evidence we had about behaviour problems in the class was observations on the children's classroom behaviour. We looked to see whether children thought by teachers to have a behaviour problem tended to spend more time in "task avoidant" behaviour in the classroom (i.e. disruptive and aggressive behaviour, and daydreaming, observed using the systematic observation schedule described in Chapter 4). This did indeed prove to be the case, although the differences were not large; for all three years "task avoidant" behaviour was higher for those children with problems than for those with no problems (see Table 8.4). For example, in the top infant year, the 55 children seen to have no problems were task avoidant in 8% of observations, whereas the 39 seen to have problems were task avoidant in 10% of observations.

However, as we described in Chapter 4, the time-sampling observations showed that disruptive and aggressive behaviour were infrequent, during classroom learning time at least. More research is required in order to clarify this apparent contradiction between the prevalence of problem behaviour identified by teachers' reports and by classroom observations.

In other results from the time-sampling observation study, reported in Chapter 4, we found that black boys were more likely to fool around with other children when the expectation was that they would be working. They also tended to receive more disapproval/criticism from teachers.

The observation results tend to suggest agreement between teachers' perceptions of behaviour problems and children's actual behaviour in class. There are at least two explanations of this. The most obvious is that teachers' perceptions are valid, and that they are reporting behaviour problems they observe in the class accurately. But it is also possible that teachers' perceptions may themselves play a causal role in affecting children's behaviour.

TABLE 8.4
Association Between Behaviour Problems and "Task-avoidant" Behaviour

	% All Observations "Task Avoidant" and numbers of children					
	1983		1984		1985	
	%	N	%	N	%	N
No problems	8	(76)	10	(59)	8	(55)
Behaviour problem (mild and definite)	9	(36)	13	(48)	10	(39)

Note: See Chapter 3 for definition of "task-avoidant" behaviour.

The processes at work are likely to be complex, and we can only speculate about their nature. One possibility is that teachers are affected by the popular view that black males are more likely to be physical and aggressive (see Chapter 1), and this would perhaps exaggerate their perception of black boys' behaviour problems. If this is true, and if the black boys become aware that they are seen by teachers as having more problems than other children, and of the extra criticism and disapproval they receive, they may in turn react to this, perhaps aggravating the very behaviours seen by teachers as problems that interfere with their learning.

Complex as this explanation might appear, it is unlikely to do justice to the cumulative effects of teachers' and children's interactions with each other over the three years of infant school. Moreover, as reviews of teachers' expectation research have shown, expectancy effects are likely to be found to occur only with some teachers (Brophy, 1983). Clearly, in order to understand better the origin and prevalence of behaviour problems in class, more detailed research is required on the associations between teachers' perceptions, children's behaviour, sex, and ethnic group.

Teachers' Views on Underlying Causes of Behaviour Problems

At the end of the middle-infant year we asked the teachers what they saw as the underlying cause of the behaviour problem for each of the children rated. By far the most common cause was seen to be factors in the home (46% of those with problems), particularly relationships in the home, e.g. lack of attention, and affection, or parents being over-strict. These reasons were more likely to be mentioned in the case of black than white children (24% of black children, 14% of white children, $P<0.05$). This may be part of a general tendency, commented on in Chapter 1, to attribute perceived school problems of black children to factors in the home. Only six children (2%) were said by teachers to have problems caused by school factors (e.g. changes of teachers within the year, conflict with another child in the same class). However, separate analysis of results from the sample of interviewed parents did show one strong association between home factors and teachers' judgements about children's behaviour problems. That is, children with single mothers were much more likely to be described as having a behaviour problem. In the top-infant year, for example, 71% of the black children with single mothers were said to have problems, compared with 41% of the black children from two-parent families. The same pattern of results was found in the reception and middle-infant years. (We had few white children from single-parent families.) However, the design of our study could not provide insights into the dynamics that might be involved, and studies of this issue are certainly required.

Information Given to Parents About Their Childrens' Behaviour Problems

In the middle-infant year we asked teachers if they had told parents about their children's behaviour problems. Only one in four of the parents had been told. Reasons given by the teachers for not telling parents were that the teacher didn't see the parents, it would make the problem worse, it wasn't serious enough, or that the parents were unco-operative or difficult. The majority of parents told were said to have responded positively; 35% of them were supportive of the teacher, or tried to help, and 36% agreed with the teacher's view. However, 25% of those told were said to have responded negatively—15% passively, in the sense that they couldn't see the problem, or said the child couldn't change, and 10% actively negative, e.g. they disagreed, or blamed the teacher.

Parents' Views on Behaviour Problems

In our last interview with parents, at the end of the top-infant year, we asked about the children's behaviour at home. Twenty-two per cent thought their child showed problems; 16% thought their child had mild problems, and 6% thought their child had definite problems. The most frequently mentioned problems were disobedience—mentioned by 9% of parents—followed by temper and emotional problems. Eleven percent of parents thought their child was at times difficult to control at home. White parents were more likely than black parents to say this (15% of white parents, 4% of black parents, $P<0.05$).

At the same point in time (end of top infants), teachers reported that 34% of the children had behaviour problems at school. There was little agreement between teachers and parents about individual children. About 30% of those children seen by teachers as a problem at school at the end of the top infants were seen by parents as a problem at home and 34% of those children seen by parents as a problem at home were seen by teachers as a problem at school. In contrast to teachers, parents did not think that black children had more behaviour problems than white, or boys more than girls.

A similar disagreement between teachers' and parents' views on children's behaviour problems was reported by Rutter et al. (1970), where agreement between teachers and parents as to which children were in the most deviant group (selected on the basis of Rutter's questionnaire) was found for only one child in every six or seven. It is likely that some types of behaviour (e.g. lack of concentration) are more of a problem in the school setting. It may also be that some behaviours are more likely to occur at school than at home; aggressiveness and fooling around, and also withdrawn and nervous behaviour, for example, may occur more often when children come together in groups.

CURRICULUM COVERAGE IN READING, WRITING, AND MATHS

We have already described in Chapter 3 the large differences we found between teachers in the 3R curriculum they presented to children in their classes. In this section we describe differences we found in the curriculum given to different children within the same class. It will be remembered that when we refer to the curriculum, or "curriculum coverage", we are referring to work in reading, writing and maths and not to the curriculum as a whole.

We collected information on children's curriculum experiences by drawing up checklists of activities in the areas of written language and maths. The same checklist was used in two ways, firstly to describe the curriculum introduced to *any* one child in the class, and secondly the curriculum activities *actually* introduced to each child. This information was collected during the summer term at the end of each school year. The checklists were first explained to teachers and two completed with the research officer present. The rest of the checklists were then left for teachers to complete later.

During pilot work it became clear that curriculum items could not be graded in advance in terms of difficulty; teachers disagreed, for example, about whether learning letter sounds or learning whole words was more difficult. For this reason we decided to focus on the range and depth—what we call "curriculum coverage"—of topics in written language and maths. It seemed important not to just add up the number of items covered by each child but, before summing, to weight each item in such a way that its score reflected the proportion of children who had been taught this item. The assumption was that activities introduced to fewer children would be perceived as more difficult and so to this extent the method of scoring reflected the difficulty of items as well as their range. This method gave a curriculum coverage score for each child. Interested readers can find more about the method we used in the paper by Farquhar et al. (1987).

Differences Between Children Within the Same Class

We selected two ways of looking at differences in the curriculum taught to different children in the same classrooms. Firstly, we looked at standard deviations (S.D.) for curriculum coverage scores in each classroom. As an example, in the reception year, these ranged from 0 to 24.7 for mathematics, and from 1.7 to 11.8 for written language. These figures show that in some classes most children receive very similar curriculum coverage scores (the S.D. scores were low), whereas in other classes children's scores varied greatly (the S.D. scores were high).

Secondly, we looked at the proportion of children who could have been taught a curriculum item—that is, who were in a class where that item was taught—and yet were not taught that item. By way of illustration we show results for subtraction in the reception and middle-infant years (see Table 8.5).

These results show that being in a class where subtraction is taught does not mean that a particular child will be taught subtraction. This reinforces the results of Bennett et al. (1984) and shows that any description of the curriculum at the class level may well overestimate the range of curriculum experiences of individual children. Later in this chapter we see whether differences between children in their curriculum experiences were related to their attainment and progress.

Explanations for Differences Between Children in Curriculum Coverage

Having found that differences existed between children within the same class in the curriculum reported to have been taught to them, it seemed important to find out why this was the case, since the decision might have important effects on their progress. At the end of the reception year we asked teachers to summarise for each child whether they thought they had covered more, or less, or about the same amount of the curriculum as other children, and, if either more or less, to explain why they thought this had happened. Teachers gave four different types of explanation: firstly, children's skills and ability on entry into school; secondly, their approach to learning (motivation, concentration, and co-operation); thirdly, home influences on learning, particularly the amount of parental help and material home conditions; and fourthly, children's attendance at school. We examined each of these four explanations to see if they were supported by our own data.

TABLE 8.5
Proportion of Children Not Introduced to Subtraction Items
Taught in Their Classes (First Two Years of Infant School)

Checklist Item	1st Year %	2nd Year %
Practical subtraction	33	10
Practical subtraction (recorded)	54	14
Written subtraction (with aids)	73	19
Written subtraction (without aids)	0	35

The first was supported by the statistically significant associations ($P<0.001$) we found between school entry skills (the nursery test results) and both language (correlation = 0.43, $P<0.001$) and maths (correlation = 0.31, $P<0.001$) curriculum coverage scores. In other words, those children who came into school with higher 3R skills were likely at the end of the year to have covered more of the curriculum than other children. The second of the explanations put forward by teachers—a poor approach to learning—was not supported by our data; those children judged by their teachers at the end of the year to have behaviour problems (which included problems of concentration, overactivity, and disobedience—all indicative of a poor approach to learning) were no more likely to have covered less of the curriculum than other children, once entry skills had been taken into account.

Similarly, once entry skills were taken into account, we found that parental help at home and a measure of material home circumstances (parental income) were not related to curriculum coverage, contrary to teachers' beliefs. Children's attendance was also not significantly related to curriculum coverage.

It seems, then, that of the reasons put forward by teachers, only the skills that children brought with them to the classroom were in fact related to the range of curriculum covered.

We looked to see whether other factors, not suggested by teachers, might be related to curriculum coverage in the reception year, over and above children's skills and abilities on entry into schools. Two factors emerged as the most important. The first was the school the child attended; we found large differences ($P<0.001$) between schools in the curriculum covered, after controlling for children's academic skills on entry. Unfortunately, we do not know why this should be the case. This is because, as we described in Chapter 2, we only studied a sample of children from each class, and hence we could not generalise about the class or school as a whole. We did not therefore attempt to collect the detailed information about the schools needed to explain differences between them.

The second factor related to curriculum coverage was teacher academic expectations for children; those children for whom teachers had higher expectations had also covered more curriculum items ($P<0.001$ for both maths and written language for all three years). This association was still significant after having controlled for children's academic skills on entry ($P<0.001$ for the reception year). In other words, the association between teachers' expectations and the curriculum given to a child did not appear simply to be a reflection of the child's academic skills. We look further at this association, and what it might tell us about how teacher expectations are mediated, later in this chapter.

Ethnic and Sex Differences in Curriculum Coverage

There was no evidence, over the three years, of any systematic differences between boys and girls, and black and white children in the curriculum they were introduced to.

ASSOCIATIONS BETWEEN FACTORS AT SCHOOL AND CHILDREN'S ATTAINMENT AND PROGRESS

Two measures had the strongest and most consistent relationship with school performance. They were teacher expectations and curriculum coverage.

Teacher Expectations

At the beginning of this chapter we looked at the mismatch between expectations and attainment collected at the same period in time. We saw that only 5% of children were seriously misclassified. To find out about the relationship between expectations and later attainment we calculated associations between teacher expectations, collected in September, and children's attainments measured the following July. Each year expectations were highly and significantly related to attainment ($P<0.001$).

The more important question is whether teacher expectations were related to achievement once the scores at the beginning of the year were taken into account, that is, to children's *progress*. These results are shown in Table 8.6.

The associations between teacher expectations and progress are expressed in terms of the range of effect in standard deviation units. To give an example, Table 8.6 shows the association between teacher expectations

TABLE 8.6
Associations Between Teacher Expectations and Progress

	Range of Effects (S.D. Units)	P
Reception		
Maths	0.4	0.01
Reading and Writing	0.6	0.001
Middle		
Maths	0.7	0.001
Reading	0.4	0.01
Top		
Maths	0.5	0.001
Reading	0.8	0.001

Note: See Appendix 3 for explanation of the statistical analyses used to produce this table.

and progress in maths during reception to be 0.4. This means that the difference in maths progress from the top of the teacher expectation scale—that is, those rated above average—and the bottom of the teacher expectation scale—that is, those rated below average is 0.4 S.D., a statistically significant difference.

Results in Table 8.6 show that expectations are significantly related to progress in each year and therefore suggest that expectations have an effect over and above simply picking up differences in ability.

The association between expectations and progress is smaller than that between expectations and end of year attainment. However it is higher on average than that reported in a recent meta-analysis of American studies (Smith, in Brophy, 1983, 0.38 S.D.) and about the same as our own estimates of the sex and ethnic group differences (see Chapter 6).

Curriculum Coverage in Reading, Writing, and Maths

We have already seen that the range of 3R curriculum coverage varied considerably for individual children, even within the same class. The range of activities in maths and written language presented to children will determine the boundaries and depth of children's experiences in these areas, and might therefore be expected to have an effect on their progress.

We found that associations between curriculum coverage scores and end-of-year attainments were highly significant ($P<0.001$) for each school year.

Again, these results may not be surprising. It may just mean that teachers are good at choosing work that matches children's abilities. The more crucial question, again, is whether curriculum coverage scores are related to end-of-year scores, once scores at the beginning of the school year are taken into account. These results are shown in Table 8.7.

These results again show a statistically significant effect, and indicate that the range of curriculum activities given to children are related to progress, over and above teachers' appropriate responses to different levels of ability.

To summarise, of the school-based measures we looked at, we found that teachers' academic expectations and children's curriculum coverage showed the strongest and most consistent associations with school progress. What do these results mean in terms of influences on children attainment and, in particular, how do expectations affect children?

One possible explanation arises out of the additional finding, discussed earlier, that teachers' expectations and children's curriculum coverage scores were associated in each of the three years, and this was so even when children's test scores at the beginning of the year were taken into account.

Attempts to explain how expectations affect children's attainment have

TABLE 8.7
Associations Between Curriculum Coverage Scores and
Progress

	Range of Effects (S.D. Units)	P
Reception		
Maths	1.1	0.001
Reading and Writing	1.6	0.001
Middle		
Maths	1.7	0.001
Reading	1.1	0.001
Top		
Maths	0.7	0.001
Reading	0.8	0.001

tended to draw on complex models involving behavioural and psychological components (e.g. Brophy & Good, 1974; Cooper, 1979; Rogers 1982). There are two processes most commonly seen at work. The first—that expectations are reflected in teachers' classroom interactions with children (e.g. Brophy & Good, 1970; Cooper, 1979; Galton & Delafield, 1981)— received little support from our results. We looked at associations between expectations and measures of teacher and child behaviour from the time-sampling observation study. We hypothesised that children for whom teachers had higher expectations would receive from their teachers more praise, less criticism, more instructional contact, have more contact from teachers about work in hand, and engage in less "task avoidant" behaviours. We found no clear or consistent evidence over the three years to support these hypotheses. It is possible that a finer categorisation of behaviour—for example of the appropriateness and type of teacher feedback on tasks, and of different types of teacher response to incorrect and correct pupil answers (see Brophy & Good, 1970), might have detected more subtle differences. The second way expectations are often believed to operate is through mediating psychological processes in the child, for example through achievement motivation and self-esteem (see review by Rogers, 1982). We did not have data on such factors and so could not test this theory.

However, our results linking expectations and curriculum coverage suggest a more direct route. That is, we found that those children for whom teachers have higher expectations tend to be given a wider range of activities in written language and maths, over and above their attainments at the beginning of the school year. This can only be a partial explanation of how expectations operate because, as we shall see in Chapter 10, expectations and curriculum coverage were independently related to progress. But there is nonetheless some degree of overlap and it appears that expectations of individual children may be one guiding force behind decisions made by teachers about what activities to give them. The curriculum given to children may therefore be one way in which teachers' expectations can operate in the classroom. (A more extended discussion of the issue can be found in Farquhar et al., 1987.)

Behaviour Problems, Underachievement and Pleasure to Teach

Of the other factors at school, the teacher judgements of children's behaviour problems, whether children were underachieving, and whether children were "a pleasure to teach" were all significantly related to children's end-of-year attainments ($P<0.01$). However, associations between these three variables and progress were not as strong as expectations and curriculum coverage (see Chapter 10).

Classroom Interaction

As we described at the beginning of this chapter, we collected information on children in schools about their classroom behaviour and interactions; for example, the amount of teacher-pupil interaction, teacher praise and criticism, and time "on-task". We saw in Chapter 1 that research over the past two decades, especially in North America, has made much of the associations between these "process" variables, taken from systematic observations, and "outcomes" in terms of attainment—so-called "process-product" studies.

The time-sampling observation study of children's behaviour during classroom work time provided the basis for the general description presented in Chapter 4. But in looking at associations between observation measures and attainment, one wants to use data about the *individual child*, and we came to the reluctant conclusion that this would not be advisable. The reason for this is technical but we believe important. It concerns the stability of observational data on individual children. We found that variation between and within days for some variables was considerable. This can be shown to affect the reliability of observations (Plewis, in press) It is likely that instability of behavioural data in this sense is a feature of most observational studies and we are sure that this has not been given the attention it deserves. It is possibly one reason for the generally inconsistent results linking measures of classroom interaction with children's school progress.[2]

---

[2] There is no place to describe fully this issue here and interested readers are referred to the papers by Blatchford et al. (1987a) and Plewis, in press.

SUMMARY

Results on the mismatch between teachers' expectations and children's attainments suggested that teachers had high expectations of black boys and low expectations of white girls in maths. One tentative interpretation put forward to account for this puzzling finding was that a tendency to underestimate girls in maths was combined with teachers not wanting to appear biased against black children. Teachers tended, therefore, to over-estimate black boys (because they were both black and boys) and under-estimate white girls (because they were both white and girls). Results on teachers' judgements of which children were underachieving suggested that teachers had higher expectations for boys. Teachers also appeared to have higher expectations than predicted from the test results of children with better W.P.P.S.I. vocabulary scores and those who were seen by teachers as a pleasure to teach.

There was no evidence that teachers had lower expectations of black children overall, or that their expectations were affected by the background factor of income or whether children were considered to have behaviour problems.

It was found that a third of children were reported by teachers to have a behaviour problem that interfered with their learning. Of these, 16% were considered to be serious problems. Boys and black children were reported to show more problems. The most common problems were aggressiveness/disobedience and distractability.

Parents reported fewer behaviour problems at home and there was little agreement with teachers about which children had problems.

We found differences in the curriculum taught to children within the same classes. These differences were significant even having controlled for children's differing levels of skills on entry to school.

We found that teachers' expectations and the range of children's curriculum coverage, and, to a lesser extent, whether children were seen to have behaviour problems, to be underachieving, and to be a pleasure to teach, were associated with children's school attainment and progress. Teacher expectations and curriculum coverage were themselves associated, and it was suggested that the range of curriculum activities given to individual children may be one way that teachers' expectations operate in the classroom.

9
The Child's Point of View

INTRODUCTION

Children are not often asked their opinions by researchers or adminis-
trators about such basic aspects of their lives as how they view school,
playtime, or holidays. Perhaps they are considered too inexperienced to be
taken seriously. Or perhaps adults prefer not to consider a viewpoint that
might cast doubt on the arrangements that they make. However, it seemed
to us that a study of infant schooling would be incomplete without an
attempt to describe the children's perception of their experience.

So, towards the end of their last term in the infant school, we interviewed 133 7-year-old children in our 33 project schools. The sample was
made up of those children whose parents we had interviewed throughout
the study, and who were not absent from school at the time of our
interviews. There were 37 white boys, 28 black boys, 38 white girls, and 30
black girls. (It will be remembered that the white children were of U.K.
origin, the black children of Afro-Caribbean origin.)

Initially, we tried out various ways of interviewing children, including
group interviews at school and individual interviews at home. In the end,
we decided to interview them individually at school. Interviewing at home
was logistically difficult, because of the uncertainty of finding the children
in, and it would not always have been possible to find a place where
children could talk privately. Group interviews at school sometimes produced interesting discussions, but again we felt that in this situation some
children did not talk freely. Further, group interviews cannot provide

systematic data on individuals. The individual interviews that we finally settled on lasted 20–30 minutes, and were carried out in a quiet corner of the school. The children's answers were recorded verbatim as far as possible. They generally seemed to enjoy the interview, although naturally they varied in their forthcomingness, and in the degree to which they needed encouraging.

The interviewers were the three researchers (JB, PB, CF) who had worked in the schools for the previous three years, and were thus to an extent familiar figures to the children. There was no ethnic matching of interviewer and interviewee—each researcher interviewed all the sample children in "their" schools.

We decided to focus the interview on five issues: the children's attitude to school and lessons; their attitude to playground experiences; their self-assessment of their academic standing; their perception of "naughtiness" in themselves and others; and the extent to which they were aware of discrimination by staff or children. This latter issue we tackled indirectly by asking whether there were any children who were punished or privileged more than others, although we did not ask directly about racial teasing. We would have liked to have asked the children their opinion of the teachers, but we felt that this was not politic in the school setting.

ATTITUDES TO ACADEMIC WORK

We showed the children a picture of children's faces, with expressions ranging from very happy to very miserable, and asked them to point to the face which showed how they felt about maths, reading to the teacher, reading to themselves, and writing. In each case we then asked "Why is that?" Not all children were able to give a reason, some simply answered "I don't know", or "I just do/don't". Maths turned out to be the most popular subject with boys. Eighty percent pointed to one of the smiling faces, compared with 62% of girls ($P<0.01$). When asked why they liked it, the usual answer was that they enjoyed "doing sums". A typical, fuller, answer was "I like adding, doing my times table, dividing and taking away. I'm quite good at it, because my brother teaches me when we're in bed". Those who did not like maths often complained that it was difficult. "I don't like maths, I just don't—I get things wrong." "We have to look on the board and I keep getting muddled up."

Reading aloud to the teacher was the next most popular activity, especially with black children. Seventy percent of black children, and 60% of white ($P<0.05$) pointed to a smiling face for this activity. Reading to oneself, on the other hand, was the most unpopular school activity, liked by only 51% of children. The children's comments gave some clues about the reasons for these preferences. A number of children explained that they did not like reading to themselves because they did not know all the words: "Everytime I don't know a word and I feel sad"; "I don't like reading "'cos sometimes you need a teacher to tell what you don't know, and she is talking to someone else and she says wait a minute"; "Everytime I don't know a word, I don't get no-one to tell me the word. My dad's always in bed 'cos he has to work at night. My big sister's upstairs doing her homework and my mum's cooking". Presumably these difficulties were not only frustrating, but made some passages unintelligible. Other children said that reading to yourself was "lonely"; part of their pleasure in reading aloud was obviously the shared social experience: "It's a little bit boring not reading to anyone. I like to read to my Mum or my Dad or my teacher, or my Gran". On the other hand, the more skilled readers much preferred to read to themselves: " 'Cos when I read to my teacher she keeps talking to other children. When I read to myself, I can just carry on reading"; "You don't get disturbed when you're reading to yourself. It's nice and quiet—you can concentrate better".

We asked the children *when* they read to themselves at home, and their answers suggested that as yet few of them were avid readers. The 9 children who said they read as soon as they got home from school may have been in this category. A quarter of the sample (32 children) said that they mainly read to themselves in bed, and some of them had reading habits like those of adults: "I usually read at night when I can't get to sleep, and then I fall asleep". More often, the children saw reading as a solitary activity of last resort, to be turned to only when they were no possibilities of more interesting activities. (This reason may, of course, also explain why some children chose to read in bed.) "I read when I'm bored"; "When there's nothing else to do"; "When I can't play out"; "When no-one will play with me"; "On Sundays, when there's nothing to watch on the telly"; "On Sundays, Sundays are boring"; "When my mum's busy and my dad's working".

Writing was only marginally preferred to reading to oneself—56% of the children pointed to a smiling face. The most frequently articulated reason for enjoying writing, given by 25 children, was the pleasure of creating: "I like writing stories. I like to write exciting stories and funny stories—but sad ones make me feel unhappy"; "I like writing because if you do something, then you can come back to school and write about it"; "I like writing, 'cos no-one else can write what I'm writing". Eleven children gave reasons that seemed to have come from adults: "It learns you lots of difficult words"; "When you're bigger you'll be able to write good". Four children enjoyed writing because they liked illustrating their stories, and two children said that they liked writing because of the teacher's praise.

The most frequently articulated reasons for *not* liking writing centred round the tedium or frustration of not being able to spell (14 children)—

"It's boring, 'cos you have to keep walking round the classroom to get a word"; "Sometimes you think you're going to be so clever, but you need a hard word, and you have to rub it out, and it looks horrible"; "I just find it a bit boring, having to queue up for the teacher when I want a word". Ten children disliked writing because of a sense of failure: " 'cos it's too hard. When Miss asks us to write stories, my stories don't make sense". Four children particularly objected to writing "news": "Sometimes for news I don't go anywhere, so I don't know what to write, so I sit there looking like that" (points to picture of sad face). One boy complained bitterly: "If I showed you my 'news', it's lies—lies about what I've done and what I've got".

It seems possible that the children liked maths because they were given a great deal of practice with familiar tasks, in which they could succeed and be rewarded with "ticks". (We showed in Chapter 4 that most maths tasks in the top infant class were in fact number work.) In contrast, reading to themselves involved dealing with unfamiliar material, with many frustrations and little or no reward if they could not make sense of the book. Reading aloud was more popular because the children were helped with the unfamiliar words, had fewer frustrating experiences, and were rewarded by the social interaction. If this interpretation is correct, children might like reading to themselves better if they were provided with more reading material at a level they could cope with. Both unconfident and fluent readers may benefit from more opportunities to read aloud to others. In some classrooms, children read to each other in pairs or small groups. This arrangement both allows for social interaction, and enables the children to puzzle out the meaning of the text together. And children might enjoy writing more at the early stages if the new "Developmental Writing" approach were used. In this approach, children are encouraged to be as independent as possible in writing, for example, when necessary inventing their own spellings. It is noteworthy that according to the parents, the great majority of children did some writing at home. Writing at home may have been more attractive because of the greater availability of help, or perhaps because the children were able to choose what to write, or to discuss it as they wrote.

ACADEMIC SELF-ASSESSMENT

We showed the children a picture of three (identical) groups of children, and told them: "This group is good at maths, they are better at it than other children. This group isn't good at maths, they are worse at it than other children. And this group in the middle is not specially good or specially bad. Can you show me which group you belong to?" We repeated the question for reading and writing.

The first point to make is that the children, especially the boys, tended to overestimate their achievements. The boys especially over-estimated their maths achievement, 83% considering themselves above average in maths, compared with 63% of the girls ($P<0.01$). These proportions are almost identical to the proportions of boys and girls who said they liked maths. In fact, on the maths tests we gave the children at about the same time, the difference between the scores of the boys and girls was very small.

Boys were also more likely than girls to say that their reading was above average, although fewer overestimated their reading achievement than their maths, and the difference was not significant. Seventy-two percent of boys thought they were above average, compared with 61% of girls ($P<0.08$). As in maths, these beliefs did not correspond to the test scores, which showed that girls were slightly better readers, and black girls were significantly better than all other children.

A similar trend emerged in writing, that is, more boys than girls rated themselves as above average—57% vs. 47%—although again this difference was not significant. It will be noted that the children tended to rate their performance lower in writing than in reading, and especially than in maths. This parallels the relative unpopularity of writing as a school subject. Again, our writing tests showed that there was no basis for the girls to rate themselves lower than boys. Girls, especially black girls, did significantly better than boys.

In all three subjects more boys than girls rated themselves as above average, and more black children than white. These differences were mainly due to the fact that the white girls were less likely to rate themselves above average than the other children. The children were generally inaccurate in their self-assessments. Children who rated themselves as "above average" were no more likely to have above average scores than those who rated themselves average, and vice versa. However, the few children who rated themselves below average did indeed tend to score below average on our tests.

It was encouraging to find that so many children felt positive about their school achievements. Only 7% rated themselves as below average in maths, 14% in reading, and 18% in writing. At first sight, it is tempting to relate these findings to the lack of streaming, competition, or ranking of children in English infant schools. However, there is evidence from many school systems that children under the age of about eight are generally poor at estimating both their physical and intellectual attainments, and tend to overestimate both. They are also less disturbed than older children by the experience of failure (Nicholls, 1978; Parsons & Ruble, 1977). It is not clear why this should be the case. Younger children are intellectually capable of comparing themselves with others, and frequently do so, for example, when comparing possessions. However, there is some evidence that young children tend to evaluate their own achievements by how well they have performed a particular task, for example, a page of number work, rather than by taking into account the performance of others. It may be that with increasing age they become more aware of the value that adults attach to competition. It may also be that more and clearer information is given to older children about their achievements relative to others, and that they are made more aware of the rewards and penalties of success and failure (Ruble, Boggiano, Feldman, & Loebl, 1980).

A number of researchers have found, as we did, that whilst girls tend to have higher school attainments than boys, they tend to assess their abilities as being lower (Parsons, Ruble, Hodges, & Small, 1976). Others have found that from about the age of four years girls show greater anxiety about failure than boys, and are more sensitive to negative information. The paradox is very marked, because not only do girls achieve better than boys, but, as we found, teachers less often find their behaviour difficult, and less often criticise them. On the face of it, their confidence should be greater than that of boys (see Parsons et al., 1976).

In trying to explain this paradox some have argued that children are influenced by gender stereotypes in society. Thus the stereotype that men are strong and competent, women are weak and incompetent may influence children's self-perceptions (Kohlberg, 1966). There is certainly U.S. evidence that by the age of five children have developed some clearly defined gender stereotypes (Williams, Bennet, & Best, 1975), but it has yet to be shown how these influence their self-perceptions. Bronfenbrenner's view (1961) is that the problem is caused by the way in which girls tend to be reared. He argues that they are given too much warmth, gentleness and protection, so that they become excessively dependent, and oversensitive to criticism and failure. Others have suggested that parents and teachers may convey to children that they have lower expectations of girls than boys. We found some evidence in our study that the teachers did have higher expectations of boys, but not that parents did (Chapter 8).

Another theory is that parents and teachers give different attributions (explanations) to boys and girls for failure. Thus, if adults convey to boys, but not to girls, that their failure is due to the difficulty of the task or to a passing bad mood, then the boys' self-concept would not be damaged, as it would be if failure were attributed to lack of ability (Parsons et al., 1976). A widely discussed current theory is that of Dweck (Dweck, Davidson, Nelson, & Enna, 1978), who argues that the very fact that boys are much more often criticised by teachers than girls for their behaviour means that the negative feedback they receive about academic work is attributed by them to the generally critical attitude of the teacher, rather than their own failings. In contrast, the lesser amount of negative feedback teachers give to girls is mainly about their work, rather than their behaviour, and is thus taken more seriously by them. Further, Dweck has shown that teachers are much more likely to tell boys than girls that they have failed through lack of effort. Hence when girls fail they have no such excuse to fall back on, and they tend to attribute their failure to lack of ability (Dweck et al., 1978).

In line with this hypothesis, we found that those groups of children who received the most criticism from the teachers (the black boys) and who the teachers said had the most behaviour problems (the white boys, and the black girls and boys) were those who rated their achievements highest. In contrast, the white girls, who were the best-behaved group, and who received the least criticism, rated themselves lowest. On the other hand, we also found that they received the least praise from the teachers, a fact which could in itself lower their self-image. Our findings certainly suggest that one should be cautious in generalising about sex differences, which may not be the same in all ethnic groups.

Whilst most current research on sex differences in academic self-perception focuses on the role of the classroom teacher, it seems likely that a complex interplay of home, school and societal influences is at work. It may thus be difficult for one of the agents concerned, for example, the teacher, to intervene effectively to alter these perceptions.

NAUGHTINESS AT SCHOOL

Bad behaviour was seen by the teachers in our study as interfering with learning, and we did indeed find that it was associated with slower school progress (Chapter 8). It seemed, therefore, worth trying to find out how the children viewed "naughtiness" at school.

We began by asking them why children got told off at school. Their answers depicted a school life nearer to a "blackboard jungle" than the relatively well-ordered classes we observed. This may be because even rare instances of bad behaviour made a big impact on them. It may also be because we did not carry out our observations in the playground, where most of the fighting seemed to occur. The most frequently described offence was, in fact, fighting, mentioned by 84 of the 133 children. "Fighting, and going out of the classroom. Miss has to drag them back in, and sometimes they try and bite her." "Running around the school, beating up people in the playground. I beat this black boy up, thumped him in the belly, because he kept saying 'Kiora, Kiora'." "Saying no, climbing on roofs, beating people up, spitting at teachers, swearing"; "climbing up cupboards, throwing crayons about, and swearing". Throwing, swearing, and shouting were mentioned by 11 children. By comparison, most of the other offences seemed trivial—"Going to the toilet when they're not supposed to"; "Blocking the toilets"; "Zoe's very bad. She folded up her work and tore it and said 'Look, a pattern'".

According to the children, the most frequent punishment for doing something really naughty was being sent to the Head or Deputy Head—66 children mentioned this. Fourteen children said that they got smacked ("They get slapped on the bottom"; "The teacher goes red and hits you"; "Miss takes them by the hand and slaps them on it"). Thirteen children said that they were isolated in some way: "They get told off, then they have to go outside the door", and 12 said that the teacher just shouted at them, or told them off ("She tells us off, and gets very cross"; "She shouts really loud and thumps hard on the table"). Eleven children said that they were kept in—"They stay in for two weeks, or one week, at playtime, and they don't get second dinners or second pudding". One or two schools had idiosyncratic punishments—"They go in the bad book"—and one child said that they were set lines to write.

We asked the children whether they themselves had ever received these punishments. More boys than girls said that they had (54% vs. 38%, $P<0.05$), and more black than white children (57% vs. 37%, $P<0.01$). The group most likely to say that they had been punished for being "really naughty" were black boys—61% said that they had; the group least likely were white girls—only 26% said that they had received this punishment. These answers were in accord with the teachers' account of who showed problem behaviour. The children themselves did not suggest that boys, or black children, were more often punished than others. At least, when we asked them whether they thought that they themselves were told off more or less than other children in the class, very few children—only 6% - said that they were, and none of the children suggested that they were discriminated against. Most—65%—thought that they were told off *less* than other children. There were no sex or ethnic differences in this respect. Thus, as with academic achievement, the children tended not to compare themselves accurately with others, and to take an over-rosy view of their behaviour.

When we asked the children whether they thought that there were some children "who got away" with being naughty, the great majority—73%—agreed that this was the case. Black boys were especially likely to agree ($P<0.05$). When asked why this should be so, most children said that the children who got away with it were those who ran off, or told lies, or put the blame on other children. Two boys suggested that there was sex discrimination ("Most of the teachers are girl teachers and they like the girls better than the boys"), one girl mentioned class ("If posh people are rude, they get away with it"), and one girl suggested that the more able children weren't punished ("Yes, definitely. Someone who writes good stories gets away with things. Tracey gets away with it. She writes good, really creative stories. And David, he gets off a lot, and he does a good story"). No one mentioned race discrimination.

PRIVILEGES AT SCHOOL

As well as trying to see whether the children felt that there was discrimination in relation to punishment, we tried to find out whether the children believed that the teachers discriminated in their distribution of privileges. We selected two activities to ask about which teachers often use as rewards, singling out a child to do a "special" job, and showing work to the headteacher.

However, we found that a fifth of the children could not think of a "special job" that their teacher gave as a reward, and a third could not think of an unpleasant "job" that the teachers gave out as a punishment. Moreover, amongst those who could, there was very little agreement about which were the attractive jobs. Further, what the teacher intended to be a reward was sometimes seen by the child in a very different light. Some children, for example, very much enjoyed taking messages round other classrooms, and some children hated it, and did not regard it as a privilege. Some liked sharpening pencils ("You can see the lovely colours in the bin"), others disliked it ("The points keep breaking"). There were children who liked tidying the room and wiping tables, although more of them disliked these jobs. It was not always very clear, when children said that they had been chosen for a "special" or for an unpleasant job, whether they meant jobs so intended by the teachers, or jobs that they themselves thought were good or unpleasant. For these reasons, the children's answers to this section of the interview are difficult to interpret. Amongst those who did describe being given "good" and "bad" jobs, there were no significant ethnic or sex differences in the proportions of children who said they were chosen to do them.

We then asked the children about another privilege, being chosen to show their work in assembly or to the Head. Seventy-six percent of the children said that they had been chosen, black children more often than white (86% vs. 68%, $P<0.05$).

We tried to find out whether the children felt that the teacher showed unfair discrimination in choosing children for special privileges, by asking whether there were some children who were not chosen. Although most—80%—agreed that some children never got chosen, their explanation for this was that these children were naughty, or silly, or did not do good work, not that they were discriminated against. (We discuss this issue later in the chapter.)

DINNER TIME AND PLAYTIMES

As we pointed out in Chapter 4, a substantial minority of the school day—28%—is taken up by dinner and playtimes. It was clear from the children's comments that these times played a very important part in determining their general attitude to school.

We started by asking them to point to a face which showed how they felt about having dinner at school. Sixty percent pointed to a smiling face, and 24% to a sad one. Mostly the children's enjoyment or otherwise depended on whether they liked the food that was served. Those who mentioned that they did (50 children) far outnumbered those who disliked the food (15). Baked beans and chips were particularly often singled out for mention: "I like dinner because we get nice things to eat—beans, sausages, burgers—chips—salad". "I like the chips, baked beans, spaghetti and stuff." For a few children the food was either the best or the worst aspect of the school day. Ten children enjoyed dinner because of the social side: "People tell jokes, and we all laugh"; "I can talk to my friends without the teacher saying 'shut up'", but more children (14) complained of the noise in the dinner hall.

Of the three playtimes, the dinner hour was the most popular—68% of children picked out a smiling face, and only 17% a sad one. Boys more often enjoyed it than girls (75% vs. 64%, $P<0.05$), but this was mainly due to the large proportion of black boys who enjoyed it—93%. In contrast, only 53% of white girls enjoyed the dinner playtime. Some children had mixed feelings: "There's some good things, you can join games, but on the other hand some people can hit you, and the playground's so big it's hardly ever seen"; "Sometimes it's very cold, and I don't like it, but sometimes I really, really like it—it's sunny, and you can run about. Sometimes you can run up to the Juniors and use their water taps". Dislike of the cold was mentioned by a number of children, all girls, in relation to playtime, even though the children were interviewed in mid-summer. Children who definitely disliked the playtime most often gave as the reason being picked on by other children, or being "beaten up" (13 children), or having no-one to play with, or having only one friend.

The mid-morning playtime was overall much less popular than the dinner hour playtime—only 53% of children enjoyed it, and 33% definitely did not. However, this difference was entirely due to the fact that fewer black children enjoyed the mid-morning playtime, usually complaining that it was too short: "I don't like little playtimes. I like the long plays, because you've got time to play what you want to play". Six children preferred the morning playtime *because* it was short: "Normally no-one hardly ever interferes with you because there's so little time, and you can relax and play around". Three children complained that they were too tired to enjoy the morning playtime: "You get up too early in the morning and still feel a bit sleepy"; and nine children complained that it was the coldest playtime.

The afternoon playtime was rather more popular—60% of children enjoyed it, and 23% definitely did not. Like the morning playtime, some children considered it too short, but it was preferred by others because it signalled the approaching end of the school day: "I like it because it's near going home"; "It's hometime soon, and you won't be doing any work after it".

It might be thought that the main reason for enjoying playtimes was a negative one—to escape from lessons. In fact, only four children gave this explanation. There was no particular tendency for the children who liked playtime to say elsewhere in the interview that they disliked lessons. Liking playtime seemed more a matter of enjoying the opportunity to run around, and play games. One girl said "We play lots of games, we skip, we sing, we can go into the nursery sometimes, do cartwheels, have races, swing the skipping rope". Boys tended to mention specific games: "The boys chase the girls and the girls chase the boys, you're excited"; "We play 'Hide and seek' and 'Had' and football".

However, this pleasure was marred for some by fear of physical or verbal aggression from other children: "You get beaten up for nothing"; "They kick and punch and throw stones". Playtime activities also tended to lead to trouble with the staff in charge. Seventy-two percent of children said that they had been told off in the playground, boys more often than girls (84% vs. 63%, $P<0.01$). Very few children—only 7%—said that they got told off more than other children. When we asked which children got told off most, the answer was generally that it was the naughtiest children. A few children said that boys got told off more than girls, but no one mentioned race discrimination.

Teasing and Fighting

When discussing playtimes, we asked if any of the children were teased. Ninety-six percent of the children said that some children got teased, and 67% said that they themselves got teased. Girls more often said they got teased than boys (78% of girls vs. 57% of boys, $P<0.01$). This sex difference was mainly due to the large proportion of white girls (84%) who said they got teased. Considerably fewer children—50%—admitted to doing the teasing, and the proportions did not differ significantly between girls and boys, and black and white children.

We asked the children what names they got called. Most of the names referred to the children's appearance, or sometimes their smell. They included Fatty, Smelly bum, Crybaby, Skinny ribs, Bighead, Piggy, Pigface, Stinky, Gollywog, Chocolate head, Nigger, Black bitch, Black shit, White pooh, White icecream. When we asked the children why they thought they were called these names, most of them either could not explain, or said it was because the teasing child disliked them, or wasn't their friend. Fifteen children seemed to accept the names as justified: "Because it's the way I look"; "Because I smell"; "Because I'm black";

"They think white's the best colour"; "Because I'm boring"; "Because I don't share my things".

In the course of their answers, a number of the children volunteered the information that certain strategies were effective in dealing with, or preventing, teasing. The most frequent, reported by both boys and girls, and black and white children, was physical aggression: "They stopped teasing me because I kick them in the head"; "They're too scared of me now, I beat them up". The next most frequently used strategy was to keep a low profile: "I don't get teased, 'cos normally I'm under the shed"; "I don't call them names back"; "I don't make trouble". A number of children said that they didn't get teased because they were popular: "I make friends with everyone in the school"; "Lots of children in my class like me". A few children relied on adult help, "telling Miss" or, in one case, "I tell my dad and he comes up to the school and sorts it out". One girl neutralised the insult: "I tells them PIG stands for Pretty Intelligent Girl". Often the children seemed to accept the insults as an unpleasant but inescapable side of school life. But although adults often believe that teasing is harmless, it was clear that a number of children found it very upsetting: "Some people think I'm horrible, and I'm not".

Yet, despite all the complaints about teasing, very few children—7%—said that they got teased more than other children. This was further evidence that young children are not good at comparing their status with that of others, and tend to over-rate themselves relative to others. We asked specifically whether any children were teased because of their colour. Sixty-five percent of the children agreed that this was the case. The great majority of both black and white children said that it was the black children who were teased, although eight white and four black children said that both black and white children teased each other, and two white and four black children said that it was mostly black children who teased white children. Most of the white children took teasing black children very much for granted: "I do. I call them monkeys that escaped from the zoo last year", and only four made disapproving comments: "People call black people blackies, but I don't, 'cause they're all original people, it doesn't matter about their colour". However, only 34% of children admitted to having been teased *themselves* because of their colour—48% of the black children, and 23% of the white ($P<0.05$). Some black children were clearly disturbed by this teasing. "They say you can't play with us 'cos you're black, but I'm not black, I'm brown"; "They say to us you're half caste, I don't like that"; "My mum says if the teacher don't do nothing we have to hit them".

We asked the children whether they ever got into fights. Sixty-seven percent said they did, boys more often than girls (79% of boys, 56% of girls, $P<0.01$). However, the children who got into fights did not necessarily admit to starting them or to liking fighting. In fact, only 14% of the children—20% of the boys, and 7% of the girls ($P<0.01$)—pointed to a smiling face when we asked how they felt about getting into fights. Those children who said they got into fights but didn't enjoy fighting either explained that they fought in self-defence: "They put gangs on me"; "They beat me up"; "They kick me in the neck", or that fighting was a response to anger: "I get very angry"; "People get angry, so do I".

In fact, life in the playground was seen by virtually all the children as both verbally and physically aggressive. Ninety-two per cent of the children at some point in the interview referred to fighting taking place at school, and white girls in particular disliked this aspect of school. Two-thirds of the children complained of being teased. Although adults often dismiss teasing as a trivial, everyday event, our interviews suggest that children feel as unhappy as adults at being called Piggy, Smelly, or Black shit, and few had developed effective strategies for dealing with the insults. Some children referred to a lack of support from adults in the playground. It was clear that, whereas some children flourished in this situation, others were placed under a degree of tension. If alternative ways of spending playtimes, or structuring and supervising playground activity could be provided, many children would be much happier at school.

GENERAL ATTITUDES TO SCHOOL, HOLIDAYS, AND THE JUNIOR SCHOOL

We ended the interview by trying to assess the children's general attitude to school. First, we asked them to choose a face which showed how they felt about going to school in the morning. Sixty two percent of the children picked a smiling face; boys were somewhat more likely to do so than girls ($P<0.08$), mainly because of the larger proportion of white boys—76%— who liked school. This finding may be related to our observation in the classrooms that white boys were more work-oriented than other groups (Chapter 4), since the children's attitude to lessons was very central to their enjoyment of school. Those children who said they felt happy about going to school were significantly more likely than other children to say that they enjoyed reading to the teacher ($P<0.01$), reading to themselves ($P<0.01$), writing ($P<0.001$), and maths ($P<0.001$). Not all these children were prepared to say that school was interesting—only 43% did so, and 26% thought it was definitely boring. Black children were somewhat more likely to say that school was interesting than white children ($P<0.09$), but this difference was mainly due to the small proportion of white girls—32%— who thought it was interesting.

Nevertheless, when we asked them what was the best thing about school, the largest group—56 children—mentioned some aspect of work: "Doing my Fletcher book"; "Maths, it's numbers really, and I always count the stairs where I live"; "Work, because you get a good education. Could become a pop star, or something, or a writer". However, nearly as many children—46—said the best thing about school was playing: "Playing with my friends"; "Football with my friends"; "Playing in the Wendy House". Twelve children chose drawing or painting as the best thing, whilst outings, T.V., swimming, science, singing, stories, and their class teacher all got one or two mentions. Three children thought the best thing about school was the food, and for two it was going-home time: "I can't wait to get home". Fewer children—only 33—thought the worst thing about school was some aspect of the work. For ten of the children this complaint was nonspecific—"The work"—but more often a specific subject was disliked, most often writing stories.

The next largest group of children—46—thought that the best thing about school was playing with their friends, but nearly as many—35— thought that the worst thing was the difficulties they had with other children. The majority of these difficulties (20) centred round fighting: "I don't like fighting, that's all"; "Fighting. Well, I can fight, I fight my own battles, but. . ."; "People beat you up. If you tell the teacher, teacher tells you to fight them back. That's what you should really do". Other complaints were less specific: "People being horrible"; "Sometimes I be horrible to people 'cos they call me names"; "I don't like playing with boys. I just like draughts and chess. I've got chess at home".

The teacher's praise, and especially her blame, was an important contributor to the children's happiness. A number of children gave as a reason for liking a subject "Miss says my work is very good", and being told off, or punished, was considered the worst aspect of school by 23 children: "The worst thing is Mrs. X.—sometimes she drags people around and slaps them round the face, and my mum comes up to school then"; "Staying in at playtime"; "Standing up in class because you've been naughty"; "Being told off. It spoils the day for me".

Five children picked out "tidying up" as the worst aspect of school, three mentioned the food, and two falling over: "I often fall over, because I play football". Two children simply didn't like being in school: "When you come back to school after an outing is the worst thing"; "The worst thing about school is that it's so long before home time"; but ten children could think of nothing bad about school: "There's nothing I don't like"; "Nothing. The thing I don't like is going home"; "I don't think there's anything worst about it. Maybe in the Juniors".

Whilst nearly two-thirds of children enjoyed going to school, a larger proportion—78%—picked a smiling face to describe how they felt about the approaching school holidays. Only 14% picked a sad face. The reason most often given for disliking the holidays was that they were boring: "There's nothing interesting to do, except watch Walt Disney films and cartoons on the video"; "I've got nothing to do, but at school we play, work, go on the apparatus, do all kinds of things"; "I sometimes feel like going to the park, but Mum says no. All you have to do is stay in the house and watch T.V.".

Only 54% of the children pointed to a smiling face to describe how they felt about going to junior school in the autumn, and 35% picked a sad face. Boys were happier about it than girls (62% vs. 47%, $P<0.05$), and this was especially true of black boys, 71% of whom were looking forward to junior school. A great variety of reasons were given for looking forward to junior school, mostly centring round the prospect of new experiences: "There's gymnastics"; "They do swimming and joined-up writing"; "They have hymn books"; "The playground's bigger". Other children were frightened or cautious about the unknown, and their capacity to cope: "I won't know where things are"; "I don't know what we'll be doing"; "I'll be shy"; "Everyone will know more than me". A number of children commented that the work would be harder, some with anxiety, and others with pleasure. One child said that he looked forward to junior school because it meant that the time when he would finally leave school would be nearer.

Thus the children's view of life in the infant school that emerged from our interview was more positive than negative, although not so positive as the picture given by the children's parents. Whereas 78% of their parents said that their child had been happy, or very happy, at school in the past year, only 62% of the children pointed to a smiling face to describe their feelings about going to school in the mornings. Similarly. whilst 73% of parents said that they had no worries about their children's forthcoming move to junior school, only 54% of children said they felt happy about it. Parents also seemed relatively unaware of the extent of teasing at school. Only 39% of parents said their child got teased, compared with 67% of the children. And only 19% of black parents and 6% of white parents said their child got teased because of their colour, compared with the 48% of the black children and 23% of the white children who told us they were teased for this reason. There is evidence from other studies that parents tend to underestimate the extent of their children's difficulties and unhappiness, perhaps because they are not discussed between them. For example, mothers have been shown to underestimate grossly the extent and intensity of their children's fears, compared with the account given independently by the children (Lapouse & Monk, 1959).

Our findings do not support the belief that black children tend to have a low self-concept in relation to their academic achievements, or their relationships with other children. It was the white girls who showed a lack of confidence in these ways. We also did not uncover evidence that the black children felt they were discriminated against by the staff, although nearly half of them said that other children taunted them because of their colour.

It may be that staff did not discriminate against them. Or it may be that the children were aware of discrimination, but unwilling to admit to it, though there were no differences in the answers to questions about discrimination, and teasing because of colour, given to the black interviewer and the white interviewers. Or it may be that some staff did discriminate, but the children were not aware of it. In discussion with black colleagues, several have told us that they do not remember any feelings that adults discriminated against them whilst they were in infant school. They might remember feeling that staff "picked on" them, but it is only now, looking back, that they interpret these experiences as having been due to racist discrimination. At any rate, on balance, the black children in our study seemed to enjoy the infant school to a similar extent to the white children, and more than the white girls.

As with any interview, we do not know how far the children's answers were influenced by the interviewing situation. Nor do we know how far the findings can be generalised beyond our sample, who were almost entirely working class, inner London children. We also do not know to what extent the children's attitudes were affected by the characteristics of the schools they attended, or the ethnic balance of the schools, since we did not interview enough children in each school to analyse these issues. However, given that there are so few accounts of young children's views on schools, we think our account provides some valuable insights into the experiences of one group of infant-school children.

SUMMARY

More than half the children enjoyed maths, reading and writing. Their attitude to school to some extent depended on their sex and ethnic group. Both black and white boys were more likely than girls to say that they enjoyed maths. The children, especially the boys, tended to overestimate their achievements: White girls were the group least likely to do so. Very few children thought their attainments were below average.

Boys, especially black boys, were most likely to say they were punished for naughtiness, both in the classroom and the playground; they were also most likely to say that they enjoyed the dinner-hour playtime. Girls, especially white girls, were the group most likely to complain of being teased, whilst boys were most likely to say that they got into fights. Two-thirds of the children said that children were teased because of their colour, and half of the black children said that they themselves were teased for this reason.

Two-thirds of the children said they enjoyed going to school, and white boys were especially likely to do so, although considerably fewer children thought that school was interesting. Only half the children felt happy about the forthcoming move to junior school.

On the whole, the majority of the children had a positive attitude to school, although less positive than their parents seemed to believe. There were significant differences in the attitude of the four ethnic-sex groups, with white boys the most positive, and white girls the least. White boys stood out as the group who most often said they liked going to school, black boys as the group who most enjoyed the long playtime. The white girls, on the other hand, seemed in a number of ways to be the group who were enjoying school least. Their self-assessments in all academic subjects were lower than those of other children, and they were less likely than the other groups to say that they enjoyed school, found it interesting, and were looking forward to junior school. They were also less likely than other children to say they had been in serious trouble with the staff, but they also more often complained of being teased. Black children complained of racial taunts from other children, but not of discrimination from the staff.

10 Progress Through the Infant School: Explanatory Models

INTRODUCTION

In previous chapters, we described how progress in reading and writing, and in maths, was related to ethnic group and sex (Chapter 6), home variables (Chapter 7), and school variables (Chapter 8). In this chapter, we bring these results together in order to try to answer two questions. First, we wanted to find out which home and school variables were related to progress over the whole infant school period, when we considered the variables from each group, and from both groups, in combination, rather than considering each variable on its own, as we previously had done. Second, we wanted to see whether the fact that children in our four different ethnic group sex groups made different rates of progress could be accounted for by the home and school variables related to progress.

We put forward statistical models for progress in reading and writing, and in maths. These models give us some indication of which variables, among those that we measured, are the best predictors of progress. However, we did not consider for inclusion in our models all possible predictors. Instead, we considered only those variables which could be given explanatory or causal interpretations as influences on progress. And so, for example, we excluded from consideration our measure of parents' satisfaction with their child's progress, even though it was related to progress (see Chapter 7), because it is likely that this association merely reflects the fact that children who make good progress at school have more satisfied parents than those who make less progress. Although the variables we included in our models can be given causal interpretations, we do not claim that the models are necessarily causal ones; as we shall see, most of the independent associations we found can be given more than one interpretation. And it is always possible that there are variables which we did not measure which could account for the associations that we found. Nevertheless, we believe that the modelling approach described in this chapter (and in more technical detail in Appendix 3) does help us better to understand the processes which influence children's academic progress at school, and which determine why some children make more progress than others.

PROGRESS IN READING AND WRITING

In earlier chapters we found that:

1. The interaction between ethnic group and sex is related to progress in reading and writing, with black boys making less progress and black girls more progress than the two white groups.
2. The amount and complexity of children's writing at home, and parental contact with and knowledge of school, are related to progress, together with a tendency for children with more experience of books to make more progress.
3. Among the school variables, curriculum coverage, teacher expectations, teacher ratings of children's behaviour and whether a child was considered a pleasure to teach were each separately related to progress.

We also found that the higher the children's vocabulary scores at the end of nursery (as measured by the W.P.P.S.I.), the more progress they made during infant school.

The three home process variables which were individually related to children's progress in reading and writing were all related to each other, and we found that only one was independently related to progress. That is, once the amount and complexity of children's writing at home was taken into account, children's experience of books and parental contact with and knowledge of school were no longer related to children's progress.

When we considered the four school variables related to progress as a group, we found our overall teacher rating of behaviour (constructed from the data for each year as described in Chapter 8) was not independently related to progress, but the other three variables were. Of these three, curriculum coverage (averaged over the three years) and teacher expectations (an overall rating for the three years) were more strongly associated with progress than "pleasure to teach".

When we put the seven variables—ethnic group, sex, the vocabulary subtest, the one home variable and the three school variables—together into one group to look at independent influences on progress, we found that we could only do this by working with a very small sample. Data were missing for a substantial number of children for one or more of these variables, and so we created two groups of variables and hence estimated two statistical models. The first subgroup included all variables except child writing at home, the second subgroup comprised child writing at home, the W.P.P.S.I. vocabulary test, ethnic group, and sex. The analysis of the first subgroup showed that curriculum coverage, teacher expectations, and the interaction between ethnic group and sex had independent associations with reading and writing progress. The results, based on a sample of 125 children, are presented in Table 10.1, and make allowances for the differences between schools, which were statistically significant (intra-class correlation $\hat{\rho} = 0.24$, $P<0.05$); this model explained just over half the variation in progress.

We found that each variable in the second subgroup was independently related to reading and writing progress and these results, this time based on a sample of 116 children, are given in Table 10.2. Again, the school differences were statistically significant ($\hat{\rho} = 0.10$, $P<0.05$). This model explained about one-third of the variation in progress. (For further information on interpreting Tables 10.1 and 10.2 see discussion of Table 10.3 on pp. 164–165.)

TABLE 10.1
Independent Associations with Reading and Writing Progress (1)

Variable	Range of Effect (S.D. Units)	P-Value
Curriculum coverage	1.2	0.01
Teacher expectations	0.9	0.001
Ethnic group and sex	0.4	0.05

TABLE 10.2
Independent Assocations with Reading and Writing Progress (2)

Variable	Range of Effect (S.D. Units)	P-Value
Child writes at home	1.4	0.001
W.P.P.S.I. vocabulary	0.7	0.05
Ethnic group and sex	0.5	0.07

Considering the results for the models together (and results from other analyses not presented here), curriculum coverage, teacher expectations and child writes at home each have an independent effect on children's progress in reading and writing, but the W.P.P.S.I. vocabulary and "pleasure to teach" do not. The balance of the evidence suggests that the school variables have a stronger relationship with progress than the one home variable. It can also be seen from Tables 10.1 and 10.2 that these groups of variables do not account for the interaction between ethnic group and sex, which is statistically significant in Table 10.1 and almost so in Table 10.2. However, the size of this interaction is a little smaller than the ones reported separately for reading and writing in Chapter 6.

PROGRESS IN MATHS

Three of the school variables—curriculum coverage, teacher expectations and "pleasure to teach"—were associated with progress in maths, but none of the home variables were. The vocabulary test at nursery was not related to maths progress, but sex was (see Chapter 6 for more details). When these four variables were considered together, we found that "pleasure to teach" was not independently related to progress, but that curriculum coverage and teacher expectations were, and that these two variables did not account for the sex difference. The results are given in Table 10.3, based on a sample of 136 children, with allowance made for statistically significant differences between schools ($\hat{\rho} = 0.15$, $P<0.05$). About one-third of the variation in progress is explained by this model.

The results in Table 10.3 can be interpreted in the following way (and the same approach can be used for Tables 10.1 and 10.2). Children with the highest mean curriculum coverage score over the three years would have a maths score at the end of top infants which would be, on average, 0.9 S.D. units higher than the mean maths score for children with the lowest mean curriculum coverage score, but who were otherwise identical in terms of their initial maths score, overall teacher expectation rating, and sex.

TABLE 10.3
Independent Associations with Maths Progress

Variable	Range of Effect (S.D. Units)	P-Value
Curriculum coverage	0.9	0.05
Teacher expectations	1.0	0.001
Sex	0.3	0.05

Moreover, boys and girls with the same initial maths score, the same teacher expectation rating and the same mean curriculum coverage score would differ, on average, by 0.3 S.D. units on the maths test at the end of top infants. However, these differences are subject to the caveats raised in the next section.

CONCLUSIONS AND SUMMARY

A number of conclusions emerge from the analyses we were able to do. The first is that, for our sample, school and teacher variables are more important than home variables in explaining differences in children's progress. (Background variables such as mother's education were associated with pre-school attainment, but not with progress through infant school.) The only home variable we found to be of any importance in predicting progress was the amount and complexity of children's writing at home (and, as we pointed out in Chapter 7, this is perhaps better regarded as a "child" rather than as a "home" variable).

Our second conclusion is a negative one: We have not been able statistically to explain the differences in reading and writing progress made by black boys and black girls, nor have we been able to explain why boys make more progress than girls in maths. Perhaps if we had had more stable data at the child level from our observations in classrooms, or if we had had more detailed information on parental practices at home, we might have been able to account for these differences. It is also possible that with a much larger data set, we would have been able to look at whether, for example, differences in progress made by black boys and girls varied across teachers and schools. Further discussion of this issue can be found in Plewis (in press). But, for the present, the differences remain unexplained.

It is clear from our models that curriculum coverage and teacher expectations have important relationships with progress (and the fact that the results for reading and writing, and for maths, are so similar gives us some confidence about their validity). We discussed in Chapter 8 just how these variables might be operating together, although they do also appear to be independently related to progress. It is possible that the effect of the curriculum coverage variable operates in two ways: within and between classrooms. Within any one class, children scoring higher on the curriculum coverage variable make more progress, either because their teachers have higher expectations of them, or because teachers go through more of the curriculum with children they find to be progressing well. We have learned (Chapter 3) that there is considerable variation between classes in the curriculum covered by the class, and it is possible that children taught by teachers who cover more of the curriculum make more progress than children in classes where curriculum coverage is less. Unfortunately, we do not have the data to test these ideas, as we did not collect either test data or curriculum coverage data for complete classes. Also, this kind of analysis is more meaningfully done for individual school years, rather than for the whole infant school period.

There are some caveats which we should attach to the results and conclusions from our models. The first is that the models are based on small samples, both in absolute size and as a proportion of the black and white nursery tested sample. Each of the models was estimated on less than half the nursery tested sample. However, the evidence presented in Appendix 5 suggests that the characteristics of those lost from the analyses were not substantially different from those retained. The size of the samples also casts some doubt on the independence of the associations of curriculum coverage and teacher expectations on progress, because very few children who were rated below average by their teachers at the beginning of the year had high curriculum coverage scores, and vice versa; in other words, there was little overlap between the distributions of teacher expectations and curriculum coverage. It is also possible that there was greater homogeneity in the parental practices we measured than would be found for national samples, and hence the influence of these variables might be smaller than the influence of school variables. Nonetheless, there was a reasonable spread of scores on all the derived home variables. Finally, our conclusions about the important influences on progress, and about the relative importance of home and school variables, might be affected by the reliability of our measures. The fact that a variable does not appear in our models does not necessarily mean that it is unimportant—it may not have been measured at all, or it may not have been measured reliably. If home variables were measured less reliably than school variables in our study then they were less likely to have appeared in our statistical models. But, as far as we could ascertain, our results hold up well when different assumptions about reliability are introduced. Further discussion of this issue can be found in Appendix 3.

To summarise, the variation in children's rates of progress during their time at infant schools is more strongly influenced by aspects of the school and the classroom than it is by characteristics of the children's homes and their parents. But the school influences that we measured do not account for the different amounts of progress made by black and white boys and girls.

11 A Summary and Some Implications

The aims of our study were to throw light on the factors in the home and the school that affect attainment and progress in the infant school, and in particular the factors that might account for differences in the school attainment of boys and girls, and black and white children.

In order to address these issues, we made a longitudinal study of children aged 4 to 7 years in 33 I.L.E.A. infant schools, starting whilst they were still in nursery classes, and following them until they started at junior school. Our sample was made up of black British children of Afro-Caribbean origin and white British children of U.K. origin who attended the same schools (Chapter 2). Every year we interviewed the children's parents and their teachers, observed the children in their classrooms, and tested their attainments. In the final year we also interviewed the children.

We will start this final chapter with a discussion of our findings about the attainment and progress of the sample as a whole. We will then go on to discuss the differential progress of the four ethnic-sex groups.

FACTORS RELATED TO ATTAINMENT AND PROGRESS IN THE INFANT SCHOOL

Pre-school Attainments

Throughout this book we have distinguished between attainment, that is, achievement at a particular point in time, and relative progress, that is, the difference in progress made by children who had similar educational attainments at school entry. If all children progressed at the same rate, then those who were doing best at school entry would continue to be doing best at the end of infant school. We found that this was, to a considerable extent, the case, and that the strongest predictor of attainment at age seven was the amount of 3R knowledge that the children had before ever they started school. In the case of reading, the strongest predictor of reading ability at age seven was the number of letters the child could identify at age four-and-three-quarters (Chapter 6, p. 109). The range of reading and maths knowledge at age four, even within a largely working-class sample, was very great. Whilst a few children could read, many did not know the basic conventions of written language. Some children could write their names neatly, others could only produce an unformed scribble (Chapter 6, p. 98). Those children with a head start tended to maintain it on the whole.

This relationship between early and later attainment is not necessarily causal. For example, it cannot be assumed that it was *because* children had some knowledge of letters at age four that they read better than their classmates at age seven. Another factor, such as the child's interest in books, or belonging to a "literary" kind of family, could have been the cause of both the early and the later attainment. In order to establish whether or not this is the case, it would be necessary to show in a controlled experiment that teaching letters to four-year-olds, irrespective of their interest in books, family characteristics, etc. leads to improved reading attainment later. Bryant and Bradley have carried out such experiments with letter sounding with six year olds. They showed that children aged six to eight who were taught letter sounds and taught to analyse the sounds in words read significantly better at age eight than children who had not received this help (Bryant & Bradley, 1985).

We ourselves would guess that knowledge of letters and other early reading skills do bear a causal relationship to later attainment, for two reasons. Firstly, although children can certainly make some progress in reading without recognising the shape or sound of individual letters, learning them involves paying attention to the structure of words, which is one component of reading. Secondly, those children assessed by the reception teacher as having some early reading skills would be likely to be given reading books earlier than the other children. Unless the teacher then gave a great deal of extra attention to the children with fewer skills, the gap between the children which was present before they started school would inevitably be reinforced. It should be added that teachers can hardly be blamed for this situation, since they are not trained or encouraged to set goals for low-attaining school entrants. Indeed, in our interview with the reception-class teachers only a fifth of them described academic progress as one of their two main aims. The majority of reception teachers seemed to believe that socialisation (by which they meant instilling classroom discipline and encouraging good relationships with other children) must take priority in the first year. Yet, as we show later in this chapter, our evidence suggests that the reception year is particularly important for progress.

We certainly would not recommend on the basis of our study that parents and teachers should concentrate on teaching letters *at the expense* of other reading-related activities. Learning to read is a complex process, involving not only recognising letters and words, but also being able to extract the meaning of a written passage. Reading aloud to children is an important way to assist this process, by arousing their interest in, and enjoyment of, books and motivating them to learn to read. But the evidence certainly suggests that as one aspect of learning to read, teaching letter sounds is likely to be helpful. There is little evidence that parents' attempts to teach reading and writing to pre-school children will interfere with, or even hold back, children's progress, and whether or not teachers approve, parents will go on making these attempts. The supposed ill effects of such teaching is the first of the current myths about infant schooling that we would wish to contest.

Since the extent of pre-school children's literacy and numeracy was so strongly related to later attainment, we tried to establish where the children had obtained their knowledge. It was not possible by this stage to discover what individual school entrants had been taught in the nursery class, but in our interviews with the nursery teachers we asked them what 3R knowledge and skills they expected children to acquire before they left the nursery. Whilst there was considerable variation amongst the teachers, in general they put little emphasis on teaching literacy and numeracy, and their expectations in these areas were often low. For example, a third of the nursery-class teachers told us that they did not expect children to be able to count above five when they left the nursery, whereas in fact we found that on average the children could count to at least ten. And only a third of the nursery teachers expected their children to know the names and sounds of any letters by the time they left the nursery (Chapter 3, p. 32), whereas we found that on average the children could identify five letters.

All the nursery classes had a plentiful supply of books, and the staff regularly read to the children. But simply introducing children to books in a happy atmosphere does not ensure that they will make a connection between meaning and print, or have any understanding of written language. We found that on leaving the nursery less than half of the children understood that in a picture book it is the print that is read, rather than the pictures. Those children whose parents did not teach them anything about written language often did not learn this in the nursery class either. We should make it clear that we are not advocating that nursery-class children should be sat down with reading primers. In an observational study in children's homes, one of us showed how some mothers of four-year-olds teach number concepts through board and card games, counting biscuits, coins, etc., and embedded learning to read and write in "real" tasks like writing to Granny, or signing a birthday card (Tizard & Hughes, 1984). The basic conventions of written language can be taught by pointing out whilst reading aloud that print goes from left to right, and down the page, and by directing children's attention to the words and numbers in their environment. It is these kinds of activities that nursery teachers should, we believe, emphasise more. Again, it needs to be stressed that the nursery teachers in our study were following the advice of inspectors, sometimes against their own inclinations. Since we began our research, a trend towards more emphasis on early literacy and numeracy has taken place in I.L.E.A. nursery classes.

Factors within the home appeared to make an important contribution to pre-school children's 3R knowledge. Social class has been found to be an important factor by other researchers. We had few middle-class parents within our sample, but we found that those mothers with higher educational qualifications tended to have more literate and numerate four-year-olds. The associations between the parent's educational practices and pre-school literacy were even stronger, especially the extent to which parents read to children and provided them with books, and also taught them about letters. But much the strongest association was with the child's own ability to define words, which no doubt reflects both innate ability and the extent to which parents talked about words and their meaning with their children (Chapter 7, p. 114–115). Again, we need to point out that, in order to show that these associations are causal, controlled experiments of the effects on later reading attainment of, for example, reading aloud to pre-school children, would be necessary.

Factors Within the Infant School

School attainment at age seven was not inexorably determined at school entry. In statistical terms, pre-school test results explained about half of the variation in top infant test scores. Although by and large those children who did best at age four did best at age seven, some children did better than would have been predicted from their pre-school scores, whereas others did worse. From an educational point of view, it is important to know what parents and teachers were doing that was responsible for a relative acceleration or slowing of progress. We found that, whereas parents had a big influence on the level of pre-school attainments, factors in the school were more important once the children started at infant school.

The two major factors in the school associated with progress were the range of 3R curriculum taught to the children, and the expectations that teachers had of them. One further factor, the particular school the child attended, was also, to a lesser extent, associated with progress. All three factors were interrelated, but all had an independent association with progress. This means, for example, that irrespective of which school a child attended, or whether or not their teacher had high expectations of them, children's attainments were higher if they had been introduced to a wider 3R curriculum (Chapter 10).

We found that the amount of progress the children made depended to a significant extent on the school they attended. The difference was most marked in writing, but it was still significant, of the order of about five points on a standardised test, in reading and maths. For reading, the difference between schools was most marked in the reception year (Chapter 6, p.107). During this year children in some schools made considerable progress, whereas in others, children with a similar level of knowledge of reading at the beginning of the year made very little progress. Since the correlations between early and later reading attainments became more marked at the end of the reception year, these findings suggest that the reception year offers an important opportunity to give special assistance to the lower-attaining children. In our opinion, a school reading policy for this important year is essential.

In the case of maths, we found no difference between schools in the amount of progress children made in the reception year, but marked differences in the middle and top infant years. These findings are not surprising, given the very small amount of maths teaching that we observed in the reception year in almost all the schools. Many teachers would object that we have underestimated the amount of maths that was going on in the reception year, since children learn a great deal of maths whilst playing in the sand tray, or with Lego. They would argue that experiences of this kind are needed before children are ready for number work. However, evidence is accumulating that children enter school with much more understanding of basic mathematical concepts and skills than is generally recognised. Many four-year-olds can judge the relative size of numbers, count objects, add and subtract small numbers, and understand the inverse relation between addition and subtraction (see review in Young-Loveridge, 1987; Hughes, 1986). Building on these skills, for example, by the use of games with playing cards, dice, etc., seems likely to be at least as fruitful as sand and water play for the development of mathematical skills. This would seem to be a promising area for collaboration with parents.

Several research studies before ours have suggested that the reception year may be of special educational importance. One U.S. researcher discovered that children who had been taught by a particular first grade teacher, Miss "A.", had higher educational qualifications and higher status jobs as adults than did adults who had been taught as children in parallel classes in the same school. It was said of Miss "A." that: "it did not matter what background or abilities the beginning pupil had; there was no way that the pupil was not going to read by the end of grade one ... She invariably stayed after hours to help the slow learners ... and could remember each pupil by name even after an interval of 20 years". The researchers found no evidence that parents had been able to select Miss "A.'s" class for their children. The initial boost that she seemed to give to the children's confidence and attainments was present at the end of elementary school, and the researchers argue that this left the children with an advantage throughout their educational career (Pederson, Faucher, & Eaton, 1978; see also for another study of a reception teacher, Rist, 1970).

Although we have said that children in different schools made different amounts of progress, we have some evidence that in fact the differences were between classes rather than schools, that is, it was the individual teacher (as in the case of Miss "A.") who made a difference to the child's progress (Chapter 6, p. 107). As to why children made more progress in some schools or classes than others, we only have clues, rather than conclusions, from our findings, because we did not set out to study differences between schools and teachers. But since we found that the 3R curriculum taught varied between schools, and was associated with progress, we suspect that it played an important role in producing these differences.

Up to now, rather little interest has been shown by educational researchers in the infant-school curriculum, that is, exactly what 3R skills and knowledge children are taught at each stage. Yet it is clear that attainment and progress depend crucially on whether children are given particular learning experiences—they cannot be expected to tell the time, for example, unless someone has taught them. We found a wide range between schools or classes in what children of the same age were taught, and this could not be accounted for by the intake of the school.

Within classes, we found a consistent relationship between the teachers' expectations of individual children at the beginning of the year and the range of the 3R curriculum they were introduced to (Chapter 8, p. 137). This was true even when controlling for the children's initial skills: That is, of two children with similar skills at the beginning of the year, the one judged by the teacher to have higher academic potential than the other would be introduced to a wider range of 3R knowledge during the year. It might be argued that this simply means that the teacher was a good judge of which child would in fact be better able to cope with a wider curriculum, but our findings suggest that the teachers were influenced by other than strictly academic considerations—for example, we found that their expectations were influenced by their opinion that a child was "a pleasure to teach".

Teachers have expectations not only of individual children, but of the class as a whole. The only way we were able to glimpse these in our study was by asking teachers why they had not introduced certain curriculum items to *any* of the children in their class. Whilst some teachers answered that these items were too difficult for children of this age, others said that they were too difficult for the children in this school. Yet we know that in other schools, with a similar intake, teachers had introduced these items. We suspect that low expectations are an important cause of the low level of attainment in many of the schools we studied. Our sample of children were, on average, well below the national norms in reading and maths, and by the end of infant school 25% were definitely poor readers. (These findings are not necessarily true of I.L.E.A. as a whole.) We found no evidence that the children "caught up" in the junior school. At the end of the first year in junior school both reading and maths scores were highly correlated with those of the year before, and the poor readers had made relatively little progress (Chapter 6, p. 109).

Low attainment in the schools was certainly not caused by a general state of chaos or confusion in the classroom. In three-quarters of our observations we found children busy working, or organising work, and disruptive or aggressive behaviour in the classroom was rare (Chapter 4, pp. 64–66). Nor was it the case that the children spent a great deal of time playing; the proportion of classroom time devoted to play ranged from 14% in the reception year to 2% in the top-infant year (Chapter 4, p. 61). It does, however, seem to us likely that the low level of reading attainment in the schools was related to the small amount of time that the children spent reading. In our observations we found that only 4% of the working time in top-infant classes (roughly 8 minutes a day) was spent by the children in any kind of reading, and quite a lot of this time was taken up with rapidly flipping through books (Chapter 4, p. 54). This figure is, of course, an average. In some classes none of the children did any reading during the days we observed them; others averaged 27 minutes per child. In nearly all these latter classes, instead of trying to hear each child read, the teachers had arranged for children to read to each other in pairs or in small groups (Farquhar, 1987). It seems important to evaluate whether this approach does, in fact, improve reading skills and the enjoyment of reading, and if it does, to bring it to the attention of more teachers.

If, as we believe, the expectations of the teachers were too low, a crucial issue for future investigation is to establish how expectations can be raised in a largely working-class area. Initially, it is obviously both desirable and feasible to raise the expectations of teachers in low-achieving working-class schools to those of teachers in higher-achieving schools in similar areas. A more ambitious, and very important, project would be to see just how high one can reasonably set expectations in a working-class area—is it possible by this process to achieve the standards of a middle-class school? The question is one of great importance in primary education, since if teachers' expectations are low, children will inevitably leave infant school with a handicap.

There was a serious mismatch between the level of the children's attainment at age seven and the expectations of the parents, especially the black parents. About a half of both the black and white parents told us that they would like their child to go to a university or polytechnic, and over a third of the black parents wanted their child to get a professional job (Chapter 5, p. 84). These are perfectly reasonable aspirations, no doubt shared by the teachers for their own children. Yet only 12% of all young people entered full-time higher education in 1984, and 70% of students accepted for university come from social classes 1 and 2 (Great Britain, 1986). Since very few of the children in our sample came from this social background, they would have to make very much more progress at school, if they were later to enter higher education than was the case at present. Of this the parents seemed unaware. Only a minority had received feedback about the standard of their children's work (Chapter 5, p. 91), the majority seemed satisfied with the schools, and 70% were satisfied with the progress their children had made.

One way to raise attainments, currently being advocated by government, is to impose a centrally controlled curriculum, and monitor standards by external assessment of the children at the age of seven. Most British infant teachers are deeply opposed to these proposals. They fear the loss of autonomy entailed, and also the consequences of "teaching to the test". That is, external assessment would be likely to result in teachers coaching children for the test, to the neglect of their wider aims, such as stimulating intellectual curiosity, encouraging a love of books, and widening children's interests. They also worry that assessment at seven would result in a return to streaming in primary schools.

These are real concerns, which we share. It would be a serious loss if innovative thinking and new educational approaches were discouraged by a government straightjacket. This is especially the case because most of the education that we saw was not very innovative. The great majority of children were, in fact, being taught a rather narrow range of subjects in a fairly traditional way. The second myth about British infant schooling that we encountered is that it encourages learning through "discovery" or play. We saw very little discovery learning, or working in groups. For much of their time, children worked on their own through maths or writing "work cards". We also saw no case for arguing that a core curriculum is necessary for infant schools, or that they should go "back to the basics". The curriculum in I.L.E.A. infant schools is already focused on "the basics". We found that two-thirds of classroom time was spent in 3R activities in the top-infant year, 21% on art and creative work, of which the largest proportion was drawing, crayoning and tracing, and only 3% of the time was spent in free play. There was very little teaching of science, other than nature work, and very little practical work. By the top-infant year maths teaching was mainly written number work, reading was usually taught through the use of "reading schemes", and a lot of time was spent on what many of the children saw as rather dull writing tasks (Chapter 9). The need would seem to be not for more time to be spent on the 3Rs, but for children to be helped to attain a higher standard in them, which we have suggested involves raising teachers' expectations and extending the range of the 3R curriculum they teach.

The objections to external assessment referred to earlier do not apply to assessments internal to the school. We believe that such assessments need not discourage innovation, if devised by the teachers themselves with the aim of seeing whether their objectives had been attained, and of discovering the strengths and weaknesses of their pupils. Assessments of this kind involve the teacher in evaluating her own work as much as the children's achievements. They should be quite frequent, rather than occurring only at the age of seven. Our findings suggest that assessing children's skills soon after entry to school, so that teachers could diagnose the areas in which children need help, would be an important way of raising standards. Such assessments would need to be linked to a much clearer setting of goals by infant teachers than is usual at the present time. Unless teachers have clear objectives of what they intend children to learn during the year, both individually and as a class, they cannot assess whether they themselves, or their children, have achieved these objectives. Setting objectives involves curriculum planning, both for the class as a whole and for individual children. Our study suggests that extending curriculum coverage is an important way of putting higher expectations into practice.

Teachers' objectives do not have to be narrow in order to be assessed. If they are concerned that use of a standardised reading test takes no account of their aim of encouraging a love of reading, for example, it is quite possible to decide on simple ways of assessing whether this aim has been achieved. Such an assessment might lead to a review of school practices, to see whether the school offers opportunities to foster reading habits in children. Is it possible, for example, to give them a chance to curl up with a book and read undisturbed for a reasonable period of time, perhaps in the school playtimes? We think there is a strong case for informing parents of the curriculum plans for the year, and also for enlisting their help in assessment at the end of the year. They would be an important source of information about their child's reading habits, interests, ability to use maths in practical situations, and so on. This process, by entailing teachers sharing their educational goals with the parents, might lead to greater home-school co-operation, and perhaps also to a change in the perspectives of both teachers and parents.

Parental Back-up in the Infant School

Some teachers are likely to be sceptical of this suggestion, and to blame the parents for their pupils' low level of achievement. We found that the majority of teachers thought that parents, and not schools, were the main influence on children's educational success (Chapter 5, p. 82). At the same time, we had plenty of evidence that the teachers did not believe that the parents they dealt with would use this influence well. When we asked the reception-class teachers whether they thought that their parents would provide the back-up at home that they would like, only a third thought that the majority of parents would do so, and 29% felt that very few, or none, of their parents would do so (Chapter 5, p. 76). This proved to be a third myth very widespread amongst teachers, and certainly not supported by our evidence. At the pre-school interview, the great majority of parents told us that they wanted to help with their child's education—only 20% said that it was a matter to be left to the teachers. Throughout the infant school most parents were deeply committed to helping their children. In the first two years of school, 40% of parents said they heard their children read five times a week (Chapter 5, p. 77). Despite the fact that very few teachers encouraged parents to help with writing and maths, a great deal of such help was being given in most of the children's homes.

It is of course possible, perhaps even likely, that the parents overestimated the frequency with which they read to their children, and heard them read. Nonetheless, the fact that we found strong associations between the frequency of these behaviours as reported by parents and the level of the children's preschool reading skills suggests that their reports had some validity.

There is another widely held belief amongst teachers, that black parents are particularly likely to fail to provide adequate educational support for their children. This, too, proved to be a myth. We found that black parents gave their children even more help with school work than white parents, and had a more positive attitude towards giving this help (Chapter 5, p. 83). Both black and white parents read aloud to their children with equal frequency—during the reception year 40% said that they read to them every day. The great majority of parents provided their children with books—at school entry, as we saw for ourselves, only a quarter of the children had as few as ten or less books—and similar proportions of black and white parents said that they borrowed children's books from the public library, and attended school meetings.

The myth of the unsupporting black family forms part of a racist stereotype. In fact, there is a long tradition of respect for education in the Caribbean, and many black parents emigrated to this country to give their children a better educational future. The black parents in our study had stayed at school longer than the white parents, and more of them had acquired at least one C.S.E. or O-level. They were well aware that, because of discrimination, they needed to be better qualified than their white peers. (See also Maughan & Rutter, 1986.)

Factors in the Home Related to Progress

We have shown that factors in the home were strongly associated with the children's pre-school attainments, and thus their attainments at age seven. But once the children had started school, in our largely working-class sample, school variables had a stronger relationship with progress than home variables (Chapter 10). The amount of parental contact with, and knowledge of, the school, was significantly associated with progress, but not after allowing for the extent of the child's writing at home. In the case of maths, the only factors independently related to progress were the teachers' expectations, the curriculum coverage, and the sex of the child. Neither the frequency with which the parents read to the child, nor the frequency with which the parents heard the child read, or helped with maths, were related to progress (Chapter 7, p. 117–121). And, despite a good deal of parental help, the reading and maths standard of our sample was below average.

These findings are in conflict with those of experimental interventions in schools, such as the Haringey project (Tizard et al., 1982), which have found that increasing the amount of parental help with reading substantially raised reading levels. We suspect that their success was due to careful organisation of the reading materials, and considerable interaction with the parents throughout the project about the child's reading. Simply sending reading primers home does not in itself seem likely to raise reading standards.

Child Characteristics and Progress

Whilst parental behaviour and attitudes were not related to progress in the infant school, certain characteristics of the children themselves were strongly related to progress. These included not only the sex and ethnic group of the children, but their W.P.P.S.I. vocabulary score at age four, the amount and complexity of the writing they did at home, and whether the teachers saw them as having behaviour problems, or as being a "pleasure to teach", by which they usually meant being eager to learn. No doubt all these characteristics were affected by home and school influences, or, as in the case of sex and ethnic group, were related to progress because of the way in which parents, teachers, and others behaved differently towards boys and girls and black and white children. Nevertheless, children are not the sum total of the influences bearing on them, and their individual thoughts, feelings, behaviours, and characteristics, which we assessed only crudely and very incompletely, made an independent contribution to their progress.

Parental Satisfaction with Infant School

Contrary to the current media view that parents are dissatisfied with schools, we found that the level of parental satisfaction was generally high (Chapter 5, p. 89). Where dissatisfactions were expressed, they were as often concerned with hygiene and playground supervision as with teaching methods or discipline. Further, two-thirds of the parents were either satisfied or very satisfied with the progress their child had made over the three-year period. Whether they were right to be satisfied is a point we return to later.

Home-school Communication

Parent-teacher communication has undoubtedly increased in recent years, but there were several indications from our study that ways need to be found to extend it. We have already suggested that the apparent ineffectiveness of parental help with reading was due to insufficient home-school liaison about the reading process. We found that children's progress in reading and writing (Chapter 7, p.117) was related to the amount of parental knowledge of, and contact with, the school. But we also found that in most schools it was very much up to the parents to obtain information about teaching methods. Written explanations, or other attempts to ensure that all parents understood the school timetable and curriculum, were very unusual. About 80% of parents told us that they had had at least one discussion with their child's teacher each year, but these discussion were often not very informative. Most of what the parents knew about the curriculum they had gleaned from looking at their children's work. Contact between parents and teachers does not seem to be enough for communication to occur. In addition, there needs to be an agreement on the importance of sharing information with *all* parents, and a clear curriculum policy or teaching plan to communicate with them.

The majority of parents, especially black parents, were not told whether their children's reading and maths attainment was average, or above, or below average (Chapter 5, p. 91). Parents of children whose attainments were below average were particularly likely not to be told. Hence many parents had an over-rosy view of their child's attainment—at the end of infant school only 16% thought their child was below average in reading, whereas we found that 65% were below average on our reading test. And by no means all the parents of children whom the teachers described to us as having behaviour or learning problems had been told this by the teachers.

Some teachers were motivated by what they saw as the child's best interests, since they feared that bad behaviour would be excessively punished by the parents, and below-average children would be over-pressurised at home. Afro-Caribbean parents were especially likely to be viewed in this way. When we asked the reception-class teachers: "What has been your experience of Caribbean parents?", only 13% said that they could not generalise, and 70% mentioned such negative attributes as that they were "overconcerned with their children's education"; "had too high expectations"; "lacked understanding of British education"; "were too authoritarian at home". (A third of the teachers, including some of those who had made critical remarks, mentioned positive attributes; Chapter 5, p. 91.) These are subjective judgements, which depend on values and perspectives. From where the parents stood, obtaining educational qualifications was essential for the future of their children in a racist society.

Another reason why teachers did not tell parents whether or not the child's work was average was their belief that children should not be compared with one another, but judged according to their own rate of progress. They felt that comparisons between children could result in labelling some as slow learners and would, in any case, be misleading, since children who made no progress in one year might "take off" in the next.

We did not find these arguments convincing. We suspect that most teachers do, in fact, compare children, and that they would want to know whether their own child was below average, or behaving badly at school. And we had strong evidence that, in general, children doing badly one year do not "take off" the next. The correlations between children's scores from one year to another were very high. For example, we found a correlation of 0.89 between reading scores in the top-infant year and the first year of junior school, that is, the children had hardly changed rank at all during the year, and poor readers remained poor readers (Chapter 6, p. 109). It seems to us that parents have a right to be informed about the standard of their child's work and behaviour, and that in the long run children would be better served by open communication between teacher and parent.

Teachers who use innovative methods are sometimes reluctant to discuss their work with parents because they are aware that parents' ideas about primary education may be different from theirs. We do not underestimate the difficulty of explaining modern methods to parents from different backgrounds, but serious attempts to do so can be rewarding. One of us showed that parental scepticism and hostility towards "learning through play" in the nursery changed to support when teachers went to exceptional lengths to explain to all the parents exactly what they were doing with the children, and why (Tizard, Mortimore, & Burchell, 1981). Teachers might also consider supplementing their own educational approach by encouraging parents to carry out the activities which they consider important. For instance, if parents think that learning the alphabet, or "tables" and mental arithmetic, are important, and teachers do not, teachers might nonetheless encourage parents to teach these activities at home, in ways that do not interfere with their own approach, e.g. by teaching letter sounds rather than letter names. There is considerable evidence that many parents will teach their children what they think is necessary, whether or not the school approves. It seems sensible to acknowledge this fact, and make it an opportunity for home-school liaison.

We do not want to suggest that every parent is a paragon, but both the present study and many others (e.g. Hannon, Long, Weiberger, & Whitehurst, 1985; Tizard et al., 1982) have found that a very high level of parent-teacher co-operation is possible if teachers set out to seek and organise it. Some teachers are worried that parents will "take over" the school, or disturb classrooms. In our experience, few parents are interested in school management or in working in the classroom. What they are primarily interested in is knowing how to help their own child.

Undoubtedly teachers are handicapped by the fact that they are not trained to work with parents, and not allocated time in which to do so. Yet parents are potentially the teachers' best allies; as we discovered, most parents, especially black parents, value schools and teachers highly, are anxious to help their children, and welcome opportunities to co-operate with teachers to this end.

ETHNIC AND SEX DIFFERENCES IN ATTAINMENT AND PROGRESS

One of the main aims of our study was to look for factors that might account for differences in the school attainments of boys and girls, and black and white children. At the pre-school stage, we found no significant ethnic differences in early reading, writing and maths skills, or in scores on the W.P.S.I. vocabulary test. The only sex differences at this stage was that both black and white girls were superior to boys in writing. This superiority continued throughout the infant school. At the end of infant school, there was still no overall ethnic difference in attainment, but the black girls had emerged as ahead of all other groups in both reading and writing, whilst black boys were doing worst. Both black and white boys made more progress than girls at maths, with white boys making the most progress. When we retested the children at the end of the first year of junior school, there were still no significant overall ethnic differences in attainment. By now there was a significant sex difference in reading, with girls definitely ahead of boys (Chapter 6, pp. 104–105).

We suspect that those studies that have found an ethnic difference in the achievement of seven- or eight-year-old children have compared black children with white children who were attending different schools in different neighbourhoods. At a later stage other factors, notably racism in all its manifestations, may play an increasing role in the underachievement of black children.

The Infant-school Experiences of Black and White Girls and Boys[1]

There were a number of indications in our findings that not only the attainments but also the experience of infant school tended to be different for these four groups of children. In our classroom observations at top infants we found that on average white boys spent a greater proportion of the school day doing maths than other groups, and this seemed to be because the teachers allocated more maths tasks to them. In general, white boys were the most "work-oriented" group. We observed that they both initiated and received a greater proportion of work contacts with teachers than the other children, and had fewer purely social contacts with other children in the classroom. In our interviews with the children, it was the white boys who most often said that they felt happy about going to school in the morning.

In contrast, black boys on average had the smallest proportion of contacts with teachers about school work. We observed that they received most disapproval and criticism from the teachers, and they were most often said by the teachers to have behaviour problems. In our classroom observations, they were the group most often seen to be "fooling around", but these incidents were relatively rare. In our interviews with them, the black boys were more likely than the other groups to tell us that they had been punished for being "really naughty", and also told off in the playground. They were the group who most enjoyed the long dinner-hour playtime, and most looked forward to the holidays.

None of this meant that they disliked school, or had a poor academic self-concept. They were more likely to say that they looked forward to the new experiences of junior school than the other groups, they enjoyed maths as much as the white boys did, and they were the group who most enjoyed reading to the teacher. Both black and white boys were more likely than girls to assess themselves as above average in all school subjects.

Whereas the black boys tended to get into trouble at school, and to do

---

The findings in this sector of the chapter are drawn from Chapter 4, 8 and 9.

poorly at reading and writing, but to remain cheerful and self-confident about most aspects of school life, white girls in many ways presented the opposite picture. To an extent, they were invisible to the teachers. As a group, they received less disapproval and criticism from the teachers than did the other children, but also less praise. They were least often said to have behaviour problems. They spent more time in the classroom than other groups on such "housekeeping" jobs as sharpening pencils and fetching materials. Like the black girls, they were less likely than boys to say they enjoyed maths, and less likely to rate themselves as above average in maths, and of all the groups, they were least likely to rate themselves above average in reading and writing. They were also the least likely to say that they found school interesting. They were the group least likely to say that they were punished for being really naughty, but most likely to complain that they got teased at school.

The black girls, it will be remembered, made the most progress in reading and writing in the infant school, and had the highest attainments in these subjects. They shared with the white girls a tendency to like maths less than the boys did, and to rate their maths achievements lower than the boys did. Like the white girls, too, they were less likely than the boys to say they got into fights at school or told off in the playground. In other respects, however, their experiences were different from those of the white girls. The teachers described them as having at least as many behaviour problems as the white boys, and many more than the white girls, although not as many as the black boys. The black girls themselves told us, almost as often as the black boys did, that they got into trouble for naughtiness. They were as self-confident in their assessments of their reading and writing attainments as the boys were, they complained of being teased no more than did the boys, and they were more likely to think that school was interesting than the white girls did.

There were important respects in which the school experiences of both black boys and girls differed from those of the white children. They were much more likely to be the subject of racial taunts from other children, and they did not have the experience of being taught by someone of the same ethnic group. Throughout the infant school, none of the black children had a black classroom teacher (although a few classes had a South Asian teacher), whereas the white children were generally taught by white teachers. Further, only 4 of the 33 schools had a black classroom "helper". It was also true that hardly any boys had the experience of being taught by a man— there was only one (white) male teacher in our study. It is difficult to know whether or how the degree of ethnic and sex match between the four groups of children and their teachers affected their behaviour and progress. The best match between teacher and child was for the white girls, who had the fewest behaviour problems but seemed to enjoy school least and have the least self-confidence.

Because we had very few middle-class children in our sample, we do not know the extent to which these generalisations would hold good in a more socially diverse group. It may be, for example, that middle-class white girls tend to be more self-confident than working-class white girls, or that middle-class black boys have fewer behaviour problems than working-class black boys. Our findings do suggest, however, that it can be very misleading to generalise about children of different ethnic groups without taking sex into account, or vice versa. From this point of view, the recent I.L.E.A. decision to analyse public examination results by ethnic group and sex is a welcome one.

Accounting for Sex and Ethnic Differences in Attainment, Progress, and Behaviour at School

The task of explaining ethnic-sex interactions in school progress and attainment is more complex than explaining straightforward ethnic or sex differences. This is particularly the case because most other studies of ethnic differences have not analysed their data about girls and boys separately, and most studies of sex differences have not included black children in their samples. We have very little data, therefore, from other research that can be used to support or refute any hypotheses that we put forward.

So far as factors in the home are concerned, the girls' superiority in writing may be linked to our finding that at the pre-school stage parents of girls were more likely to say that they had taught them to write other words as well as their names than parents of boys (Chapter 5, p. 79). At the infant-school stage, girls were read to more often, and had more books, than boys (Chapter 5, p. 81). They also wrote more often at home, and at a higher level, than boys. The causal connections could, however, be in either or both directions. For example, perhaps the girls wrote more at home, and were more often taught to write at home, not because parents encouraged girls more, but because girls found writing easier than boys did; or perhaps they enjoyed writing more than boys, and hence practised it more at home, and in the process got better at it.

We found no evidence from our interviews with parents to account for the finding that boys made more progress in maths than girls. That is, we found no evidence that parents helped boys with maths more than they did girls. Possibly our measures were insufficiently sensitive, or possibly in some way parents conveyed the attitude that maths is particularly a masculine skill, without necessarily giving boys more help in it.

As to the ethnic-sex interactions we found, some readers might like to be reminded that there were no significant ethnic or sex differences in W.P.P.S.I. vocabulary scores between the four groups at the pre-school stage. Thus the greater progress in reading of the black girls, for example, cannot be attributed to their early superiority in language skills. It is often suggested by teachers that black boys' low attainment and behaviour problems at school are in some way related to the childrearing practices of the undoubtedly higher proportion of black single mothers. The mothers are either seen as allowing the boys to run wild, or, contrariwise, as exerting such tight discipline on the boys that they rebel and in either case do not settle down to school learning. However, the children in our sample from single-parent families (most of whom were black) did not in fact have lower attainments or make less progress than those from two-parent families (Chapter 7, p. 112, 117). But we did find that black children from single-parent families were much more likely to be described by the teachers as having behaviour problems than black children from two-parent families (Chapter 8, p.133). The numbers are too small to say whether this difference applied equally to boys and girls, and there were insufficient white children in single-parent families to say whether they also were seen as having an excess of behaviour problems.

So far as factors at school are concerned, here, too, we found few clues to explain the sex differences and the sex-ethnic interactions. We did find that the white boys, who made the fastest progress at school in maths, spent more time doing maths, at least at top infants, than the other groups, apparently because the teachers allocated more maths to them (Chapter 4, p. 58). There was also some evidence that teachers had higher expectations of boys than girls, especially in maths, although they did not introduce them to a wider curriculum than girls (Chapter 8, pp. 124–128). We found no evidence that teachers had higher expectations of white children than black children.

We were not able to explain the relatively fast progress of the black girls in reading and writing, and the relatively slow progress of the black boys. The difference in progress was substantial, equivalent to six points on a standardised test in reading, and eight points in writing (Chapter 6, p. 101–102). It is tempting to relate the slower progress of the black boys to our finding that the teachers described them as having more behaviour problems than any other group. However, the black girls, who were also said to have behaviour problems (although less often than the black boys), nonetheless made the most progress in reading and writing of any of the four groups. Further, in the sample as a whole behaviour problems were not independently related to progress once other factors, such as teacher expectations, were taken into account. This may, of course, mean that the way in which behaviour problems affected progress was by influencing the expectations the teacher had of the child. It may also be that behaviour problems had different implications for learning for black boys and girls. We suspect that there is a complex interaction between ethnic group, sex, behaviour problems and progress which we had insufficient data to analyse further.

Indeed, research on sex differences in attainments and attitudes at school, discussed in Chapter 1, suggests that very subtle patterns of teacher-child interactions may affect the classroom behaviour and attitude to academic work of boys and girls. This may prove to be equally true of ethnic-sex effects. Before school entry our four groups of children had equivalent attainments, except for the girls' superiority in writing. By the end of infant school marked differences in attainment had developed between the groups. There were also marked differences in the behaviour of the children in these groups. It seemed that factors in the school, as well as in the home, had already shaped the children towards conforming to gender roles which differed between black and white children. We are not able to explain how this came about, because our study was not geared to examine the complex dynamics likely to have been involved.

These complex dynamics are likely to have involved factors in society as a whole. Our research design, which focused on factors in the school and the home, and to some extent in the child, omitted influences in the wider society which reach children via the media, books, neighbours, relations, and their own street experiences; these may be very important.

The Children's Point of View

We found that, by and large, children enjoyed school, and tended to feel positive about their school achievements (Chapter 9). This was most true of the white boys, and least true of the white girls. This is not to say that the children found lessons particularly interesting; less than half did so, and some of their reasons for not finding them interesting are worth considering. Reading was seen by some children as a frustrating and solitary activity, with no-one to help with unfamiliar words. Writing could be equally frustrating because of the constant need to ask for "spellings". We suspect that maths was popular not only for its intellectual challenge, but also because it offered tangible success for easy repetitive tasks. Since the experience of success plays a key role in feeling positive about learning, it is important to consider how reading and writing could give this experience more often. The new "developmental" primary teaching approaches, for example, allowing children to read to each other in pairs or small groups, and encouraging them to be more independent in the early stages of writing and to invent their own spelling, may prevent some of these frustrations.

Our study was not addressed to children's social experiences at school, but for the children these were often the worst or the best side of school life. This finding is not surprising, given that playtimes and dinner hour occupied 28% of the whole school day, compared with 29% spent studying the 3Rs, of which 2% was spent reading (Chapter 4, p. 51). Life in the playground was seen by virtually all the children as both verbally and physically aggressive. Some children could cope with this environment and thoroughly enjoyed playtimes, but white girls were especially likely to dislike the long dinner playtime and to complain of being teased. Several teachers told us that they had to spend considerable time and energy at the beginning of lesson periods sorting out problems that had arisen during playtime. Some schools, not in our study, have introduced a variety of arrangements to modify this situation; for example, "staggering" play-times, so that there are fewer children in the playground at any one time, or allowing children to stay in the classroom if they wish, or providing organised recreation in the playground. There is a need to evaluate the effectiveness of these innovations. At present, "playtime" does not seem high on the agenda of parents, teachers, or politicians, although we suspect that many children would see it as an important issue. We found that parents tended to underestimate greatly the extent to which children had problems with their social life at school.

RESEARCH ISSUES

As the reader will have noted, there are many under-researched issues in infant education. Most educational research, like our own, has looked for associations between early and later attainment, or between home and school factors and the child's attainment. Such studies can only suggest what the causal connections might be; they need to be followed by control-led experiments, although this happens all too rarely. The issues thrown up by our own research which are in particular need of experimental investi-gation include the effect of pre-school 3R teaching and experience with books on pre-school and later attainments; the effect of raising the expec-tations of teachers in working class areas; the effect of extending the range of the 3R curriculum on attainment; the effect of increasing the amount of time children spend reading in school on reading attainment; the effect of increasing parents' knowledge about the school and of increasing feedback about their children's behaviour and progress on home-school relations and on children's behaviour and progress; the effectiveness of different types of home-school collaboration on reading and maths; the effect of providing alternative playtime regimens on the level of children's aggres-sion and on the contentedness of the children. We found relatively few leads to explain the sex and ethnic-sex differences in progress and behaviour that we recorded. In our opinion, these issues require detailed ethnographic studies within the school to attempt to understand the dynamics responsible for the differences. It would also be useful to survey a much larger number of schools, to see if there are any schools where sex and ethnic-sex differences in behaviour and attainment do not develop, and if so, to analyse the characteristics of these schools.

THE TEACHER'S SITUATION

Despite the reservations we have expressed about infant schools and teachers, it should be stressed that we saw some very good teachers, and that most parents were satisfied with the schools, and most children were happy at school. Nevertheless, our discussion should end with a consideration of the teacher's situation, because there is a sense in which in every discussion of education "the buck stops" with the teacher. It is in the classroom that the crucial face-to-face educational interactions occur, and in Britain, because primary teachers have considerable autonomy, it is where the crucial educational decisions are made. A policy decision may be made by central or local government, or by the head teacher of the school concerned, but unless the teachers support it, they will not necessarily put it into effect in their classrooms.

But teachers do not exist in a vacuum, and their attitudes inevitably reflect those of the wider society. If they hold gender and ethnic stereotypes, so do the majority of British people. If their expectations of both parents and children in working-class areas are low, they only reflect widely-held views. Moreover, teachers are constrained by the amount of support made available to them by heads, advisors, and educational authorities. If teachers do not work closely with parents, they can fairly retort that they have not been trained to do so, that they are given no extra time for such work, and that the inspectors and headteachers do not provide them with the necessary support and training. If they do not give sufficient individual attention to the low-attaining children, they can reasonably point to the difficulties of doing so whilst managing the rest of the class.

For these reasons it seems clear that if schools are to improve, teachers need a great deal of support, in terms of in-service training, and also adequate time to think about, evaluate, and discuss their work, decide on objectives and assess their success, and work with parents. For example, if they were freed half a day a week for individual discussions with parents, where necessary by home visits in the evening, they could ensure an exchange of information with all the parents in their class every term, and in the process foster friendly home-school relationships. A second half day a week free from teaching would allow them time to plan objectives for individual children, and evaluate the extent to which they are attained, and visit other schools where innovations have been made. Secondary-school staff expect regular periods free from teaching to plan their work, but "noncontact" teaching time is rarely available for infant-school teachers. The very fact that these proposals sound like "pie in the sky" to infant teachers is an indication of the low esteem accorded them. This low esteem is reflected in the marked difference between the career and pay structures in secondary and primary schools.

Although lip service is often paid to the role of the infant school, our study suggests that infant education deserves and needs a great deal more discussion and support. Once the children had started school, within our largely working-class sample, factors within school were much more strongly related to progress than factors within the home, and differences between schools or teachers were also important for progress. Not only our study, but many others (e.g. Morris, 1966), suggest that children who are poor readers when they leave the infant school are likely to be poor readers throughout their educational careers. The same is likely to be true for maths and writing.

There is no reason to suppose that this state of affairs cannot be changed, and every reason to believe that resources spent on improving standards in infant schooling would be a key educational investment. The best way of effecting changes within schools is not yet well understood. It seems likely that changes in both initial and in-service training would be required, as well as supporting teachers in the classroom, providing opportunities for them to develop their professional skills, and finding ways of fostering more effective home-school collaboration. All these measures require that increased resources be devoted to this sector of the state education system.

References

Aitkin, M., Bennett, S.N., & Hesketh, J. (1981). Teaching styles and pupil progress. *British Journal of Educational Psychology, 51,* 170–186.

Aitkin, M. & Longford, N. (1986). Statistical modelling issues in school effectiveness studies. *Journal of the Royal Statistical Society, 149,* 1, 1–43.

A.M.M.A. (Assistant Masters and Mistresses Association) (1984). Report of a survey carried out for A.M.M.A.'s Primary and Preparatory Education Committee.

Ashton, P. (1978). What are primary teachers' aims? In C. Richards (Ed.) *Education, 3–13 1973–77.* Driffield, North Humberside: Nafferton Books.

Barker Lunn, J.C. (1970). *Streaming in the primary school.* Windsor: N.F.E.R.

Baron, R.N., Tom., D.Y.H., & Cooper, H. (1985). Social class, race, and teacher expectations. In J.B. Dusek (Ed.), *Teacher expectancies.* Hillsdale, N.J.: Lawrence Erlbaum Associates Inc.

Bassey, M. (1978). *Nine hundred primary school teachers.* Windsor: N.F.E.R.

Beez, W. (1968). Influences of biased psychological reports on teacher behaviour and pupil performance. *Proceedings of the 76th Annual Convention of the American Psychological Association, 3,* 605–606.

Bennett, N., Andreae, J., Hegarty, P., & Wade, B. (1980). *Open-plan schools.* Windsor: N.F.E.R.

Bennett, N., Desforges, C., Cockburn, A., & Wilkinson, B. (1984). *The quality of pupil learning experiences.* London: Lawrence Erlbaum Associates Ltd.

Blatchford, P., Burke, J., Farquhar, C., Plewis, I., & Tizard, B. (1985). Educational achievement in the infant school: The influence of ethnic origin, gender, and home on entry skills. *Educational Research, 27,* 1, 52–60.

Blatchford, P., Burke, J., Farquhar, C., Plewis, I., & Tizard, B. (1987a). A systematic observation study of children's behaviour at infant school. *Research Papers in Education, 2,* 1, 47–62.

Blatchford, P., Burke, J., Farquhar, C., Plewis, I., & Tizard, B. (1987b). Associations between pre-school reading related skills and later reading achievement. *British Educational Research Journal, 13,* 1, 15–23.

Bloom, W. (1987). *Partnership with parents in reading.* London: Hodder & Stoughton.

B.M.D.P. statistical software manual (1985). Berkeley: University of California Press.

Boehm, A. (1971). *Boehm Test of Basic Concepts manual.* New York: The Psychological Corporation.

British Ability Scales. Windsor: N.F.E.R.-Nelson.

Bronfenbrenner, U. (1961). Some familial antecedents of responsibility and leadership in adolescents. In D. Petrollo & B.M. Bass (Eds.), *Leadership and interpersonal behaviour.* New York: Holt, Rinehart, & Winston.

Brophy, J.E. (1979). Teacher behaviour and its effects. *Journal of Educational Psychology, 71,* 6, 733–750.

Brophy, J.E. (1983). Research on the self-fulfilling prophecy and teacher expectations. *Journal of Educational Psychology, 75,* 5, 631–661.

Brophy, J.E. & Evertson, C.M. (1977). Teacher behaviour and student learning in second and third grades. In G.D. Borich (Ed.), *The appraisal of teaching: Concepts and process.* Reading, Mass.: Addison-Wesley.

Brophy, J. & Good, T. (1970). Teachers' communication of differential expectations for children's classroom performance: Some behavioural data. *Journal of Educational Psychology, 61,* 365–374.

Brophy, J.E. & Good, T.L, (1974). *Teacher-student relationships: Causes and consequences.* New York; Holt, Rinehart, and Winston.

Brown, C. (1984). *Black and white Britain.* The Third P.S.I. Survey. London: Heinemann.

Bryant, P. & Bradley, L. (1985). *Children's reading problems.* Oxford: Basil Blackwell.

"The Bullock Report" See Great Britain, Department of Education and Science.

Carew, J.V. & Lightfoot, S.L. (1979). *Beyond bias: Perspectives on classrooms.* Cambridge, Mass.: Harvard University Press.

Carter, T. (1986). *Shattering Illusions.* London: Lawrence & Wishart.

Central Advisory Council for Education (England) *Children and their primary schools* ("The Plowden Report"). London: H.M.S.O.

Clarricoats, K. (1978). Dinosaurs in the classroom. *Women's Studies International Quarterly, 1,* 353–364.

Clay, M. (1979). *The early detection of reading difficulties: A diagnostic survey with recovery procedures.* Auckland, New Zealand: Heinemann.

Clift, P. (1981). Parental involvement in primary schools. *Primary Education Review, 10,* 2–4.

Coard, B. (1971). *How the West Indian Child is made educationally sub-normal in the British school system.* London: New Beacon Books.

"The Cockcroft Report" See Committee of Inquiry into the Teaching of Mathematics in Schools.

Committee of Inquiry into the Education of Children from Ethnic Minority Groups (1981). *West Indian children in our schools.* Interim Report of the Committee of Inquiry into the Education of Children from Ethnic Minority Groups ("The Rampton Report"). London: H.M.S.O.

Committee of Inquiry into the Education of Children from Ethnic Minority Groups (1985). *Education for all.* The Report of the Committee of Inquiry into the Education of Children from Ethnic Minority Groups ("The Swann Report"). London: H.M.S.O.

Committee of Inquiry into the Teaching of Mathematics in Schools (1982). *Mathematics Counts.* Report of the Committee of Inquiry into the Teaching of Mathematics in Schools ("The Cockcroft Report"). London: H.M.S.O.

Cooper, H. (1979). Pygmalion grows up: A model for teacher expectations communication and influence. *Review of Educational Research, 49,* 389–410.

Cooper, H. (1985). Models of teacher expectation communication. In J.B. Dusek (Ed.), *Teacher expectancies*. Hillsdale, N.J.: Lawrence Erlbaum Associates Inc.

Crano, W.D. & Mellon, D.M. (1978). Causal influence of teachers' expecations on children's academic performance: A crossed lagged panel analysis. *Journal of Educational Psychology, 70*, 1, 39–49.

Croll, P. (1986). *Systematic classroom observation*. London: Falmer.

Davie, R., Butler, N., & Goldstein, H. (1972). *From birth to seven*. London: Longman.

Delamont, S. (1980). *Sex roles and the school*. London: Methuen.

Douglas, J.W.B. (1964). *The Home and the School: A study of ability and attainment in the primary school*. London: MacGibbon & Kee.

Dunkin, M.J. & Biddle, B.J. (1974). *The study of teaching*. New York: Holt, Rinehart, & Winston.

Dusek, J.B. & Joseph, G. (1983). The bases of teacher expectancies: A meta-analysis. *Journal of Educational Psychology, 75*, 3, 327–346.

Dusek, J.B. & Joseph, G. (1985). The bases of teacher expectancies. In J.B. Dusek (Ed.), *Teacher expectancies*. Hillsdale, N.J.: Lawrence Erlbaum Associates Inc.

Dweck, C.S., Davidson, W., Nelson, S., & Enna, B. (1978). Sex differences in learned helplessness. *Developmental Psychology, 14*, 268–276.

Earls, F. & Richman, N. (1980). Behaviour problems in pre-school children of West Indian-born parents: A re-examination of family and social factors. *Journal of Child Psychology and Psychiatry, 21*, 2, 107–117.

Essen, J. & Wedge, P. (1982). *Continuities in childhood disadvantage*. London: Heinemann Educational Books.

Farquhar, C. (1987). Little read books. *Times Educational Supplement*, 8 May.

Farquhar, C., Blatchford, P., Burke, J., Plewis, I., & Tizard, B. (1985). A comparison of the views of parents and reception teachers. *Education, 3–13, 13*, 17–22.

Farquhar, C., Blatchford, P., Burke, J., Plewis, I., & Tizard, B. (1987). Curriculum diversity in London infant schools. *British Journal of Educational Psychology, 57*, 151–165.

Firkowska, A., Ostrowska, A., Sokolowska, M., Stein, A., Susser, M., & Wald, I. (1978). Cognitive development and social policy. *Science, 202*, 1357–1362.

Fogelman, K. & Goldstein, H. (1976). Social factors associated with change in educational attainment between 7 and 11 years of age. *Educational Studies, 2*, 95–109.

French, J. (1984). Gender imbalance in the classroom. *Educational Research, 26*, 2, 127–136.

Fuller, M. (1980). Black girls in a London comprehensive school. In R. Deem (Ed.), *Schooling for women's work*. London: Routledge & Kegan Paul.

Galton, M. & Delafield, A. (1981). Expectancy effects in primary classrooms. In B. Simon & J. Willcocks (Eds.), *Research and practice in the primary classroom*. London: Routledge & Kegan Paul.

Galton, M. & Simon, B. (1980). *Progress and performance in the primary classroom*. London: Routledge & Kegan Paul.

Galton, M., Simon, B., & Croll, P. (1980). *Inside the primary classroom*. London: Routledge & Kegan Paul.

Gilroy, P. (1986). *There ain't no black in the Union Jack*. London: Hutchinson Education.

Goldstein, H. (1987). *Multilevel models in educational and social research*. London: Griffin.

Good, T. (1979). Teacher effectiveness in the elementary school. *Journal of Teacher Education, 30*, 2, 52–64.

Grant, C.A. & Sleeter, C.F. (1986). Race, class, and gender effects. *Review of Educational Research, 56*, 2, 195–211.

Great Britain, Central Statistical Office. (1982d). *Social Trends (1982). No. 12. A publication of the Government Statistical Service*. London: H.M.S.O.

Great Britain, Central Statistical Office. (1986). *Social Trends (1986). No. 16. A publi-cation of the Government Statistical Service.* London: H.M.S.O.

Great Britain, Central Statistical Office. (1987). *Social Trends (1987). No. 17. A publi-cation of the Government Statistical Service.* London: H.M.S.O.

Great Britain, Department of Education and Science (1975). *A language for life.* ("The Bullock Report"). London: H.M.S.O.

Great Britain, Department of Education and Science. Assessment of Performance Unit (1982a). *Mathematical developments. Secondary Survey Report No. 3* (by D.D. Foxman, M. Martini, & P. Mitchell). London: H.M.S.O.

Great Britain, Department of Education and Science. Assessment of Performance Unit (1982b). *Mathematical development. Primary Survey Report No. 3* (by D.D. Foxman, G.J. Ruddock, M.E. Badger, & R.M. Martini). London: H.M.S.O.

Great Britain, Department of Education and Science. (1982c). *Education 5 to 9. An illustrative survey of 80 first schools in England.* London: H.M.S.O.

Great Britain, Department of Education and Science (1987). *The national curriculum 5–16: A consultation document.* London: H.M.S.O.

Gundara, J. (1986). Education for a multicultural society. In J. Gundara, C. Jones, & K. Kimberly (Eds.), *Racism, diversity and education.* London: Hodder & Stoughton.

Hannon, P. (1987). Parent involvement—a no-score draw. *Times Educational Supplement*, 3 April, p.23.

Hannon, P.W. & Cuckle, P. (1984). Involving parents in the teaching of reading: A study of current practice. *Educational Research, 26,* 1, 7–13.

Hannon, P., Long, R., Weiberger, J., & Whitehurst, L. (1985). *Involving parents in the teaching of reading: Some key sources.* Division of Education, University of Sheffield: U.S.D.E. Papers in Education, No. 3.

Hewison, J. & Tizard, J. (1980). Parental involvement and reading attainment. *British Journal of Educational Psychology, 50,* 209–215.

Hidiroglou, M.A., Fuller, W.A., & Hickman, R.D. (1980). *SUPER CARP* (6th Edition). Iowa: Statistical Laboratory, Iowa State University.

H.M.I. (1978). *Primary education in England: A survey by H.M. Inspectors of Schools.* London: H.M.S.O.

Hoffman, L. (1974). The effects of maternal employment on the child. A review of the research. *Developmental Psychology, 10,* 204–228.

Hughes, M. (1986). *Children and number.* Oxford: Basil Blackwell.

Huston, A.C. (1983). Sex-typing. In P.H. Mussen (Ed.), *Handbook of Child Psychology* (4th Edition). New York: Wiley.

Inner London Education Authority (I.L.E.A.) (1983). *Race, sex and class: 2. Multi-ethnic education in schools.* County Hall, London: I.L.E.A.

Inner London Education Authority (I.L.E.A.) (1983). *Race, sex and class: 3. A policy for equality: Race.* County Hall, London: I.L.E.A.

Inner London Education Authority (I.L.E.A.) (1983). *Social and ethnic characteristics of I.L.E.A. pupils,* 1981–82. April 1983 (RS 873/83). Statistical Information Bulletin No. 8. London: I.L.E.A. Research & Statistics Branch, Addington Street Annexe, County Hall, London SE1 7UY.

Inner London Education Authority (I.L.E.A.) (1985a). *Parents and primary schools* (RS 987/85). London: I.L.E.A. Research & Statistics Branch, Addington Street Annexe, County Hall, London SE1 7UY.

Inner London Education Authority (I.L.E.A.) (1985b). *Socio-economic background, parental involvement and attitudes and children's achievements in junior schools* (RS 982/85). London: I.L.E.A. Research & Statistics Branch, Addington Street Annexe, County Hall, London SE1 7UY.

Inner London Education Authority (I.L.E.A.) (1986). *The Junior School Project Part A: Pupils' progress and development.* London: I.L.E.A. Research & Statistics Branch, Addington Street Annexe, County Hall, London SE1 7UY.

Inner London Education Authority (I.L.E.A.) (1987). *Ethnic background and examination results 1985 and 1986* (RS 1120/87). London: I.L.E.A. Research and Statistics Branch, Addington Street Annexe, County Hall, London SE1 7UY.

Jackson, B. & Marsden, D. (1962). *Education and the working class.* Harmondsworth: Penguin.

Kelly, A. (in press). Gender differences in teacher-pupil interaction: A meta-analytic review. *Research Papers in Education.*

Koch, G.G., Landis, J.R., Freeman, J.L., Freeman, D.H. Jr., & Lehnen, R.G. (1977). A general methodology for the analysis of experiments with repeated measurement of categorical data. *Biometrics, 33,* 133–158.

Kohlberg, L. (1966). A cognitive-developmental analysis of children's sex-role concepts and attitudes. In E.E. Maccoby (Ed.), *The development of sex differences.* Stanford: Stanford University Press.

Lapouse, R. & Monk, M.A. (1959). Fears and worries in a representative sample of children. *American Journal of Orthopsychiatry, 29,* 803–18.

Levy, P. & Goldstein, H. (1984). *Tests in education: A book of critical reviews.* London: Academic Press.

London Borough of Redbridge (1978). *Cause for concern: West Indian pupils in Redbridge.* London: Redbridge Community Relations Council and Black Parents Association.

Mabey, C. (1981). Black British literacy: A study of reading attainment of London black children from 8 to 15 years. *Educational Research, 23,* 2, 83–95.

Maccoby, E.E. & Jacklin, C.N. (1974). *The psychology of sex differences.* Stanford: Stanford University Press.

MacFarlane, J.V., Allen, L., & Honzik, M.P. (1954). *A developmental study of behaviour problems of normal children.* Berkeley: University of California Press.

McGee, R., Williams, S., Share, D.L., Anderson, J., & Silva, P.A. (1986). The relationship between specific reading retardation, general reading backwardness, and behavioural problems in a large sample of Dunedin boys: A longitudinal study from 5 to 11 years. *Journal of Child Psychology and Psychiatry, 27,* 5, 597–610.

McMichael, P. (1979). The hen or the egg? Which comes first—antisocial emotional disorders or reading disability? *British Journal of Educational Psychology, 49,* 226–235.

Maughan, B. & Rutter, M. (1986). Black pupils' progress in secondary schools. *British Journal of Developmental Psychology, 4,* 19–29.

Milner, D. (1983). *Children and race: Ten years on.* Harmondsworth: Penguin.

Morris, J.M. (1966). *Standards and progress in reading.* Windsor: N.F.E.R.

Morrison, D.F. (1967). *Multivariate statistical methods.* New York: McGraw-Hill.

National Foundation for Educational Research (N.F.E.R.) (1971). *Basic Mathematics Test B.* Windsor: N.F.E.R.-Nelson.

Newson, J. & Newson, E. (1968). *Four-year-olds in an urban community.* London: George Allen & Unwin.

Nicholls, J.G. (1978). The development of the concepts of effort and ability, perception of academic attainment, and the understanding that difficult tasks require more ability. *Child Development, 49,* 800–814.

Office of Population Censuses and Surveys (O.P.C.S.) (1978). *General Household Survey.* London: H.M.S.O.

Office of Population Censuses and Surveys (O.P.C.S.) (1980). *General Household Survey.* London: H.M.S.O.

Office of Population Censuses and Surveys (O.P.C.S.) (1982). *General Household Survey.*

London: H.M.S.O.

Office of Population Censuses and Surveys (O.P.C.S.) (1983). *General Household Survey*. London: H.M.S.O.

Osborn, A.F. & Milbank, J.E. (1987). *The effects of early education*. Oxford: Clarendon Press.

Parsons, J.E. & Ruble, D.N. (1977). The development of achievement-related expectancies. *Child Development, 48*, 1075–79.

Parsons, J.G., Ruble, D.N., Hodges, K.L., & Small, A.V. (1976). Cognitive-developmental factors in emerging sex differences in achievement-related expectancies. *Journal of Social Issues, 32*, 3, 47–61.

Pattison, P. & Grieve, N. (1984). Do spatial skills contribute to sex differences in different types of mathematical problems? *Journal of Educational Psychology, 76*, 4, 678–689.

Pedersen, E., Faucher, T.A., & Eaton, W.W. (1978). A new perspective on the effects of first-grade teachers on children's subsequent adult status. *Harvard Educational Review, 48*, 1, 1–31.

Plewis, I. (1985). *Analysing change*. Chichester: Wiley.

Plewis, I. (1987). Social disadvantage, educational attainment and ethnicity: A comment. *British Journal of the Sociology of Education, 8*, 1, 77–81.

Plewis, I., (in press). Assessing and understanding the educational progress of children from different ethnic groups. *Journal of the Royal Statistical Society*, Series A.

Plewis, I. (in press). Estimating generalisability in systematic observation studies. *British Journal of Mathematical and Statistical Psychology*.

"The Plowden Report" See Central Advisory Council for Education.

Pollak, M. (1972). *Today's Three-year-olds in London*. London: Heinemann.

Pollak, M. (1979). *Nine years old*. Lancaster: M.T.P. Press.

Pugh, G. & De'Ath, E. (1984). *The needs of parents—practice and policy in parent education*. Basingstoke: Macmillan.

"The Rampton Report" See Committee of Inquiry into the Education of Children from Ethnic Minority Groups.

Richards, C. (Ed.) (1985). *The study of primary education: A source book, Vol. 2*. Lewes: Falmer Press.

Richman, N., Stevenson, J., & Graham, P.J. (1982). *Pre-school to school: A behavioural study*. London: Academic Press.

Rist, R. (1970). Student social class and teacher expectations: The self-fulfilling prophecy in ghetto education. *Harvard Educational Review, 40*, 411–451.

Rogers, C. (1982). *A Social Psychology of Schooling: The expectancy process*. London: Routledge & Kegan Paul.

Rosenshine, B. (1977). Review of teaching variables and student achievement. In G.D. Borich (Ed.), *The appraisal of teaching: Concepts and processes*. Reading, Mass.: Addison-Wesley.

Rosenthal, R. & Jacobson, L. (1968). *Pygmalion in the classroom*. New York: Holt, Rinehart, & Winston.

Ruble, D.N., Boggiano, A.K., Feldman, N.S., & Loebl, J.H. (1980). Developmental analysis of the role of social comparison in self-evaluation. *Developmental Psychology, 16*, 2, 105–115.

Rutter, M., Tizard, J., & Whitmore, K. (1970). *Education, health and behaviour*. London: Longman.

Rutter, M., Maughan, B., Mortimore, P., & Ouston, J. (1979). *Fifteen thousand hours: Secondary schools and their effects on children*. London: Open Books.

Rutter, M., Yule, W., Berger, M., Yule, B., Morton, J., & Bagley, C. (1974). Children of West Indian immigrants—I: Rates of behavioural deviance and of psychiatric deviance. *Journal of Child Psychology and Psychiatry, 15*, 241–262.

Rutter, M., Yule, B., Morton, J., & Bagley, C. (1975). Children of West Indian immigrants—III: Home circumstances and family patterns. *Journal of Child Psychology and Psychiatry, 16* 105–123.

Scarman, L. (1981). *The Brixton disorders 10–12 April 1981.* Report of an inquiry by Lord Scarman presented by the Secretary for the Home Department. ("The Scarman Report"). London: H.M.S.O.

Scarr, S., Capanulo, B.K., Ferdmass, M., Tower, R.B., & Caplan, J. (1983). Developmental status and school achievements of minority and nonminority children from birth to 18 years. *British Journal of Developmental Psychology, 1,* 31–48.

Schaffer, D., Meyer-Bahlburg, H., & Stokman, C. (1980). The development of aggression. In M. Rutter (Ed.), *Scientific foundations of developmental psychiatry.* London: Heinemann Medical Books.

Sharpe, S. (1976). *Just like a girl.* Harmondsworth: Penguin.

Soar, R. (1977). An integration of findings from four studies of teacher effectiveness. In G.D. Borich (Ed.), *The appraisal of teaching: Concepts and processes.* Reading, Mass.: Addison-Wesley.

"Social Trends": See Great Britain, Central Statistical Office.

S.P.S.S.X. (1983). *User's guide.* New York: McGraw Hill.

Stallings, J.A. (1975). Implementation and child effects of teaching practices in Follow Through classrooms. *Monographs of the Society for Research in Child Development,* Serial No. 163, 40, 7–8.

Stone, M. (1981). *The education of the black child: The myth of multicultural education.* London: Fontana.

"The Swann Report" See Committee of Inquiry into the Education of Children from Ethnic Minority Groups.

Taylor, M.J. (1981). *Caught between: A review of research into the education of pupils of West Indian origin.* Windsor: N.F.E.R.-Nelson.

Terman, L. & Tyler, L. (1954). Psychology and sex differences. In L. Carmichael (Ed.), *Manual of child psychology.* New York: Wiley.

Tizard, B. & Hughes, M. (1984). *Young children learning.* London: Fontana.

Tizard, B., Mortimore, J., & Burchell, B. (1981). *Involving parents in nursery and infant schools.* London: Grant McIntyre.

Tizard, J., Schofield, W.N., & Hewison, J. (1982). Collaboration between teachers and parents in assisting children's reading. *British Journal of Educational Psychology, 52,* 1–15.

Tomlinson, S. (1983). *Ethnic Minorities in British Schools: a review of the literature, 1960–82.* London: Heinemann Educational (for Policy Studies Institute).

Tomlinson, S. (1984). *Home and school in multicultural Britain.* London: Batsford Academic.

Troyna, B. & Williams, J. (1986). *Racism, education and the State.* Beckenham, Kent: Croom Helm.

Wechsler, D. (1967). *W.P.P.S.I. manual (Wechsler Preschool and Primary Scale of Intelligence).* New York: The Psychological Corporation.

Weiner, G. (1980). Sex differences in mathematical performance. In R. Deem (Ed.), *Schooling for women's work.* London: Routledge & Kegan Paul.

Wells, C.G. (1985). *Language, learning and education: Selected papers from the Bristol Study: "Language at Home and at School."* Windsor: N.F.E.R.-Nelson.

Whitbread, N. (1972). *The evolution of the nursery-infant school.* London: Routledge & Kegan Paul.

Wikeley, F. (1986). Communication between parents and teachers. In M. Hughes (Ed.),

Involving parents in the primary curriculum, Perspectives 24. Exeter: School of Education, University of Exeter.

Williams, J.E., Bennett, S.N., & Best, D.L. (1975). Awareness and expression of sex stereotypes in young children. *Developmental Psychology, 11,* 635–642.

Wolkind, S. & Rutter, M. (1985). Sociocultural factors. In M. Rutter & L. Hersov (Eds.), *Child and adolescent psychiatry: Modern approaches* (Second edition). Oxford: Blackwell Scientific.

Young, D. (1978). *Group mathematics test.* Sevenoaks, Kent: Hodder & Stoughton.

Young, D. (1980). *Group reading test* (2nd edition). Sevenoaks, Kent: Hodder & Stoughton.

Young-Loveridge, J.M. (1987). Learning mathematics. *British Journal of Developmental Psychology, 5,* 155–167.

Yule, W., Berger, M., Rutter, M., & Yule, B. (1975). Children of West Indian immigrants—II: Intellectual performance and reading attainment. *Journal of Child Psychology and Psychiatry, 16,* 1, 1–18.

Yule, W. & Rutter, M. (1985). Reading and other difficulties. In M. Rutter & L. Hersov (Eds.), *Child and adolescent psychiatry: Modern approaches* (Second edition). Oxford: Blackwell Scientific.

REFERENCE NOTES

1. Shuard, H. (1983). *The relative attainment of girls and boys in mathematics in the primary years.* Paper presented at G.A.M.M.A. Conference, May.

Appendices

APPENDIX 1

Definitions of Parent Variables

1. Child's Experience with Books

1982: How often family read to child, *how* child was read to (e.g. complete story/discussion of pictures, etc.), number of books suitable for child at home (as shown to interviewer).
1983: How often family read to child, type of books read (as shown to interviewer).
1984: How often family read to child, type of books read (as shown to interviewer).
1985: How often family read to child, how often child read alone.

2. Teaching of Reading at Home

1982: How family taught reading (incidentally/games/books/flashcards/etc.), how often family taught reading.
1983: How often family heard child read.
1984: How often family heard child read, if child used home computer for reading, if child used electronic games for reading.
1985: How often family heard child read, if child used home computer for reading, if child used electronic games for reading.

3. Teaching Writing at Home

1982: What child taught (name/other words, etc.), if taught capital and/or lower-case letters.
1983: No questions.
1984: No questions.
1985: What child taught: punctuation/use of capitals, spelling, handwriting/letter formation, layout.

4. Teaching Maths at Home

1982: If/how taught counting.
1983: If taught counting, if taught number series, if taught number symbols, if taught addition, if taught subtraction.
1984: If played games with child involving number, if taught counting, if taught number symbols, if taught addition, if taught subtraction, if involved child in weighing/measuring, if/to what level taught clock face, if taught digital clock, if/to what level taught money, if child used home computer for maths, if child used electronic games for maths.
1985: If/to what level taught addition, if/to what level taught subtraction, if/to what level taught multiplication, if/to what level taught division, if taught tables, if involved child in weighing/ measuring, if/to what level taught clock face, if child used home computer for maths, if child used electronic games for maths.

5. Child Writes at Home

1982: No questions.
1983: What child wrote at home (name/sentences/etc.), how often child wrote.
1984: What child wrote at home, how often child wrote.
1985: What child wrote at home, how often child wrote

6. Parental Contact with and Knowledge of School

1982: If parent had been round infant school, if had met child's future teacher, if could describe nursery programme, if could describe reception programme.
1983: If attended any P.T.A. meetings, if attended any meetings with staff (open days/coffee mornings/workshops etc.), if had an individual discussion re child's work with teacher, if/how helped in school, if teacher had explained teaching of reading, if teacher had explained about writing (capitals/lower-case letters), if teacher had explained teaching of maths, if parent knew child's reading book/scheme, if could explain how reading taught, if could explain what maths taught, if knew reception class programme, if teacher sent reading home, if told child's reading level (cf. peers).
1984: If/how frequently attended any meetings with staff, if/how frequently had an individual discussion re child's work with teacher, if/how helped in school, if could explain how reading taught, if could explain what maths taught, if teacher had explained teaching of reading, if teacher had explained teaching of maths, if parent knew middle-infant programme, if had approached staff with worries re teaching/children's work, if/how frequently teacher sent reading home, if teacher sent reading card /P.A.C.T. card, if told child's reading level (cf. peers).
1985: If informed of any schoolwork problems, if/how frequently attended any meetings with school staff, if/how frequently had an individual discussion re child's work with teacher, if/how helped in school, if had approached staff with worries re teaching/children's work, if/how frequently teacher wrote on reading/P.A.C.T. card, if/how frequently parent wrote on reading/P.A.C.T. card, if received a written report, if could explain what maths taught, if teacher explained maths teaching, if/how frequently teacher sent reading home, if told child's reading level (cf. peers), if told child's maths level (cf. peers).

7. Parental Attitude to Helping Child at Home

1982: If felt able to give child time/attention needed, if felt child's infant education could be left to teachers.
1983: If reported difficulty in finding time to help child, if believed it necessary to help, if reported worries about helping, if believed it important to read to child.

1984: If reported difficulty in finding time to help child, if believed it necessary to help, if reported worries about helping, if believed it important to read to child.

1985: If reported difficulty in finding time to help child, if believed it necessary to help, if reported worries about helping, if felt child's junior education could be left to teachers.

8. Parental Satisfaction with Child's Progress

1982: No questions.

1983: If pleased with child's progress.

1984: If pleased with child's progress, if felt child doing as well as capable of.

1985: If pleased with child's progress, if felt child doing as well as capable of, if pleased with child's progress over three years, if satisfied with child's reading level, if satisfied with child's maths level.

9. Parental Satisfaction with School

1982: If happy with choice of school.

1983: If had any worries/problems re the school, if child happy at school, if/to what extent child got on with class teacher, if felt could approach staff with worries re teaching/children's work, if would like anything altered/improved, if felt reading sent home often enough, if felt reading sent home was right level.

1984: If child happy at school, if/to what extent child got on with class teacher, if any worries/problems re child at school, if felt could approach staff with worries re teaching/ children's work, if had approached/satisfied with response, if would like anything altered/ improved, if felt reading sent home often enough, if felt reading sent home was right level.

1985: If child happy at school, if/to what extent child got on well with class teacher, if any worries/problems re child at school, if felt could approach staff with worries re teaching/ children's work, if had approached/satisfied with response, if had discussed child's work with teacher in as much detail as needed, if mentioned any satisfactions with school, if mentioned no dissatisfactions, if felt reading sent home often enough, if felt reading sent home was right level, if felt any important academic areas had not been covered by infant school, if felt any important nonacademic areas had not been covered by infant school.

APPENDIX 2

Basic Results for Attainment Tests

TABLE A2.1
Basic Results for Nursery Tests

	Mean	Standard Deviation	Possible Range	% at Minimum	% at Maximum
Word matching	3.8	2.4	0-10	6	1
Concepts about print	2.5	2.7	0-10	41	2
Letter identification	2.4	3.5	0-10	50	12
Word reading	n.a.	n.a.	0-10	97	0
READING (Total)	9	7	0-40	2	0
Writing name	2.5	1.8	0-5	18	24
Copying phrase	2.0	1.4	0-5	23	1
WRITING (Total)	4.5	2.9	0-10	12	1
READING AND WRITING[a]	27	17	0-80	1	0
Reading numbers	4.0	3.5	0-10	23	4
Placing and giving	5.8	3.8	0-10	21	26
Counting; 1 to 1 matching	6.1	3.1	0-10	2	14
Boehm concepts	5.7	2.8	0-17	3	0
MATHS (Total)	21	11	0-37	1	0
W.P.P.S.I. vocabulary[b]	12	5	0-44	5	0

All these results are based on n=343.
[a] Writing is given a weight of 4 when combined with reading.
[b] These are raw scores.

TABLE A2.2
Nursery Tests: Means and Standard Deviations

	White Boys (n=90)		Black Boys (n=51)		White Girls (n=81)		Black Girls (n=55)	
Reading	8.9	(7.0)	8.5	(6.5)	8.9	(5.7)	9.5	(7.2)
Writing	3.9	(3.1)	4.1	(2.9)	5.2	(2.7)	5.2	(2.9)
Maths	21.8	(11.0)	20.5	(10.0)	23.5	(10.2)	22.2	(11.1)
Vocabulary	13.2	(6.1)	12.1	(4.2)	12.3	(4.8)	12.7	(4.7)

TABLE A2.3
Basic Results for Reception Tests

	Mean	Standard Deviation	Possible Range	% at Minimum	% at Maximum
Concepts about print	6.5	2.4	0-10	4	15
Letter identification	14	9	0-26	4	5
Word reading	11	9	0-30	9	3
READING (Total)	31	18	0-66	1	1
WRITING	15	4	2-26	0	0
READING AND WRITING[a]	61	23	4-118	0	0
MATHS[b]	18	6	0-52	0	0

All these results are based on n=470.
[a] Writing is given a weight of 2 when combined with reading.
[b] These are raw scores.

TABLE A2.4
Basic Results for Middle-infants Tests

	Mean	Standard Deviation	Possible Range	% at Minimum	% at Maximum
Young's Reading[a]	15	8	0-45	(n=1)	0
Young's Maths[a]	19	9	0-60	0	0

These results are based on n=448.
[a] These are raw scores

TABLE A2.5
Basic Results for Top-infants Test

	Mean	Standard Deviation	Possible Range	% at Minimum	% at Maximum
Young's Reading[a]	23	10	0-45	0	(n=2)
Writing quality	23	6	7-35	1	1
Independent vocabulary	33	24	n.a.	n.a.	n.a.
Transcription and grammar	14	4	5-25	(n=2)	(n=1)
Sentences	18	9	0-60	5	(n=1)
WRITING (Total)	87	38	n.a.	n.a.	n.a.
READING AND WRITING[b]	44	18	n.a.	n.a.	n.a.
Young's Maths[a]	29	11	0-60	0	0

Reading and maths are based on n=369; writing results are based on n=331, as children who had moved from the project schools were not given a writing test.

[a] These are raw scores.

[b] Writing is given a weight of 0.25 when combined with reading.

APPENDIX 3

Statistical Models for Progress

In Chapter 2, we explained what we meant by progress and how it differed from attainment. Here we give a more formal definition of progress and show how it can be extended to define relative progress.

Let the test score at a particular occasion be x_1 and let the test score for the same attainment (not necessarily on the *same test*) at any later occasion be y. Then the relationship between x_1 and y can be modelled using linear regression with

$$y = \alpha + \beta_1 x_1 + \varepsilon \qquad\qquad 1$$

where α is the intercept and β_1 the slope of the straight line linking x_1 to y, and ε is an error term which represents the variation in y not explained by x_1.

Relative Progress

Suppose we want to know whether one group (for example, boys) make more progress than girls. Then we extend the basic model to

$$y = \alpha + \beta_o x_o + \beta_1 x_1 + \varepsilon \qquad\qquad 2$$

which is the same as model (1) except for the inclusion of x_o; x_o takes two values, 0 for boys, say, and 1 for girls. Then the value of β_o obtained from least squares estimation of (2), called $\hat{\beta}_o$, is our estimate of relative progress, or relative change. If β_o is greater than 0 then girls make more progress than boys, if $\beta_o = 0$ then the two groups make the same amount of progress, and if β_o is less than 0 then boys make more progress than girls. The statistical significance of this relative change is assessed by comparing $\hat{\beta}_o$ with its standard error using a t-test in the usual way.

We were looking for answers to three questions in Chapter 6: did boys make more progress than girls in reading, writing and maths; did white children make more progress than black children, and was there an interaction between ethnic group and sex in the amount of progress made by the four groups? And so model (2) must be extended to

$$y = \alpha + \beta_{o1}x_{o1} + \beta_{o2}x_{o2} + \beta_{o3}x_{o3} + \beta_1x_1 + \varepsilon \qquad 3$$

where x_{o1} is the variable for sex (0 = boys, 1 = girls), x_{o2} is the variable for ethnic group (0 = white, 1 = black) and x_{o3} represents the interaction between sex and ethnic group and is simply defined as the product of x_{o1} and x_{o2}.

However, model (3) is incomplete because it does not recognise that our sample children were clustered into 33 schools and between 40 and 70 classes. If we ignore this clustering or, to put it another way, if we ignore the hierarchical or multilevel nature of our data, then we run the risk of misrepresenting the statistical significance of the differences between the groups. Moreover, differences between schools, and differences between teachers within schools, are of interest to educational researchers, and therefore they need to be represented in the statistical models used by them. As we have explained in Chapter 2, we were not able to look at school and teacher differences in great detail, but we could not ignore them if we were properly to analyse relative progress. Therefore, we extended model (3) to

$$y_{ij} = \alpha + \beta_{o1}x_{o1} + \beta_{o2}x_{o2} + \beta_{o3}x_{o3} + \beta_1x_1 + u_i + \varepsilon_{ij} \qquad 4$$

where i (i = 1...33) represents schools and j (j = 1...n_i) represents children within schools, and omitting, for convenience, the subscripts for x_o and x_1. In this model, u_i is a random variable, or random effect, with a mean of zero and variance σ_u^2; σ_u^2 is the variation between schools in the progress made by children. Model (4) is a two-level model (schools and children); a three-level model (schools, classes, and children) is possible, but our data were not sufficiently extensive to consider it here.

Simple least squares estimation of model (4) is not possible. The results in Figs. 6.1, 6.2 and 6.3 came from a maximum likelihood method of estimation incorporated into the P3V program of the B.M.D. suite (B.M.D.P., 1985).

School differences

Model (4) was also used for the results on school differences in Chapter 6. The intra-class correlation used there is defined as the ratio of the between school variation to total variation, i.e.

$$\frac{\sigma_u^2}{\sigma_u^2 + \sigma_e^2} \qquad 5$$

where σ_e^2 is the pooled variance between children within schools.

The school differences are calculated as follows. For each child, there is an actual attainment score at the second occasion (i.e. y), and a predicted score based on that child's score at the first occasion (i.e. x_1), their sex and ethnic group. The difference between the actual and predicted scores is the residual and, for the sample as a whole, the mean of these residuals is zero. However, mean residuals can also be calculated for each school; for theoretical reasons (see, for example, Aitkin & Longford (1986)), these mean residuals are shrunk towards zero by a factor:

$$\frac{n_i \hat{\rho}}{1 + (n_i - 1)\hat{\rho}} \qquad 5a$$

And so, the smaller the size of the sample is for school i (i.e. n_i) and the smaller the intra-class correlation is (i.e. $\hat{\rho}$), the more the mean residual for the school is shrunk towards zero. After shrinking, the school differences were transformed to standard deviation units so that they could be compared across tests and across years.

More detailed discussion of models for relative progress can be found in Plewis (1985); Goldstein (1987) deals with multilevel models in educational research.

Explanatory Models for Progress

In Chapters 7 and 8, we presented associations between home and school variables and progress. The model we used was

$$y = \alpha + \beta_1 x_1 + \delta_1 z_1 + \varepsilon \qquad 6$$

where y and x_1 are defined as in equation (1) and z_1 is the home or school variable under consideration. The statistical significance of δ_1 was used to determine whether that variable was related to progress.

In Chapter 10, we considered the relationships between combinations of home and school variables and progress. The model used then was

$$y_{ij} = \alpha + \beta_1 x_1 + \sum_i \delta_i z_i + u_i + \varepsilon_{ij} \qquad 7$$

where the z_i are the home and school variables found to have been separately related to progress using equation (6). Variables in equation (7) whose coefficients, δ_i, were statistically significant were said to be independently related to progress, and were given explanatory, or causal, interpretations in Chapter 10.

Using equations (6) and (7) in this way usually provides reasonable results in practice. However, it does have some theoretical disadvantages; it is possible for a variable, say z_1, to be unrelated to progress on its own, but to be related to progress for fixed values of another variable, say z_2. It is also possible for z_1 and z_2 to be unrelated to progress on their own, but for their interaction, $z_1 z_2$, to be related. However, relationships of this kind are rarely found in social and educational research. Furthermore, a variable may be related to progress on its own (in equation 6), but not when considered with other variables (in equation 7). This variable could, nevertheless, have an indirect rather than a direct causal link with progress. For example, behaviour problems were found not to be independently related to progress in reading and writing, but they might have been an indirect cause, perhaps through their influence on teacher expectations. For this reason, both the separate and the independent associations with progress are of interest, and alternative interpretations of our results are possible, as are alternative analyses of our data.

To see whether the home and school variables which were related to progress accounted for the ethnic group and sex differences in progress, we combined equations (4) and (7)

$$y_{ij} = \alpha + \beta_1 x_1 + \sum_i \delta_i z_i + \sum_j \beta_{oj} x_{oj} + u_i + \varepsilon_{ij} \qquad 8$$

We found that those coefficients, β_{oj}, which were statistically significant in equation (4) were also statistically significant in equation (8). In other words, the home and school variables did not account for the ethnic group and sex differences.

One of the problems with models like (7) and (8) is that methods of estimation which ignore measurement error, or unreliability, in the explanatory variables lead to biased estimates of their coefficients (see Plewis [1985, Ch.5] for the reasons for this). In our study, we did not have estimates of reliabilities for some of our variables, particularly the variables from the parent interviews, although we had estimates for the tests (given in Chapter 6), and for the curriculum coverage variables. Split-half estimates of reliability for the latter were 0.95 for reading and writing, and 0.97 for maths for the combined, three year, variables. Various estimates of reliabilities were tried, using methods incorporated into the computer program SUPERCARP (Hidiroglou, Fuller, & Hickman, 1980), but they did not lead to any important differences from the results and conclusions given in Chapter 10. It was not, however, possible to allow both for measurement error and clustering within schools.

APPENDIX 4

Structural Equation Models for Progress

For the results presented in the main body of Chapter 6, each child's test scores were obtained by adding subtest scores in the way described in Appendix 2. The possible range of scores for each subtest was about the same. No attempt was made to divide the Young's reading and maths tests into subtests, but they could be treated as each having two subtests; reading divided into matching words to pictures and completing sentences, maths divided into oral and computation, and these do not necessarily have to be equally weighted. The chosen weights were clearly arbitrary. It would, for example, have been possible to have standardised each subtest to have the same standard deviation (say, one), and then to have added them. We would then have been forcing the standard deviations, rather than the ranges, to be the same. We could also have used the weights from a factor analysis of the relevant subtests, allowing just one factor in the model.

Each of these methods has advantages and disadvantages, but they would all have been based on cross-sectional weights. However, as our main interest was in progress, we decided to consider alternative weighting methods within the context of the longitudinal data, in order to explore further the structure of our data, and also to see whether our conclusions were altered if the weights were changed. This could have been done by using the weights from a canonical correlation analysis (Morrison, 1967) which would have maximised the correlation across time between linear combinations of the subtests. However, a statistically more complete analysis was obtained using structural equation modelling.

Structural equation modelling is used here to try to obtain reliable measurements, at more than one occasion, of an underlying and unobservable variable such as maths ability, using a number of measured indicators (or tests) of that ability, with possibly different tests used at different occasions to measure the same underlying ability, and then to estimate the correlation of the ability over time. This correlation is sometimes know as the "true" correlation and, in that sense, the method can be seen as a way of dealing with problems posed by the unreliability of tests when estimating correlations over time.

More generally, the method has two components: a measurement model, relating the measured indicators to the unobserved variables, and a structural model, relating the unobserved variables in some kind of causal framework. The method is flexible and powerful, allowing different models to be fitted to the observed covariances until a reasonable fit is found between these covariances and the covariances generated by the parameters of the model. An introduction to structural equation modelling for longitudinal data is given in Plewis (1985, Ch. 5), and the February 1987 issue of the journal Child Development has a special section devoted to applications of, and various methodological issues in, structural equation modelling. The models in this appendix were estimated using version six of Jöreskog and Sörbom's computer program LISREL, as incorporated into the S.P.S.S.X. package (S.P.S.S.X., 1983).

Two models are given here—one for progress in reading and writing, and one for progress in maths, over the whole infant period. The results are illustrated in Figs. A4.1 and A4.2, and described next. Reading and writing were combined and regarded as one underlying ability for the reasons described earlier. Alternative analyses, in which they were kept separate, would have been possible.

Reading and Writing Progress

The results in Fig. A4.1 can be described as follows: the rectangles are the observed subtests (five at nursery, and six at top infants), the circles represent the underlying ability (RW = reading and writing) at the two occasions, which is not directly measurable, the numbers on the lines from the circles to the rectangles can be regarded as the weights for each subtest (a little like factor loadings); the numbers above the rectangles are the reliabilities of each of the subtests if used as the only measure of the underlying ability, and the number on the path between the two circles is the true correlation over time for reading and writing ability. The curved lines at the top of the figure show which error covariances are included in the model. (A positive error covariance between two tests implies that if the measurement error for a child on the first test is positive [negative], then the measurement error for that child on the second test is also likely to be positive [negative]. If the error covariance is zero then the measurement errors for the two tests are unrelated across individuals.)

At the end of nursery, the weights used in all our analyses were 1 for "write name" and "copy phrase", and 0.25 for the other three subtests. The new analysis produced weights of 1 for letter identification, about 0.66 for "write name", and about 0.5 for the other three subtests. (Word reading was omitted because so few children were able to read any words at the end of nursery.)

The original weights for the six top-infants' subtests were 1 for the two reading subtests and 0.25 for the four writing subtests. The weights for this analysis are 1 for independent vocabulary, about 0.33 for writing sentences, about 0.25 for quality and Young's sentence completion, and less than 0.1 for transcription and Young's pictures. It is interesting to find that the weights for the two parts of the Young's test are quite different.

The reliabilities indicate that if just one subtest were chosen at each

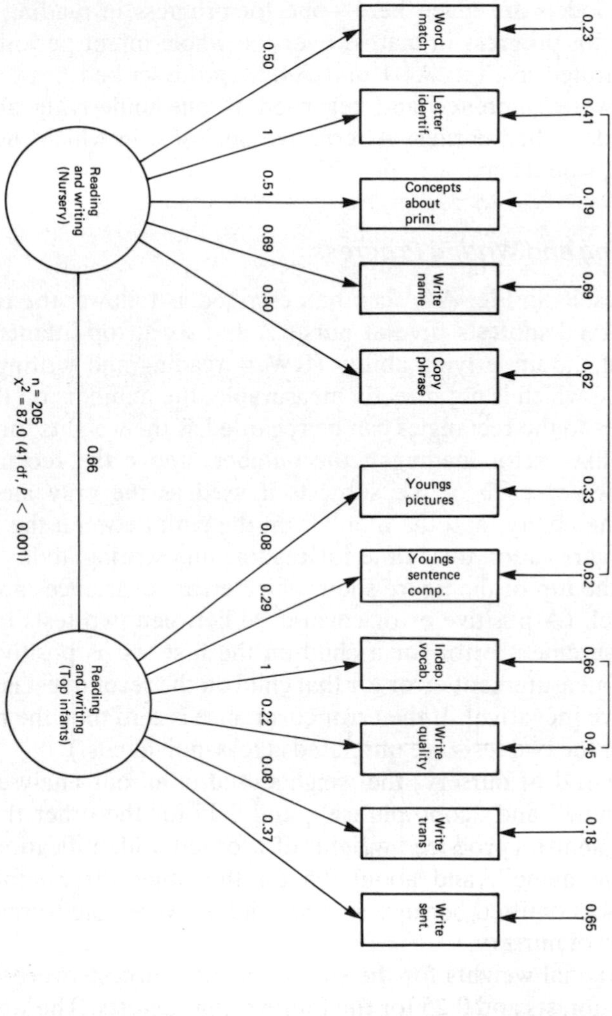

FIG. A4.1 Structural equation model: reading and writing (nursery) vs. reading and writing (top infants).

occasion then "write name" would be the most reliable at nursery and independent vocabulary at top infants. The true correlation over time (0.66), which takes account of measurement error, is higher than the observed correlation (0.58).

The model does not fit particularly well (the χ^2 value is high); not an uncommon finding with this approach, when samples are reasonably large as they are here. (The results are based on all children tested at both occasions.) A better fit could have been obtained by including more error covariance terms, but there seems no real need for this as the results with no error covariances in the model, and with just one error covariance, were very close to those presented here with two error covariances included. Alternatively, more than one underlying ability (or factor) could have been permitted at each occasion, but this would have conflicted with our wish to treat reading and writing ability as just one underlying variable, rather than separately, as two underlying variables.

Maths Progress

The results are given in Fig. A4.2. The original weights for the four nursery subtests were all 1; the new weights are about 1 for reading

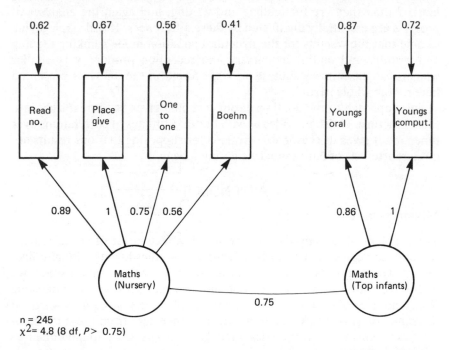

n = 245
χ^2= 4.8 (8 df, P> 0.75)

FIG. A4.2 Structural equation model: maths (nursery) vs. maths (top infants).

numbers and placing and giving, about 0.75 for one-to-one matching (which includes counting), and just over 0.5 for the Boehm test. The weights for the two parts of the Young's maths test at top infants are close. The true correlation is 0.75 compared with an observed correlation of 0.66 and the model fits well without any error covariances.

Conclusions

It should be stressed that all weighting schemes are arbitrary to some extent (as, indeed, were the scoring systems adopted for the subtests). Hence, one hopes to find results which are not affected by changes in the weights.

We have found that the weights for reading and writing from the structural equation modelling are different from the original weights. For example, the weights for letter identification at nursery and for independent vocabulary at top infants are considerably higher than the weights for the other tests. However, although the weights are different, the results for the associations between ethnic group, sex, and school on the one hand, and reading and writing progress on the other, are little affected.

The differences between the two sets of weights for maths are less marked than they are for reading and writing, and again the analyses of progress are essentially unaffected by these differences. It is also reassuring to note that the weights for the structural equation models linking reading and writing, and maths, at nursery and reception produce very similar weights for the nursery subtests as were found in the analyses presented here for the whole period.

This approach to the analysis of our test data gives us some insight into their structure. It also provides us with better estimates of correlations over time, and it gives us reasonable grounds for supposing that our results are not just artefacts of our original weighting scheme.

APPENDIX 5

Missing Data

The problem of missing data is one which affects a lot of social science research and can be particularly difficult with studies having a longitudinal design, when subjects are lost from the sample over time. In our study, we had to face not only sample attrition but also the fact that our data came from a number of different sources, and the planned sample sizes were not the same for all sources. When we put together data from these different sources to construct our statistical models for progress, we found ourselves working with rather small samples. In this appendix, we look at some of the characteristics of our different samples to see whether there was any evidence to suggest that they differed from the larger tested samples. If there were no evidence of this kind then we would have some confidence that we would have obtained similar results with more complete data.

Table A5.1 gives the means and standard deviations for the combined reading and writing tests and the vocabulary subtest, for the black and white groups, for the nursery tested sample (n=277), for those tested at top infants (n=251, including some children not tested at nursery), for those tested both at nursery and at top infants (n=165), and for those included in the two progress models (n=125 and n=116).

Table A5.2 gives the corresponding results for the maths tests. The sample sizes were 277 for the nursery test, 292 for the top-infants test, 205 for those tested at nursery and top infants, and 136 for the model.

These two tables show that, at least for their means and standard deviations, the test score statistics for the different samples are close, with no strong evidence that sample loss, and our criteria for inclusion in

TABLE A5.1
Test Scores for Different Samples: Means and Standard Deviations for Reading and Writing, and Vocabulary

Test	Nursery	Top Infants	Nursery and Top Infants	Progress Model 1	Progress Model 2
Reading and writing, nursery	27.3 (16.7)	–	26.6 (16.4)	27.8 (16.2)	27.0 (16.5)
Reading and writing, top	–	44.6 (18.1)	45.3 (17.4)	45.8 (17.3)	45.6 (17.2)
W.P.P.S.I. vocabulary	12.6 (5.1)	–	12.4 (5.5)	12.7 (5.2)	12.4 (5.2)

TABLE A5.2
Test Scores for Different Samples: Means and Standard Deviations for Maths

Test	Nursery	Top Infants	Nursery and Top Infants	Progress Model
Maths, nursery	22.1 (10.6)	–	22.0 (10.8)	23.2 (10.5)
Maths, top	–	29.9 (11.4)	30.6 (11.5)	31.0 (11.6)

particular samples, led to subsamples which were different from the main sample.

It is possible for the means and standard deviations to remain relatively constant across samples but for the covariances to change. Table A5.3 gives the covariances for the reading and writing and vocabulary tests for: (a) the sample tested at nursery and top infants; (b) the first progress model: and (c) the second progress model.

TABLE A5.3
Covariances: Reading and Writing and Vocabulary Tests

	(a)		(b)		(c)	
	RW, Nursery	RW, Top	RW, Nursery	RW, Top	RW, Nursery	RW, Top
RW, Top	166	–	167	–	159	–
Vocabulary	45	40	41	39	39	36

Again, we find no marked variation between samples, nor was there for maths: the covariances between the nursery and top-infant tests were 82 for all black and white children tested on both occasions, and 78 for those included in the progress model.

We cannot be sure, on the evidence presented here, that our longitudinal and progress model samples are unaffected by missing data. However, these results do not give us any grounds for supposing that missing data led to serious biases in our analyses.

Indices

AUTHOR INDEX

SUBJECT INDEX